COASTAL TRADE AND MARITIME COMMUNITIES IN ELIZABETHAN ENGLAND

COASTAL TRADE AND MARITIME COMMUNITIES IN ELIZABETHAN ENGLAND

Leanna T P Brinkley

THE BOYDELL PRESS

© Leanna T P Brinkley 2024

All Rights Reserved. Except as permitted under current legislation no part of this work may be photocopied, stored in a retrieval system, published, performed in public, adapted, broadcast, transmitted, recorded or reproduced in any form or by any means, without the prior permission of the copyright owner

The right of Leanna T P Brinkley to be identified as the author of this work has been asserted in accordance with sections 77 and 78 of the Copyright, Designs and Patents Act 1988

First published 2024
The Boydell Press, Woodbridge

ISBN 978 1 83765 188 7

The Boydell Press is an imprint of Boydell & Brewer Ltd
PO Box 9, Woodbridge, Suffolk IP12 3DF, UK
and of Boydell & Brewer Inc.
668 Mt Hope Avenue, Rochester, NY 14620-2731, USA
website: www.boydellandbrewer.com

A CIP catalogue record for this book is available from the British Library

The publisher has no responsibility for the continued existence or accuracy of URLs for external or third-party internet websites referred to in this book, and does not guarantee that any content on such websites is, or will remain, accurate or appropriate

CONTENTS

List of illustrations		vi
Acknowledgements		ix
List of abbreviations		x
	Introduction	1
1.	The Elizabethan maritime economy	4
2.	Commodities, markets and trade routes	18
3.	The dynamics of the coastal trade	56
4.	Business networks, seafaring communities and commercial models	79
5.	The socio-economic position of coastal traders	136
6.	Conclusions	196
Appendix A: Port books entered into the database		205
Appendix B: Commodities traded between ports		208
Appendix C: Wealth of merchants and mariners in Bristol, Southampton and Hull		214
Appendix D: Indicative voyages showing difference in value between Hull's Newcastle trade and Hull's London trade		225
Bibliography		227
Index		243

ILLUSTRATIONS

Figures

2.1.	Number of voyages between Hull and King's Lynn	29
2.2.	Origin ports of ships trading between Southampton and the Channel Islands	43
2.3.	Residences of merchants trading between Southampton and the Channel Islands	43
2.4.	Shipments of frieze cloth into Bristol across the five periods	46
4.1.	A network of merchants and mariners who traded through Southampton in 1575	87
4.2.	A network of merchants and mariners who traded through Southampton in 1577	88
4.3.	A network of merchants and mariners who traded through Southampton in 1579	88
4.4.	Levels of trade and cross-country integration in Southampton	100
4.5.	Number of voyages undertaken between Southampton and Sussex by period	102
4.6.	Percentage of Southampton voyages that went to/from Sussex	102
4.7.	Networks of Gloucestershire and Worcestershire trowmen and maltmakers operating in the port of Bristol in 1569	105
4.8.	Networks of trowmen trading through Bristol in 1576	108
4.9.	Coastal networks of the Swanley family in 1572	111
4.10.	Levels of trade and cross-country integration in Bristol	118
4.11.	Shipmaster-centric and large London networks of Hull (shipmasters in black, merchants in white)	120–22

Maps

5.1a–b.	Ward residences of merchants and shipmasters living in Southampton	180–81
5.2.	Ward residences of merchants and shipmasters living in Bristol	183
5.3.	Ward residences of coastal traders living in Bristol, organised by occupation	187

Table

2.1.	Commodities traded between Southampton, Bristol and the South West	34

ACKNOWLEDGEMENTS

There are a great many people to whom I owe a debt of gratitude, but foremost thanks must go to Professor Craig Lambert, without whom this research would rest on a fraction of the data and corresponding analysis and whose support made the creation of this manuscript possible.

Thanks are also due to: Dr Gary Baker for his role in photographing the E190 documents that are utilised in this research; Professor Cheryl Fury for her ongoing support and guidance; and those involved in the Laurence Arthur Burgess scholarship and the Society of Nautical Research.

I would also like to thank Drs Evan Jones and Richard Stone for first introducing me to Tudor maritime history and for teaching me to transcribe, and Dr David Harry for his words of wisdom as well as his words of warning. I would be remiss not to also mention Mr Michael Tumber, whose passion for the subject first sparked in me a desire to pursue historical studies.

In my personal life, thanks must go to my wonderful husband for his tireless support, his eagerness to understand, and his devotion to my well-being; as well as to my son, Cameron, whose recent arrival spurred me on to finish the manuscript.

Finally, I dedicate this book to my parents, who have not only supported me unwaveringly, but who gave my sister and me our passion for knowledge, our drive for self-betterment, and an appreciation for the satisfaction that comes from hard work.

ABBREVIATIONS

BRO	Bristol Record Office
GIS	Geographic Information System
HHC	Hull History Centre
HNR	Historical Network Research
MP	Member of Parliament
SNA	Social Network Analysis
TNA	The National Archives

Introduction

The research upon which this volume rests primarily focuses on data extracted from the national customs records collected after 1564 (known as the port books and indexed under TNA series E190). 1564 is an important year in the history of the customs system, since it was the turning point at which the crown elected to seriously address the smuggling problem that had been wreaking havoc on maritime customs for centuries. In that year, the crown issued a wide-reaching Exchequer Order which not only set specific rules on the lading and unlading of goods, but also expanded the system of 'Legal Quays' that had been introduced in London in 1559. After 1564, the Legal Quay system was applied to every port in the kingdom, meaning that each region was allocated a head port, which was to be staffed with a customer, controller, and searcher in order to cross-check record keeping. The Order also forced customs officials to record all trade that passed through their ports in blank books issued directly by the Exchequer. This meant that, for the first time, the system was expanded to include goods that were exempt from tax, most notably goods that were carried coastwise. In short, the port books were generally more thorough, more consistent in their format, and more reliable than the customs information previously recorded in the 'particular accounts'.[1]

That being said, while the new regulations of 1564 undoubtedly improved the system, there was still space for fraudulent record keeping and, if so inclined, customs officials could extensively manipulate the records. This typically meant recording falsified volumes of goods in order to reduce duties payable, or, in the case of the coastal accounts (where no duty was payable), falsifying coastal cockets for the purposes of evading tax on overseas imports and exports.[2] Nonetheless, details of the ships that docked, the shipmasters

---

[1] Alan Bryson, 'The Legal Quays: Sir William Paulet, First Marquis of Winchester', Tudor Ports of London Conference (2008), 6; B. Y., *A Sure Guide to Merchants, Custom-House Officers, &C., or the Modern Practice of the Court of Exchequer; in Prosecutions Relating to His Majesty's Revenue of the Customs* (London: In the Savoy, Printed by E. and R. Nutt, and R. Gosling for H. Lintot, 1730), p. 6; Donald Woodward, 'Short Guide to Records: 22. Port Books', *History*, 55 (1970), 207–10.

[2] A coastal cocket was a dated receipt issued at the port from which the ship embarked. This was handed to the customs officials at the receiving port as confirmation that the ship had (as claimed) travelled only by coast and was not entering

that commanded them, and the merchants carrying cargo on board were both harder to falsify and less useful to manipulate than volumes and types of goods, which are of limited interest to this study. Likewise, the falsification of coastal cockets was particularly challenging, especially on routes where a bond was required, and, at least in Bristol, this does not appear to have been the typical means through which early modern merchants undertook illicit trade (although it may have been more common in ports very close to foreign lands, such as Southampton).[3] In addition, Evan Jones has argued that particularly short journeys were not always recorded by customs officials in the coastal port books since they were deemed irrelevant to the integrity of the collection of customs.[4] However, in many cases, such routes were a vital part of the commercial landscape of the region and are well documented in other sources and in the historiography, such as in the case of trade between Hull and York. For the purposes of this volume, data from the port books was transcribed into a purpose-built relational database, which now contains details of 4,135 voyages, 1,479 unique ships, 1,905 unique merchants and 1,430 unique shipmasters, and was cross-referenced with other sources of an economic, social and political nature. Details of the port books entered into the database are displayed in Appendix A.[5]

In particular, this volume also relies heavily on data extracted from the lay subsidy returns. Cross-referencing the port book data with lay subsidy returns has proven extremely fruitful, and the wealth and inner-town residences of over 135 merchants and shipmasters have been ascertained. However, wealth assessments must be approached with caution. In particular, since the documents that survive are the final composite records written by commissioners from reports received from local appointees, they do not contain details of how personal valuations were made. There were a number of regulations in place to ensure assessment was fair, but these were very much open to manipulation. For merchants and traders whose goods were fluid, their assessment at a particular time might not have been representative of their general level of wealth. Indeed, they may have made an effort to sell goods before an

---

the port from overseas (meaning that no duty was payable); the cocket would then be signed by the officials at the receiving port as confirmation of the completed journey. In some cases, the merchant would also be required to lodge a bond at the port from which it embarked, which would be cancelled once the completed signed cocket was presented. Duncan Taylor, 'The Maritime Trade of the Smaller Bristol Channel Ports in the Sixteenth Century' (doctoral thesis, University of Bristol, 2009), p. 12.

[3] Evan T. Jones, *Inside the Illicit Economy: Reconstructing the Smugglers' Trade of Sixteenth Century* (Farnham: Ashgate, 2012), pp. 39–40, 48–49, 114–25.

[4] Ibid., pp. 19–37, 39–40; George D. Ramsay, 'The Smugglers' Trade: A Neglected Aspect of English Commercial Development', *Transactions of the Royal Historical Society*, 2 (1952), 138–51.

[5] TNA E190/1128/12, 13, 14, E190/1129/1, 18, 20, 22, E190/1130/2, E190/814/5, 6, 7, 11, 12, E190/815/1, 2, 8, E190/305/1, 11, 12, E190/306/1, 4, 16, 17, E190/307/2, 3, 9, 16.

assessment in order to reduce the tax payable.[6] Likewise, Richard Hoyle has argued that the records of the 1560s and 1570s were often compiled on the basis of how wealthy the collectors perceived individuals to be, rather than on the basis of any actual calculation.[7] Nonetheless, since the same criteria for wealth were applied in each local assessment, any inaccuracies should at least have been consistent within the specific return, and so make it possible to compare individuals within each town. By looking at individuals on a case-by-case basis and cross-referencing multiple sources, it is possible to gain an overall idea of wealth and societal status, even if individual assessments may not have been accurate to the last shilling. Such additional sources include Books of Remembrance, Court Leet Books, Brokage Books, probate inventories and wills, Admiralty Court Books, records of litigation and disputes, records of merchant societies, Weigh House accounts, Bench Books, Burgess Registers, and various other local civic sources.

It is important to note that the combining of such a range of documentary evidence can raise issues regarding the language used to describe and explain the early modern maritime world. Indeed, as we shall see, strict definitions of terms like 'merchant', 'shipmaster' and 'ship' can be illusive, particularly across records that span different bureaucratic procedures and geographic regions. As such, it is important to note that reference in this volume to ships, shipmasters and merchants almost always refers to the three principal recurring data points present in each port book record. Those represent (1) a vessel, (2) an operator and (3) an individual to whom the goods on the vessel belonged. While the 'ships' listed here may, in some cases, be no more than a trow or a barge, and the 'shipmasters' and 'merchants' may not fit into the traditional image of an early modern merchant or seafarer, these terms are used for simplicity and consistency throughout the text. Where appropriate, instances in which traders were characterised as mariners or merchants by a civic authority are delineated by use of the titles 'occupational mariner' and 'occupational merchant'.

Through detailed analysis of this extensive body of data, this volume examines an often-forgotten but vital element of the Elizabethan maritime economy. We will explore the dynamics of domestic exchange in terms of the trade routes followed, the vessels utilised, and the commodities transported, we will delve into the business networks and commercial models exploited by coastal traders, and we will discover the economic and social positions that individual coastal traders could achieve through their engagement in domestic enterprise. Although each of the case study ports had significant regional differences, common threads ran through all three regions, and these may be considered indicative of broader trends, revealing much about the wider nature of maritime England during the Elizabethan period.

---

[6] Richard Hoyle, *Tudor Taxation Records: A Guide for Users* (London: PRO Publications, 1994), pp. 2–3.

[7] Ibid., pp. 15–16.

1

The Elizabethan maritime economy

Although the specific stimuli for and precise nature of economic growth during this period has been a topic of much debate, it is difficult to deny the importance of the maritime industry to England's (and later Britain's) historic commercial successes.[1] Indeed, although there were clearly other factors at play which set England apart from, say, maritime Holland, it was, at least in part, through its ability to trade successfully across Europe and, later, into territories in North Africa, Russia, and across the Atlantic that the kingdom was able to grow as an economic power and, ultimately, build a global empire.[2] Regardless of the other perspectives one may take, it cannot be considered an exaggeration to state that the maritime activities of Elizabethan seafarers have, to some extent, impacted global history to the present.

Indeed, when Elizabeth I took the throne in 1558, she took on a royal court dominated by ambitious seafaring men on the precipice of global maritime domination. Increasing engagement in the Atlantic economy contributed to an ongoing struggle for power between major European kingdoms, and many influential English merchants and mariners sought to benefit. This wrangling for domination on both the European stage and within the royal court resulted in the forging of new trade routes in all directions. Trade routes were either sought or established into Russia, Guinea, China, and North Africa, and circumnavigation became a key achievement pursued by ambitious seafarers like Francis Drake.

---

[1] Though somewhat beyond the scope of this volume, it is worth noting that this debate has been raging since at least the 1860s, with a number of key scholarly threads being traceable back to Deane and Cole's 1967 text, *British Economic Growth, 1688–1959: Trends and Structure* (Cambridge: Cambridge University Press, 1967). More recent work has sought to both expand on and rebut claims put forward by Deane and Cole, perhaps most notably in Patrick O'Brien, 'Exports and the Growth of the British Economy, 1688–1802', in *Slavery and the Rise of the Atlantic System*, ed. by Barbara Solow (Cambridge: Cambridge University Press, 1991); and Stephen Broadberry et al., *British Economic Growth 1270–1870* (Cambridge: Cambridge University Press, 2015).

[2] Stanley Engerman and Patrick O'Brien, 'The Industrial Revolution in Global Perspective', in *The Cambridge Economic History of Modern Britain*, ed. by Roderick Floud et al. (Cambridge: Cambridge University Press, 2004).

In the process of reaching for ever-more bold forms of global expansion, merchants, seafarers and genteel investors formed powerful companies and sought security in numbers, building great fleets comprising great ships. Such men came together in major commercial hubs, in London and Seville, forging valuable connections and expanding their global networks. They sought out partners for their expensive and risky journeys to unknown lands, and rubbed elbows with the rich and famous, hoping for investment in potentially perilous journeys with promise of unimaginable riches.[3] Such activity was not without success and English commercial interests were inflated rapidly in Europe, the Americas, and beyond. By 1570, just ten years after the port books were first introduced, vessels were travelling somewhat regularly between England and the Barbary Coast, Tangier, Newfoundland and the Levant, in addition to the more traditional trading regions such as France, Spain, Iberia, Portugal, the Low Countries, Poland, Ireland and Denmark.[4]

Nonetheless, the policies of English kings and queens towards their merchant communities were highly inconsistent. Monarchies were easily distracted from the matter of commercial enterprise, and they often preferred to concentrate their efforts (and their coffers) on shows of military strength and on political manoeuvring within the European landscape, sometimes to the detriment of the kingdom's economic position.[5] The presence of men like Lord Burghley, Francis Walsingham, John Hawkins and Francis Drake at the court of Elizabeth I undoubtedly led to important changes in the later Tudor years, including the implementation of a new customs system in 1564, and Elizabeth no doubt invested in her fair share of explorative commercial voyages, yet even she was willing to embark on commercially damaging wars to ensure political power on the European stage. Thus, despite general efforts from the Elizabethan court to improve relations with the mercantile elite, the situation in Europe had a constantly disruptive effect on English trading capabilities.

In addition to Elizabeth's turbulent relationships with France and Scotland, which resulted in treaties being drawn up and discarded on an almost-annual basis, the queen had a tendency to interfere in religious matters on the continent and held a deep fear of a Catholic invasion, bringing confusion and inconsistency to the maritime economy, and resulting in a near-constant threat of open war. Between repeated debasements of coinage across Europe, embargoes coming and going as frequently as parliamentary demands, the continual fluctuation of rates of exchange, and frequent outbreaks of plague and disease, traders across Europe had a difficult time ensuring the safety of

---

[3] Alison Games, *The Web of Empire: English Cosmopolitans in an Age of Expansion, 1560–1660* (Oxford: Oxford University Press, 2008), pp. 81–115.

[4] Craig Lambert and Gary Baker, 'The Medieval and Tudor Ships Project' (2017), www.medievalandtudorships.org (accessed 15 September 2019).

[5] David Loades, *England's Maritime Empire: Seapower, Commerce, and Policy, 1490–1690* (Harlow: Pearson Education, 2000), p. 13.

their businesses during the Elizabethan years.[6] At a time when individuals could be bankrupted over a single voyage, the trading community had to be a resilient group. They were willing to risk collateral in the hope of reaping greater profits, they were enterprising in their ventures and were often prepared to turn a blind eye to the political and religious affiliations of their trading partners to ensure the success of their commercial activity.[7]

Importantly, the disruption and alteration of European trading patterns impacted coastal trading, particularly in areas that were highly dependent on overseas import and export, and the appearance of a large overseas vessel in a port had a knock-on effect on domestic exchange. In particular, in southern ports that were reliant on the export of wool and cloth, interruption of the Antwerp mart and commencement of the Anglo-Spanish war forced changes to the trajectory of trade routes and altered types, quantities and values of cargo available for domestic exchange. However, as we shall see throughout this volume, coastal commercial activity was highly adaptive, and much was undertaken by dedicated coastal traders who were open to occupying various domestic routes, carrying a range of commodities, and forming business partnerships with diverse individuals. Many coastal traders maintained their role as key distributors of domestic goods but shifted their priorities to suit the requirements of the specific time or place.

Moreover, owing to the low threshold for participation (in terms of both skill and wealth required), the loss of an individual (for example, to the plague) rarely had a significant impact on the broader landscape of domestic exchange, since there was a large body of highly flexible traders available to react to demand. Nonetheless, while the risks (and indeed the rewards) associated with domestic commercial activity may have been less extensive than those associated with overseas trade, the role of coastal commerce within the wider economic landscape was hugely important. Without domestic shipping, the internal distribution of commodities would have been impossible. At a time

---

[6] Patrick O'Brien and others, *Urban Achievement in Early Modern Europe: Golden Ages in Antwerp, Amsterdam and London* (Cambridge: Cambridge University Press, 2001), pp. 15–17; Loades, *England's Maritime Empire*, pp. 51–55, 70–73, 79–102; David Loades, *The Mid-Tudor Crisis, 1545–1565* (Basingstoke: Macmillan, 1992), pp. 42–72.

[7] Pauline Croft, 'Trading with the Enemy 1585–1604', *The Historical Journal*, 32 (2009), 300–02; Martha C. Howell, *Commerce before Capitalism in Europe, 1300–1600* (Cambridge: Cambridge University Press, 2010), pp. 17–25; Vincent Patarino, 'The Religious Shipboard Culture of Sixteenth and Seventeenth-Century English Sailors', in *The Social History of English Seamen, 1485–1649*, ed. by Cheryl A. Fury (Woodbridge: Boydell Press, 2012), pp. 141–92 (pp. 164–70); Richard G. Stone, 'The Overseas Trade of Bristol in the Seventeenth Century' (doctoral thesis, University of Bristol, 2012), pp. 80–101.

when road-travel was high-risk, coastal enterprise enabled the kingdom to function, and this was particularly true in regions that depended heavily on bulky cargoes such as coal and salt, for which overland trade was especially costly and slow moving, as was the case in Bristol, Southampton and Hull.[8]

Given the significance of the Elizabethan maritime industry to our wider understanding of global social, political and economic events, historians have long sought to understand how merchant and maritime communities operated in the years preceding British imperial rule. Indeed, we have gained an excellent overview of England's overseas trade links and the 'gentrification' of the merchant class during the medieval and early modern periods.[9] Likewise, the allure of exploring the seeds of industrialisation has led numerous noteworthy scholars to explore the world of overland trade, perhaps most notably in the case of Michael Hicks.[10] However, coastal trade is an often-overlooked feature of England's commercial and maritime past. Indeed those few studies that have investigated coastal commerce have focused on commodities and cared little to understand the socio-political or socio-economic position of coastal traders or to establish the means through which they ran their businesses.

In the 1960s and 1970s, T. S. Willan published two analyses of England's internal trade, one offering a broad overview of the methods of domestic trade (including overland, riverine and (to a lesser extent) coastal activity) and one specifically exploring coastal shipping.[11] These works helped us to understand the commodities favoured for domestic transportation within particular regions

---

[8] For details of the costs associated with overland, river, and seaborne travel, see James Masschaele, 'Transport Costs in Medieval England', *The Economic History Review*, 46 (1993), 270–74; Thomas S. Willan, *The English Coasting Trade: 1600–1750* (Manchester: Manchester University Press, 1967), pp. xii–xiii.

[9] For example, see Robert Brenner, *Merchants and Revolution: Commercial Change, Political Conflict, and London's Overseas Traders, 1550–1653* (London: Verso, 2003); Franz J. Fisher, 'Commercial Trends and Policy in Sixteenth-Century England', *The Economic History Review*, 10 (1940); James A. Galloway, *Trade, Urban Hinterlands and Market Integration, c.1300–1600: A Collection of Working Papers Given at a Conference Organised by the Centre for Metropolitan History and Supported by the Economic and Social Research Council, 7 July 1999* (London: Centre for Metropolitan History, Institute of Historical Research, 2000); Jenny Kermode, 'The Merchants of York, Beverley and Hull in the Fourteenth and Fifteenth Centuries' (doctoral thesis, University of Sheffield, 1990); George D. Ramsay, *English Overseas Trade during the Centuries of Emergence: Studies in Some Modern Origins of the English Speaking World* (London: Macmillan, 1957).

[10] Michael Hicks, ed., *Southampton and Its Region – English Inland Trade 1430–1540* (Oxford: Oxford University Press, 2015).

[11] Thomas S. Willan, *The Inland Trade: Studies in English Internal Trade in the Sixteenth and Seventeenth Centuries* (Manchester: Manchester University Press, 1976); Willan, *The English Coasting Trade: 1600–1750*.

and highlighted some specific operational features of coastal trading that existed within particular ports. In addition, some local studies have incidentally included examination of specific coastal merchants, but this has usually focused on individuals engaged in large-scale overseas trade, who were of social, financial and political importance within particular towns, and has been generally confined to those for which a substantial body of maritime literature exists, overlooking some key provincial ports.[12] Moreover, studies that have focused on only elite overseas merchants and mariners have tended to see mariners and seafarers as a markedly separate socio-economic group from merchants and traders, a preconception that this volume will strongly refute. Some research has been undertaken that specifically examines coastal trading in Hull, but this has been largely confined to the fourteenth and fifteenth centuries and studies extending beyond 1500 or starting before 1800 have been sparse.[13] The result of this lacuna has been to create a skewed perception

[12] Of the three case study ports, merchants in Bristol and Southampton have been the focus of the most detailed examination: see, among others, James Brown, 'The Landscape of Drink: Inns, Taverns and Alehouses in Early Modern Southampton' (doctoral thesis, University of Warwick, 2007); Eleanora M. Carus-Wilson, 'The Merchant Adventurers of Bristol in the Fifteenth Century', *Transactions of the Royal Historical Society*, 11 (1928); Eleanora M. Carus-Wilson, 'The Overseas Trade of Bristol', in *Studies in English Trade in the 15th Century*, ed. by Eileen E. Power and Michael M. Postan (London: Routledge, 1933), pp. 183–247; Eleanora M. Carus-Wilson, *Medieval Merchant Venturers: Collected Studies* (London: Methuen, 1954); Susan Flavin and Evan T. Jones, *Bristol's Trade with Ireland and the Continent 1503–1601: The Evidence of the Exchequer Customs Accounts* (Dublin, Ireland: Four Courts Press for the Bristol Record Society, 2009); Evan T. Jones, 'The Bristol Shipping Industry in the Sixteenth Century' (doctoral thesis, University of Edinburgh, 1998); Evan T. Jones, 'Bristol "Particular" Accounts and Port Books of the Sixteenth Century, 1503–1601' (2009), dx.doi.org/10.5255/UKDA-SN-6275-1; Jones, *Inside the Illicit Economy: Reconstructing the Smugglers' Trade of Sixteenth Century*; David Frank Lamb, 'The Seaborne Trade of Southampton in the Seventeenth Century' (doctoral thesis, University of Southampton, 1971); Allan Merson, 'Elizabethan Southampton', in *Collected Essays on Southampton*, ed. by J. B. Morgan and Philip Peberdy (Southampton: Southampton County Borough Council, 1961), pp. 57–75; Colin Platt, *Medieval Southampton: The Port and Trading Community, A.D. 1000–1600* (London: Routledge, 1973); Alwyn Ruddock, 'Alien Merchants in Southampton in the Later Middle Ages', *The English Historical Review*, 61 (1946); Alwyn Ruddock, 'London Capitalists and the Decline of Southampton in the Early Tudor Period', *The Economic History Review*, 2 (1949); Alwyn Ruddock, *Italian Merchants and Shipping in Southampton, 1270–1600* (Southampton: University College, 1951); L. E. Tavener, 'The Port of Southampton', *Economic Geography*, 26 (1950); Taylor; Edwin Welch, 'The Admiralty Court Book of Southampton, 1566–1585' (Southampton: Southampton Record Series, 1968).

[13] Wendy Childs, *The Trade and Shipping of Hull, 1300–1500* (Yorkshire: East

of the inner workings of the maritime community, a likely underestimation of the scale of England's merchant fleet and little more than estimations of the nature of coastal trading, typically characterising domestic shipping as scattered, disorganised, and low-status.

This volume will seek to challenge that view, arguing that coastal trade was not only an integral part of the kingdom's commercial, social and political success, allowing overseas trade to function by providing an active market for incoming goods and supplying the export trade, but that it was often composed of career coastal workers, who approached their trade with sensible business strategies and an entrepreneurial spirit. Prosopographical research into the lives and careers of merchants beyond the so-called 'mercantile elite' will provide a better understanding of England's commercial history and of the broader socio-economic composition of Elizabethan society. Coastal traders were not just small-scale bargemen on the periphery of the seafaring trades, they were the lifeblood of England's extensive maritime industry.

While the historiography is calling out for a kingdom-wide survey of Elizabethan coastal trading, the scope of such an endeavour would be substantial and is too ambitious for a single volume. Yet, on the other hand, examination of only a single port would be inadequate to identify overarching trends. As such, investigation into three comparable, yet economically, socially and politically distinctive, regions provides a satisfying compromise. Southampton, Bristol and Hull were selected as the case study ports since they offer diversity in their geopolitical, economic, and cultural situations, in addition to offering a consistent run of customs records that record both overseas and coastal trade. That both branches of trade are represented is of importance since the dynamics of coastal trade were often shaped by overseas markets. Between them, these ports offer a balanced geographic spread of known overseas trading networks – western advancement into Iberia and beyond (Bristol), English Channel trade (Southampton), and trade with the Low Countries and Scotland (Hull) – enabling a representative sample to be analysed.

Moreover, these ports were of relatively similar size during the sixteenth century, were each head ports covering a substantial geographic area, and each played an important role in English commercial, political, and social development. Yet, as we shall see below, they were all unique in their specific social, political, and economic make-up, allowing for examination of similar commercial activity within the context of specific regional characteristics. Indeed, individual regions experienced their own successes and failures and were impacted differently by the economy of the realm and by events in Europe

---

Yorkshire Local History Society, 1990); William G. East, 'The Port of Kingston-upon-Hull during the Industrial Revolution', *Economica* (1931); Jenny Kermode, *Medieval Merchants: York, Beverley and Hull in the Later Middle Ages* (Guildford: Cambridge University Press, 2002).

and beyond. As such, before we fully immerse ourselves into the world of the Elizabethan coastal trader, it is important to provide a broad overview of the social and economic history of the case study ports, albeit with the obvious caveat of neglecting domestic exchange.

Southampton

It is well documented that, after the 1530s, Southampton experienced significant commercial and political upheaval. The loss of the Italian merchant community to London (following improvements to the Thames harbour) pulled the wealthiest traders away from the south coast and left the area with a significant commercial deficiency. In the words of Olive Coleman, native shipping in fifteenth-century Southampton was 'a poor second' to the overseas trade plied by Italian merchants, so when that community made tracks to London there was a significant gap to fill.[14] As a result, many early historians argued that sixteenth-century Southampton was in utter destitution, and that argument is supported by the reduction of the town's fee farm in 1552, as well as by comments from the commissioners of a 1565 port survey that noted the port was no longer 'frequentid and hauntid [...] with the repayre of the [...] greate shippes of venice', causing 'great hindrannce and decaye [to] the [...] Towne'.[15]

However, more recent research has revealed that Southampton adapted fairly well to the loss of the Italian merchant community, especially considering the scale of the disaster the town appeared to face. Indeed, as James Brown notes, there were numerous alternative trading options and the local community embraced these to the full.[16] The town continued to rely to some degree on foreign traders, embracing Dutch merchants and the Walloon refugee community, who brought the new draperies to the market. However, local merchants also expanded their trade with France and, as shown by Michael Hicks, carters altered their overland trade to accommodate the lack of exotic Mediterranean products, focusing instead on the transportation of foodstuffs, wine, salt, iron, and tin.[17] Southampton during the second half of

---

[14] Olive Coleman, 'Trade and Prosperity in the Fifteenth Century: Some Aspects of the Trade of Southampton', *The Economic History Review*, 16 (1963), 19.

[15] Ibid., pp. 9–22; Leanna T. Parker, 'Southampton's Sixteenth-Century Illicit Trade: An Examination of the 1565 Port Survey', *International Journal of Maritime History*, 27 (2015), 282; Ruddock, *Italian Merchants and Shipping in Southampton, 1270–1600*, p. 268.

[16] Brown, pp. 12–14.

[17] Michael Hicks, 'The Trading Calendar', in *Southampton and Its Region – English Inland Trade 1430–1540*, ed. by Michael Hicks (Oxford: Oxford University Press, 2015), pp. 35–42 (p. 42).

the sixteenth century was indeed of lower standing than during the century before, but it was not in crisis; trade continued and the town adapted to the shift in its merchant population. Moreover, as we shall see throughout this volume, Southampton's coastal traders continued to develop broad commercial networks and to facilitate a great deal of trade with towns across the kingdom, including as far north as Newcastle and as far west as South Wales.[18]

The unique nature of Southampton's commercial situation created a specific socio-political climate, which also deserves brief mention and is important in understanding the nature of coastal commerce explored below. In particular, Southampton's long history of engagement with foreign traders meant that foreign merchants operated much more freely and cheaply in Southampton than in other port towns.[19] This openness to outsiders waned a little with the influx of Dutch and Walloon communities, who were perceived as a threat by local artisans. However, foreign merchants (as opposed to craftspeople) were generally embraced and continued to occupy a privileged position within the town. Interestingly, this attitude was in stark contrast to the town's relations with other ports in the region who failed to enjoy the same level of community spirit. There existed a tense relationship between Southampton's corporation and the local ports under its jurisdiction, particularly Lymington, that resulted in the out-ports refusing to pay their share of petty custom, and openly unlading goods outside the designated areas.[20] Nonetheless, in spite of the town's unusual socio-political composition, the corporation did benefit from a special relationship with the crown due to its strategically significant position on the Channel coast, and this resulted in Southampton's burgesses being granted an unusually high level of autonomy from royal officials.[21]

Moreover, Southampton's geographic features played a wider role in the formation of its commercial and socio-political character. Its position on the south coast naturally allowed easy access to ports in continental Europe and, as we shall see in Chapter 2, this greatly influenced the commodities available and the flexibility of Southampton traders in engaging in overseas trade. Likewise, its central position between London and the South West contributed to Southampton's far-reaching coastal and inland connections and enabled the town to act as a central meeting point for overseas and domestic commodities, making it vital to the economy of the surrounding area. Southampton Water also benefited from a so-called 'double high-tide'. This rare environmental phenomenon resulted in a longer period of high water, which provided more

---

[18] TNA E190/814/7 fol.4v, E190/814/11 fol.2r, 7r, E190/815/2 fol.2r, E190/815/1 fol.8v, E190/815/8 fol.1v–2r.

[19] Ruddock, 'Alien Merchants in Southampton in the Later Middle Ages', pp. 1–7.

[20] Parker, pp. 275–77.

[21] Michael Hicks, 'Southampton and Its Region – English Inland Trade 1430–1540' (Oxford: Oxford University Press, 2015), p. 11.

time for lading and unlading, and allowed access for particularly large ships. Nonetheless, there were also practical barriers on the part of the customs officials, as described in a survey of the port undertaken in 1565. Indeed, Southampton's port house had a duty to oversee trade spanning fifty-four miles of the south coast of England, plus an additional nine miles along the north coast of the Isle of Wight. This presented a problem for the customs officials who struggled to intervene quickly in any potential illegal activity. In addition, the majority of the coast was sheltered by the dense woodland of the New Forest, providing handy cover for smugglers and a good hiding place for pirates planning an ambush. This landscape, combined with the regional disputes between Southampton and the surrounding area, made for a region open to illicit trading.[22] As explained below, the impact of smuggling on the analysis undertaken in this study is minimal; however, it is important to note that relationships in the local region were often turbulent and these specific regional traits affected the operational nature of trade undertaken through the port.

Bristol

As in Southampton, early historians argued that Bristol suffered significant economic stagnation during the sixteenth century. David Sacks stated that after 1575 there was a 'general decline in the city's commercial well-being', and Jean Vanes referred to the period after 1560 as the 'sad days'.[23] Nonetheless, both scholars acknowledged that there was also a general restructuring of commercial enterprise in Bristol between 1575 and 1630. During that time, links with Ireland and the Iberian Peninsula were strengthened and the trade in wine, luxury goods, heavy industrial wares, and new draperies brought jobs and wealth to the town.[24] Furthermore, recent scholars have challenged Sacks' methods, arguing that Tudor Bristol was in a strong economic position and that local merchants were able to expand on those various trading elements to maintain extensive overseas trade links.[25] Moreover, Bristol's merchants have long been characterised as shrewd investors and enterprising businesspeople,

---

[22] Parker, pp. 272–73.

[23] David Harris Sacks, *The Widening Gate: Bristol and the Atlantic Economy, 1450–1700* (California: University of California Press, 1991), pp. 21–53; Jean Vanes, 'Documents Illustrating the Overseas Trade of Bristol in the Sixteenth Century' (Kendal: Bristol Record Society, 1979), p. 26.

[24] Mary D. Lobel and Eleanora M. Carus-Wilson, 'Bristol', in *Historic Towns: The Atlas of Historic Towns: Volume 2: Bristol: Cambridge: Coventry: Norwich*, ed. by Mary D. Lobel (Yorkshire: Scolar Press, 1969), pp. 1–27 (pp. 14–21); Sacks, pp. 54–84; Vanes, pp. 1–27.

[25] Richard G. Stone, 'The Overseas Trade of Bristol before the Civil War', *International Journal of Maritime History*, 23 (2011), 215–18.

as evidenced by their ability to adapt to changing commercial landscapes and their involvement in voyages of discovery.[26] Tudor Bristol boasted healthy overseas, overland and coastal trade links and contributed significantly to England's maritime successes. Sixteenth-century Bristol saw significant population growth as well as the construction of various costly new buildings, demonstrating that the port was in an era of reasonable economic stability.[27]

In terms of its socio-political character, Bristol was quite unlike Southampton and was home to a powerful class of local merchants. Various scholars have explored Bristol's mercantile elite in depth and have shown that they dominated the highest ranks of society over many centuries, often being extremely wealthy and substantially involved in local politics, traits that Evan Jones argues allowed for a high level of corruption and smuggling.[28] With such local power came a level of detachment from crown policy decisions that challenged the government's ability to enforce regulation. Dana Durkee has argued that the majority of provincial ports 'enjoyed a good measure of political autonomy from the crown' during the Tudor years and this was especially true of Bristol.[29] While Southampton relied heavily on crown help to ensure its survival, Bristol developed a local political and cultural identity that was bolstered by its separation from London and the crown court. This is neatly demonstrated in a 1565 survey of smuggling in Bristol in which the crown-appointed commissioners appear to have deliberately omitted evidence that may have led to the prosecution of any merchant or mariner. As argued by Jones, this was probably due to the social and economic proximity of the town's customs officials to the merchants and seafarers in question.[30] In other words, Bristol's civic elite would prioritise protecting the interests of

---

[26] Kenneth R. Andrews, *Trade, Plunder and Settlement: Maritime Enterprise and the Genesis of the British Empire, 1480–1630* (Cambridge: Cambridge University Press, 1984), pp. 43–63; Eleanora M. Carus-Wilson, 'The Iceland Trade', in *Studies in English Trade in the 15th Century*, ed. by Eileen E. Power and Michael M. Postan (London: Routledge, 1933), pp. 155–82; Carus-Wilson, 'The Overseas Trade of Bristol'.

[27] Lobel and Carus-Wilson, pp. 17–21.

[28] Carus-Wilson, 'The Merchant Adventurers of Bristol in the Fifteenth Century', pp. 68–82; Flavin and Jones, *Bristol's Trade with Ireland and the Continent 1503–1601: The Evidence of the Exchequer Customs Accounts*, pp. xiii–xiv; Jones, *Inside the Illicit Economy: Reconstructing the Smugglers' Trade of Sixteenth Century*, pp. 138–83.

[29] Dana Durkee, 'A *Cursus* for Craftsmen? Career Cycles of the Worsted Weavers of Late-Medieval Norwich', in *Cities and Solidarities: Urban Communities in Pre-Modern Europe*, ed. by Justin Colson and Arie van Steensel (Oxon: Routledge, 2017), pp. 151–69 (p. 151). See also James Matthew Lee, 'Political Communication in Early Tudor England: The Bristol Elite, the Urban Community and the Crown, c.1471–c.1553' (doctoral thesis, University of the West of England, Bristol, 2006), pp. 17–58.

[30] Jones, *Inside the Illicit Economy: Reconstructing the Smugglers' Trade of Sixteenth Century*, pp. 138–46.

local merchants over the interests of the crown. We shall see throughout this volume that these socio-political characteristics had a direct and significant impact on the nature of Bristol's coastal commercial activity.

As was the case in Southampton, many of these features can be credited in part to the geographic landscape in which Bristol existed. Its successes in overland, coastal, and overseas trade were bolstered by its rich hinterland, which allowed for the production of wool, cloth, and industrial/agricultural goods. Moreover, Bristol's position within an estuary ensured the town became a central hub for trade networks that linked the River Severn ports to the wider world, including to Ireland, Iceland, the Iberian Peninsula and Gascony.[31] However, the geographic landscape also helped to facilitate illicit trading and the political independence of the port was assisted to some degree by its physical distance from the capital. Moreover, Bristol customs officials too had a significant and complex area to cover, the boundaries of which changed frequently and were often confused, making it difficult to create an established power structure.[32] Finally, like Southampton, Bristol also benefited from a rare tidal phenomenon, in this case having the second largest tidal range in the world, which allowed shipmasters to navigate large vessels into small creeks and rivers during high tide, creating a greater opportunity for trade. However, the exceptionally high tide also meant that individuals engaging in illicit activity could very quickly make an escape from any approaching customs officials. Those who knew the rivers well, who understood the tidal patterns, and had knowledge of the local area could evacuate an illicit drop-off with speed and precision.[33]

Hull

Unlike the other ports, there is no single comprehensive study of Hull that covers the period between 1500 and 1800. However, several works have provided a good base of knowledge for the earlier period and others have covered the Tudor years in limited depth. During the early fourteenth century, the town benefited from a healthy wool and cloth industry. However, in the late fourteenth and early fifteenth centuries, Hull, like much of England, saw steep economic decline. Struggles with eastern markets and the rapid expansion of London had a catastrophic impact on Hull that did not subside until the

---

[31] Carus-Wilson, 'The Overseas Trade of Bristol', pp. 183–247; Jones, 'The Bristol Shipping Industry in the Sixteenth Century', p. 34; Lobel and Carus-Wilson, pp. 16, 21.

[32] As evidenced by the town's frequent disputes with the customs officials of Gloucester: see Taylor, pp. 85–89, 104–12.

[33] Jones, *Inside the Illicit Economy: Reconstructing the Smugglers' Trade of Sixteenth Century*, pp. 63–85.

mid-sixteenth century.[34] Nonetheless, as noted by Wendy Childs, the traders and seafarers who remained in Hull during the years of recession maintained enough wealth and skill that when new opportunities presented themselves in the 1550s, they were able to take full advantage.[35] Largely, this meant exploiting the growing Baltic and eastern trade routes and focusing on the trade in raw materials.[36] The importance of Baltic trade to east coast towns like Hull cannot be overstated and Peter Nash has succinctly summarised the impressive struggle won by the east coast traders against their German counterparts for dominance over the Baltic trade routes.[37] Moreover, Jenny Kermode and Wendy Childs have alluded to the possibility that Hull had an extensive and profitable coastal trading system during the period before 1565, but that is very difficult to verify for the pre-port book era.[38] Tudor Hull was a far cry from the destitute town of the fifteenth century, and those who have briefly covered the Tudor years have characterised it as a period of remarkable recovery.[39] William East has regarded this period as an era of transition from a town fully dependent on its agricultural hinterland to a highly industrialised region, depending on trade in raw materials and essential goods, namely coal and fish.[40]

The socio-political landscape of Hull has likewise only been explored in depth for the years before 1500 and after 1800. Nevertheless, these studies highlight a number of features present in Hull's mercantile community that warrant brief examination. In the decades after Hull gained its farm in 1331, local merchants dominated town politics and while there was a slight reduction in merchant involvement in the second half of the sixteenth century, the mercantile elite in Hull remained highly influential throughout the early modern

---

[34] Alan Dyer, *Decline and Growth in English Towns 1400–1640* (Cambridge: Cambridge University Press, 1995), pp. 18–21; Kermode, 'The Merchants of York, Beverley and Hull in the Fourteenth and Fifteenth Centuries', pp. 88–90.

[35] Childs, p. 41.

[36] Alan Dyer, p. 47; Ramsay, *English Overseas Trade during the Centuries of Emergence: Studies in Some Modern Origins of the English Speaking World*, pp. 96–122.

[37] Peter Nash, 'The Maritime Shipping Trade of Scarborough, 1550 to 1750', *Northern History*, 49 (2012), 213–16.

[38] Childs, p. 6; Kermode, 'The Merchants of York, Beverley and Hull in the Fourteenth and Fifteenth Centuries', pp. 55, 136, 82–84.

[39] Childs, p. 41; Alan Dyer, pp. 46–48; Kermode, 'The Merchants of York, Beverley and Hull in the Fourteenth and Fifteenth Centuries', p. 66; Ramsay, *English Overseas Trade during the Centuries of Emergence: Studies in Some Modern Origins of the English Speaking World*, pp. 101–06.

[40] East, p. 191.

period.[41] While the existence of a wealthy and politically active mercantile class was undoubtedly good for the local economy, their strong position created tension with other regional mercantile groups. As Hull controlled access to the inland Yorkshire region, local merchants often felt cheated of trade by Hull and demanded tax exemptions and reductions. Interestingly, this included a particularly bitter dispute with Southampton merchants in the fifteenth century, who successfully fought for trading privileges in the region.[42] Nonetheless, as we shall see throughout this volume, Hull merchants were able to carve out an important position in London trade and many gained substantial wealth and socio-political influence.

Finally, just as in Bristol and Southampton, many of these traits can be attributed to the geography of the region. Hull's position at the mouth of the Humber established it as a key place of trading early on and it had long surpassed its neighbours as a centre for overseas commerce.[43] Likewise, Hull benefited from an extensive hinterland and inland river network, which both provided and absorbed a broad range of commodities.[44] While Hull's harbour itself was of poor quality, ships landing at Hull traditionally laid anchor some distance downstream on the Humber, at a point known as the Old Harbour. The Old Harbour benefited from an exceptionally deep approach, which changed little over the period and allowed large ships easy access, providing a suitable landing point for the sizeable vessels that were needed to accommodate the region's extensive trade in industrial goods and raw materials.[45] So important was this tradition to Hull's trade that the region was exempted from allocating a Legal Quay, which, incidentally, also created an environment open to smuggling.[46] These geographic characteristics allowed ships easy access to open seas but also provided physical protection from erosion, and forced merchants from neighbouring towns to pass through Hull in order to trade, enabling the port to act as a gateway to the North East.[47]

---

[41] Kermode, 'The Merchants of York, Beverley and Hull in the Fourteenth and Fifteenth Centuries', p. 58.

[42] Ibid., pp. 62–63.

[43] Childs, p. 5; Kermode, 'The Merchants of York, Beverley and Hull in the Fourteenth and Fifteenth Centuries', pp. 88–151.

[44] Kermode, 'The Merchants of York, Beverley and Hull in the Fourteenth and Fifteenth Centuries', pp. 53–57.

[45] East, p. 190.

[46] The Legal Quays were first established in London in 1559 under a ruling that made it illegal to land or unload goods outside the allocated quays, which were under the direct supervision of a number of customs officials. This system was expanded in 1565 when head ports were allocated around the entire coast, as discussed in more detail below. See Bryson, pp. 6–11; East, pp. 191–92.

[47] Childs, p. 5.

Nonetheless, while all three ports experienced very different economic fluctuations, influenced by their differing political, social and geographic characteristics, we shall see throughout the following chapters that common themes ran through their coastal economies. Regional differences undoubtedly shone through, and those will become evident in the explorations that follow, but many features of coastal exchange were universal, and many of the same threads run through the customs data for each port. As with all historical study, there is a fine line between recognising situational and personal differences and revealing those common themes that bind us. This volume will attempt to toe that line, revealing the characteristics that made each of these ports unique and that influenced the lives and careers of the individuals who lived in them, and at the same time establishing the themes that ran through coastal exchange in all three towns, allowing us to view domestic trade with a wider lens and understand its broader implications for our understanding of the Elizabethan world.

2

Commodities, markets and trade routes

Before moving on to examine the trade routes and commodities of domestic exchange in detail, it is important to establish what exactly fits into the definition of 'coastal trade' utilised here, since the inclusion or exclusion of certain forms of trade within this definition has a significant impact on findings. Whether or not to include riverine trade and fishing trade has a universal impact on data outputs, and each region also had specific commercial and political features that impacted individual ports differently. We must decide, for example, whether Welsh trade is included in analysis of Bristol's coastal trade or whether Channel Island trade is included in analysis of Southampton's coastal exchange. Indeed, trade with both the Welsh ports and the Channel Islands fits into a space between domestic and foreign commercial activity, and whether it was deemed internal or external trade by officials changed over time, as we shall see below.

In most cases, the research underpinning this book has been guided by the decisions made by contemporary customs officials. Thus, this volume covers all trade that was recorded in the coastal customs records, but none that was included in overseas port books. This has resulted in some surprising research strands. For example, in Southampton, customs officials recorded all trade with the Channel Islands that included taxable goods in the overseas port books, but recorded any shipments of goods that were tax exempt (owing to the specific relationship between England and the Islands) in the coastal books. This type of very specific, centrally determined decision making regarding record keeping is relatively easy to account for, since it was predefined and consistent in its application. However, some more implicit forms of inconsistent record collection are more difficult to adjust for. For example, while customs officials were officially required to record all trade that passed through every port, there was some inconsistency in the thoroughness applied by specific officials.

In particular, inclusion of very small-scale trade that was tax exempt appears to have been considered a fruitless exercise by some. In Hull, this resulted in shipments made further inland on the River Humber being excluded from record keeping, while in Bristol and Southampton inland shipments were dutifully recorded (as explained in more detail below). That being said, outside of the trade inland from Hull, customs officials seem to have generally been very thorough in their record keeping, including vessels as small as just two tons, carrying small volumes of goods that were both tax exempt and of particularly low value.[1] Where riverine trade of this type, or indeed fishing trade, was recorded it has been included in the analysis that follows. For the most part, trade that was not recorded in the coastal customs records has been excluded, except in particular cases where evidence of a large body of trade exists in other sources, such as Hull's Humber trade.

The big picture

As a result of the extensive record keeping of early modern customs officials, a large volume of coastal data is available and some 4,000 ship-voyages have been obtained for this volume alone. Yet, in spite of the plentiful records that survive, coastal trading has been largely overlooked in the historiography. As noted above, while many commercial features of the case study ports have been established by previous scholars, those pertaining to coastal activity have been limited. In particular, several authors have given broad overviews of the commodities traded coastwise through Southampton and Bristol during the medieval and early modern periods, and various historians have observed much about the nature of coastal commerce in Hull for the earlier centuries. However, examination of Hull's trade after 1500 has been generally neglected, and studies into coastal commerce in Bristol and Southampton have remained limited.[2] More broadly, examination of coastal commercial activity has been overlooked in favour of investigation into overseas trade.[3] In this chapter, we will lay the groundwork for more detailed examination of the individuals

---

[1] For example, TNA E190/305/1 fol.3r, E190/307/9 fol.2v, E190/814/12 fol.4v, E190/815/1 fol.2r, E190/815/8 fol.2r, E190/1128/12 fol.7v, E190/1129/18 fol.4v.

[2] For example, see: Childs; Brown; Coleman; Ralph Davis, *The Trade and Shipping of Hull, 1500–1700* (Yorkshire: East Yorkshire Local History Society, 1964); Flavin and Jones, *Bristol's Trade with Ireland and the Continent 1503–1601: The Evidence of the Exchequer Customs Accounts*; Hicks; Jones, 'The Bristol Shipping Industry in the Sixteenth Century'; Jones, *Inside the Illicit Economy: Reconstructing the Smugglers' Trade of Sixteenth Century*; Kermode, *Medieval Merchants: York, Beverley and Hull in the Later Middle Ages*; Lobel and Carus-Wilson; Taylor; Ruddock, 'London Capitalists and the Decline of Southampton in the Early Tudor Period'; Alwyn Ruddock, 'Merchants and Shipping in Medieval Southampton', in *Collected Essays on Southampton*, ed. by J. B. Morgan and Philip Peberdy (Southampton: Southampton County Borough Council, 1961); Ruddock, *Italian Merchants and Shipping in Southampton, 1270–1600*; Sacks.

[3] T. S. Willan is the clear exception, whose work has provided a broad overview of the coasting trade throughout the kingdom over the sixteenth and seventeenth centuries, including limited examination of the three ports of interest in this study: see Willan, *The English Coasting Trade: 1600–1750*; Willan, *The Inland Trade: Studies in English Internal Trade in the Sixteenth and Seventeenth Centuries*.

engaged in coastal trading. We will explore the coastal trade routes that extended from the three case study ports, establishing the breadth of their domestic networks of exchange, pinpointing key markets, and identifying the commodities that flowed through them.

At first glance, the data analysed appears to support the existing historiographical narrative that, apart from a few isolated exceptions, the ports of Bristol, Southampton and Hull typically interacted with the regions that were most easily reachable by water. Southampton traded mostly with London and the south coast, Bristol's traders focused primarily on Gloucestershire and South Wales, and Hull principally engaged in trade with Newcastle and London. However, some surprising trends also emerge when this data is examined in more detail and each port benefited not only from domestic markets that appear to have been somewhat universal, but also some specialist markets, the characteristics of which resulted from the social, geographic and political particulars of the region.

For example, at macro level, it is evident that the ports with which Hull had a coastal connection were substantially less diverse than in Bristol or Southampton. While Bristol had coastal links to seventy-seven separate domestic locations, and Southampton to sixty-nine, Hull traded coastwise with only forty-one separate ports. Moreover, two of those ports, Newcastle and London, accounted for approximately 80% of Hull's coastal voyages, whereas in Bristol and Southampton the top two trading locations accounted for only 40–50% of the total shipments.[4] In Southampton, trade with Dorset and Hampshire was consistently high owing to the close proximity of those regions and the constant need for foodstuffs, raw materials and finished goods in local ports. However, the town's trade links spread much further than just the immediate surrounding area and a steady stream of traffic flowed into the broader region. Most notably, into Sussex and the Channel Islands, which also accounted for an especially large proportion of Southampton's coastwise commerce. Much the same can be said of Bristol, where the ports of the River Severn and South Wales were the most consistently visited trading places, again owing to the demand for essential products, and yet the town's regular coastal routes extended much further afield. In particular, coastal shipments frequently flowed between Bristol and the ports of Cornwall, Devon, and more occasionally as far as northern Wales and northern England.

Interestingly, while Newcastle and London consistently served as Hull's largest domestic trading partners, the importance of the less prevalent ports shifted over time, and to a much greater extent than the ports with which Bristol or Southampton traded. This was most notable in the case of the East

---

[4] TNA E190/305/1, E190/305/11, E190/305/12, E190/306/1, E190/306/4, E190/306/16, E190/306/17, E190/307/2, E190/307/3, E190/307/9, E190/307/16.

Anglian ports, and especially King's Lynn and Great Yarmouth, whose role in Hull's coastwise commercial activity fluctuated substantially across the period, as we shall see below. This suggests that Bristol and Southampton were both major centres for the collection and redistribution of products from England, Wales, and overseas, whereas Hull had a more limited role in the local region, primarily travelling to large commercial centres in order to supply its own hinterland. While such trade may not have been as lucrative as overseas voyages, it nonetheless brought cash to the corporation in the form of local port customs and charges paid for use of infrastructure such as wharfs and cranes, thus improving the local economy by providing income and secondary jobs. Moreover, coastal trade was primarily in the hands of English traders and was largely free from foreign competition, meaning that, oftentimes, locals were able to reap the financial rewards. In this chapter, we will establish the commercial and economic character of coastal activity in England (and to a lesser extent Wales) during this period, laying a vital backdrop for a broader understanding of the individual merchants and mariners that plied that trade.

Common commodities and their markets

There were common threads that ran through the coastal commercial activity undertaken in each port and this applied not just to the practical dynamics of the trade, but also to the markets each port sought access to and the commodities they exchanged. In the first part of this chapter, we will cover each of those common threads in turn, before moving on to examine particular trends that were specific to each region. A detailed list of the commodities transported between each port/region is provided in Appendix B for reference.

Local distribution of foodstuffs and essential goods

In the Elizabethan period, as now, any populated centre required a constant stream of essential goods, such as foodstuffs, metal products, fuel, and goods for use in local industries. The larger the centre, the more essential goods were required, and when that centre reached a certain size and a certain level of commercial autonomy, a proportion of those goods flowed into the port directly from overseas, as was the case in Bristol, Southampton and Hull. There were exceptions, and some specific goods almost universally travelled via London, and more so in Hull than elsewhere, but each port received a large proportion of its commodities directly from foreign ports. As a result, each of the ports under investigation here supplied their local area with a steady stream of essential goods. Large vessels incoming from overseas would dock in Southampton, Bristol or Hull and the goods on board would then be broken down into smaller vessels before being shipped onwards to the lesser ports in the area.

In Southampton, such trade was undertaken with sixteen separate Dorset and Hampshire ports, eight of which received only one or two shipments over the full dataset, and eight of which represented key trading regions for the town. Those eight principal trading regions were: the Isle of Wight (including Ryde, Newport, and Yarmouth), Lyme Regis, Poole, Portsmouth, and Weymouth (including Melcombe Regis).[5] The furthest of these from Southampton was Weymouth at around sixty nautical miles, and the nearest was Portsmouth at just 1.6.[6] The situation in Bristol was fairly similar, with trade in essential goods being undertaken between Bristol and eleven separate ports in the modern regions of Gloucestershire, Worcestershire and the West Midlands. Of those, five accounted for a large enough proportion of commercial activity to warrant detailed exploration: Bewdley, Bridgnorth, Worcester, Tewkesbury and Gloucester.[7] The furthest of these ports from Bristol was Bridgnorth, at around eighty nautical miles, and the nearest was Gloucester at around 31. Importantly, unlike in Southampton, where the sixteen ports were spread along the south coast, in Bristol, most of these towns were inland on the River Severn, a feature that we shall see had a significant impact on the practical nature of the trading activities.

This was also true in Hull, where most of the local trade was undertaken inland on the port's extensive river system, navigable via the Humber estuary, and eventually onto the rivers Trent and Ouse. However, as discussed in more detail below, this data is unfortunately absent from Hull's coastal accounts owing to a particular set of political circumstances surrounding the collection of customs in Hull. Nonetheless, although we cannot ascertain the precise nature of the trade undertaken inland from Hull, details of the commodities that entered the port from elsewhere, cross-referenced with an approximation of the population size of Hull during this period, can give us an idea of the extensive trade undertaken on that route, and other sources (such as the 1565 port survey of Hull) confirm that Hull traded extensively with the town of York, as well as various other smaller towns on those river systems. Moreover, and again like Bristol, ports on those routes were somewhat obstructed from

---

[5] The sixteen ports were Christchurch, Fareham, Hurst Castle, Hythe, Isle of Wight (where no specific port was identified), Lyme Regis, Melcombe Regis, Newport (Isle of Wight), Poole, Portchester, Portsmouth, Purbeck, Ryde (Isle of Wight), Titchfield, Weymouth, and Yarmouth (Isle of Wight).

[6] Calculations of distance throughout this volume come from MarineTraffic, 'Voyage Planner', *MarineTraffic* (2018), www.marinetraffic.com/en/voyage-planner/ (accessed 27 July 2018). Although these calculations are based on the modern landscape, they can give a rough idea of the distance between coastal ports.

[7] The eleven ports were Bewdley, Bridgnorth, Frampton-on-Severn, Gloucester, Hanley Castle, Lydney, Newnham, Ross-on-Wye, Shrewsbury, Tewkesbury, and Worcester.

broader commercial ties owing to Hull's advantageous position at the mouth of the estuary, ensuring that much essential trade was forced through Hull into those inland regions. Indeed, the established historiography attests to the extensive need for essential goods within Hull's vast hinterland.[8]

In all three regions, it is clear at least that the supply of essential commodities to the local region represented an important element of coastal enterprise, evidenced by the extensive and, in some cases, far-reaching local trade routes extending from these three head ports. Although a rudimentary means of assessing commercial impact (as it does not account for the volumes or values of commodities), a simple tally of voyages between ports suggests that this was especially true in Bristol, where trade with Gloucestershire, Worcestershire and the West Midlands typically accounted for some 40% of coastwise voyages through the town year-on-year. That figure was a little lower in Southampton, with trade into Dorset and Hampshire typically accounting for 20–30% of coastwise voyages through the port. This difference likely owed to the geographic location of the ports inland on the River Severn, which were effectively blocked off from foreign trade by Bristol and its powerful mercantile class. Conversely, ports on England's south coast were in close proximity to London, other large provincial ports such as Plymouth and Exeter, and the French coast, giving them greater autonomy over the sourcing of essential goods. In addition, the restrictive nature of travel on the narrow, winding and often obstructed River Severn limited the size of the vessels that could be utilised, resulting in a higher frequency of smaller-volume shipments than in the Southampton region, where larger ships could more easily dock along the coast. Such a figure is much more difficult to ascertain for Hull, since the Hull customs officials did not routinely record shipments made inland on the Humber (such as to the major town of York). However, as we shall see, it is likely that the supply of essential goods to ports in the Hull region accounted for a large proportion of overall coastal trade, and possibly a figure higher even than in Bristol, owing to Hull's important role as a supplier of essential goods, such as coal and salt sourced from Newcastle, and an array of commodities sourced from London.

Indeed, although each of the ports examined here received and supplied commodities that must be considered 'essential goods', the specific nuances of their trade warrant more detailed examination. In particular, it is important to note that, in many cases, ports in the local region exchanged those essential products for goods in which they specialised, either due to the presence of a particular industry in their town or owing to monopolisation of particular overseas commodities. For example, in Southampton, Weymouth was well positioned to offer a steady supply of wine from La Rochelle and Gascony,

---

[8] Childs, p. 5; Willan, *The English Coasting Trade: 1600–1750*, pp. 102–03.

in exchange for a healthy stock of firewood.[9] Although the wood of the New Forest was semi-protected, Southampton could draw on reserves of firewood from the wider area, and the established historiography places Weymouth (and particularly Melcombe Regis) at the centre of the import market for continental wine.[10] Similarly, since both Poole and the Isle of Wight ports had established trade links with a wide selection of European markets, the exchange of goods with those towns was more diverse. Poole offered primarily wine and Azores woad in exchange for mixed cargoes of lead, wine, Cornish tin, iron, hops, Spanish salt, and Normandy glass, and the ports of the Isle of Wight supplied Southampton with French wine, malt, and wool in exchange for salt, gunpowder, wine, currants, and iron. Nonetheless, the commodities traded were specific to the regions in which they were gathered. Southampton's important links to the Sussex iron and Cornish tin trades are well documented in the port books, and the particular links that Poole and the Isle of Wight had to the Channel Islands and northern France are evident from both the established historiography and from the commodities listed in Appendix B.[11]

Southampton's trade with Lyme Regis was a little different from the other local ports with which Southampton had coastal ties, since Lyme Regis did not receive essential goods from Southampton but instead received a supply of Azores woad and alum. Lyme Regis received most of its essential supplies from Exeter, and only turned to Southampton in order to obtain specialist items required to serve its thriving cloth industry.[12] The overseas customs accounts show a vibrant trade link between Southampton and the Azores during the

---

[9] TNA E190/814/5 fol.2v, 9r, 10v, 11r, 13r, E190/814/6 fol.1r, 2v, 6r-v, E190/814/7 fol.1r, 4v, 5r, 6r–7r, 9r, E190/814/11 fol.1r, 2v, 3r, 8r, E190/814/12 fol.1v, 6r, 8r-v, E190/815/1 fol.1r-v, 3r, 4r-v, 6r, 6v, 7r–8r, E190/815/2 fol.4r, 5r, 7r, E190/815/8 fol.6v.

[10] Mark Forrest, 'The Development of Dorset's Harbours in the Fourteenth and Fifteenth Centuries', *Proceedings of the Dorset Natural History & Archaeological Society*, 138 (2017), 19–20, 29–30; Richard Reeves, *To Inquire and Conspire, New Forest Documents 1533–1615* (Hampshire: New Forest Centre, 2008), pp. xii–xv; William B. Stephens, 'English Wine Imports, c. 1603–40, with Special Reference to the Devon Ports', in *Tudor and Stuart Devon: The Common Estate and Government: Essays Presented to Joyce Youings*, ed. by Todd Gray, Margery Rowe and Audrey Erskine (Exeter: University of Exeter Press, 1992), pp. 141–72 (p. 147).

[11] Helen Victoria Basford, 'The Isle of Wight in the English Landscape: Medieval and Post-Medieval Rural Settlement and Land Use on the Isle of Wight' (unpublished doctoral thesis, University of Bournemouth, 2013), pp. 48–49; Robert Tittler, 'The Vitality of an Elizabethan Port: The Economy of Poole, 1550–1600', *Southern History*, 7 (1985), 95–118.

[12] Susan Flavin and Evan T. Jones, 'A Glossary of Commodities, Weights and Measures Found in the Sixteenth-Century Bristol Customs Account', *University of Bristol, ROSE* (2009), 107; William B. Stephens, 'The Cloth Exports of the Provincial Ports, 1600–1640', *The Economic History Review*, 22 (1969), 232–40.

1560s and 1570s that allowed the town to act as a vital meeting point for dye products, which, in turn, supplied the cloth industry of the broader region.[13] Nonetheless, like the other ports examined here, Lyme Regis too provided Southampton with a local specialist product, in this case green glass. While there is little evidence of a large glass industry in Lyme Regis during this period, the customs records reveal that green glass was an important outgoing cargo for its traders. It is difficult to say for certain where this supply of green glass originated, but it is possible that the town had links to the glass trade of Bristol and Gloucester, or to glass supplied from the continent, given Dorset's close ties to northern France.

Likewise, trade between Southampton and Portsmouth also took on a somewhat different character from the other ports examined here. While as many as three or four ships per year travelled into Portsmouth from Southampton, traffic in the reverse direction was substantially lower, at just three shipments over the full dataset.[14] As an important naval town, Portsmouth had a great need for iron, ordnance, and shipbuilding materials, which it received from Sussex, Kent and London *via* Southampton. Some of these ships entered Southampton only briefly to collect coastal cockets, but others embarked from Southampton directly.[15] Given the very short distance between Southampton and Portsmouth (just 1.6 nautical miles by modern calculations) and the relatively high value of ordnance, it seems plausible that merchants would consider it worthwhile to undertake the voyage to Portsmouth without the promise of a return cargo and returned to Southampton in ballast. Interestingly, Wiggs proffered in 1955 that no Sussex iron entering Southampton was 're-exported coastwise', offering no explanation as to its destination other than it being absorbed into the hinterland.[16] The data evaluated here clearly counters that assertion and explains the seemingly heavy absorption rate of iron into Southampton.

Aside from Portsmouth, however, Southampton's relationship with the lesser ports in its region was largely reciprocal, and much the same can be said of Bristol. Like Southampton, Bristol received from its closest ports commodities produced in those regions and, in return, supplied goods imported both domestically and from overseas. More specifically, Gloucester received a range of mixed commodities from Bristol in order to supply its extensive hinterland, and the other Severn ports received mostly wine, a commodity to which they had limited access owing to their substantial distance from

---

[13] Lambert and Baker, www.medievalandtudorships.org.

[14] TNA E190/814/6 fol.1r-v, E190/814/7 fol.8v.

[15] TNA E190/814/5 fol.12v, 13v, 14r, E190/814/6 fol.2r, 8v, E190/814/7 fol.3v, E190/814/11 fol.1r, 3r, E190/814/12 fol.7r, 9v, 10v, E190/815/1 fol.6v, E190/815/2 fol.3r, E190/815/8 fol.2r, 3r.

[16] Joan L. Wiggs, 'The Seaborne Trade of Southampton in the Second Half of the Sixteenth Century' (MA thesis, University of Southampton, 1955), pp. 129–30.

continental Europe and the strong foothold Bristol's mercantile elite had on overseas trade in the region.[17] In exchange, Gloucester and Tewkesbury supplied Bristol with much-needed grains, and the other ports supplied textile products, which were largely destined for overseas export. Gloucestershire's role in grain production is well established and Duncan Taylor has noted that Gloucester claimed to be the 'origin of three quarters of all grains sent to Bristol, Devon, Cornwall, Wales and Ireland'.[18]

Likewise, the abundance of textile products in Bewdley, Bridgnorth and Worcester is well known and this data simply reaffirms the established historiography.[19] However, the abundance of Manchester cottons shipped into Bristol from Bewdley deserves particular mention as it is indicative of a strong trade link between Manchester and Bewdley, which would continue for at least the succeeding two centuries. Indeed, in 1766 it was estimated that some 150 packhorses arrived in Bridgnorth and Bewdley weekly from Manchester, carrying textile products.[20] This trade also highlights the exceptional inland reach of the River Severn. While Bewdley was not the northernmost navigable port on the river system, the voyage between Bristol and Manchester by coast was around 330 nautical miles, yet one could travel overland between Bewdley and Manchester in some 60–100 miles, owing in part to the fact the River Dee was navigable via the Mersey estuary to at least thirty or forty miles south of Manchester.[21] Therefore, even in spite of the high cost of overland transportation, in some cases, it made logistical sense for goods to be transported overland before travelling onwards by river. Thus, the physical landscape of the region could dramatically expand the geographic reach of a port and provide traders with sought-after or hard-to-access commodities at surprising locales.[22] In the case of both Bristol and Southampton, these towns

---

[17] Jones, 'The Bristol Shipping Industry in the Sixteenth Century', p. 187; John S. Moore, 'Demographic Dimensions of the Mid-Tudor Crisis', *The Sixteenth Century Journal*, 41 (2010), 1058; Taylor, pp. 85–89.

[18] Taylor, p. 99.

[19] For discussion on the wool trade during this period, see Peter J. Bowden, *Wool Trade in Tudor and Stuart England* (Oxon: Taylor & Francis, 2013), pp. 41–76; Peter J. Bowden, 'Wool Supply and the Woollen Industry', *The Economic History Review*, 9 (1956). And for figures on the import and export of wool from Bristol, see Jones, 'The Bristol Shipping Industry in the Sixteenth Century', pp. 171–82; Stone, 'The Overseas Trade of Bristol before the Civil War', pp. 227, 32.

[20] Barrie Trinder, *Barges and Bargemen: A Social History of the Upper Severn Navigation 1660–1900* (Chichester: Phillimore & Co., 2005).

[21] Customs records show ships travelling south on the Dee as far as Aldersey during the sixteenth century. See Lambert and Baker, www.medievalandtudorships.org; MarineTraffic, www.marinetraffic.com/en/voyage-planner/.

[22] John Oldland, 'The Economic Impact of Clothmaking on Rural Society,

were able to act as a central meeting point for a broad array of commodities and were well placed to draw on the regional specialisms of ports from across the kingdom, not least those in their immediate vicinity.

As mentioned above, it is impractical to attempt to examine the intricacies of Hull's role in supplying the ports inland with essential goods owing to deficiencies in the customs records. However, some analysis of the links those ports had to the Newcastle coal trade is attempted below, and the sources scrutinised in that context suggest that a great number of small vessels travelled along the Ouse and the Trent in order to provide essential goods to the region. Moreover, population data for Hull suggests that the absorption rate of the town itself was likely far lower than the volumes of essential commodities that entered the port, suggesting that such commodities travelled onwards either on land or by river or, in some rarer cases, overseas. Thus, analysis here will focus on the essential supplies that Hull received from ports outside of its immediate surrounding area, and will work on the assumption that at least some proportion of those goods travelled onwards by river to towns such as York, Selby, Goole, and Keadby, as was the case with coal, discussed separately below.

As in any town, Hull and its surrounding area required a constant supply of grain and fish, both of which were supplied by the ports of East Anglia. It has been well established that the East Anglian ports were the foremost suppliers of grain during this period and, in particular, King's Lynn often shipped 'more corn in a month than most ports shipped in a year'.[23] Likewise, East Anglia was at the centre of English fishing, allowing ports such as Great Yarmouth, Dunwich, and Southwold to act as key suppliers of fish, most notably herring.[24] As a result, traders seeking a market for grain and fish found motivation to travel to Hull to access its vast hinterland. However, unlike Southampton and Bristol, Hull did not have a great deal to offer those grain traders in return and, indeed, the East Anglian ports (especially Great Yarmouth and King's Lynn) had extensive overseas trade links of their own, as well as strong ties to London, through which they obtained a plethora of essential and luxury commodities.[25]

1300–1550', in *Medieval Merchants and Money*, ed. by Martin Allen and Matthew Davies (London: University of London, School of Advanced Study, Institute of Historical Research, 2016), pp. 229–52 (p. 232); George D. Ramsay, 'The Distribution of the Cloth Industry in 1561–2', *The English Historical Review*, 57 (1942).

[23] Neville Williams, *The Maritime Trade of the East Anglian Ports, 1550–1590* (Gloucestershire: Clarendon Press, 1988), p. 151.

[24] Ibid., pp. 5–7.

[25] Stephen Hipkin, 'The Structure, Development, and Politics of the Kent Grain Trade, 1552–1647', *The Economic History Review*, 61 (2008), 100–02; Williams, pp. 150–51.

Therefore, vessels embarking from Hull to collect grain or fish from East Anglia travelled via southern ports such as Boston or Rochester, and those embarking from East Anglia to deliver to Hull continued north to Newcastle or Berwick-upon-Tweed, presumably to source coal or fish.[26] This is evidenced further by the high number of ships from King's Lynn that engaged in the trade between Hull and Boston, which probably resulted from the geographic proximity of those two ports. While some of the vessels that delivered grain to Hull may have entered King's Lynn in ballast, and a proportion continued north from Hull to Newcastle or Berwick-upon-Tweed, some ships travelled to King's Lynn from Hull via Boston, carrying commodities such as grocery wares and fish. As King's Lynn was well serviced by London, it seems that merchants travelling to Hull to sell grain occasionally made the decision to collect goods that were saleable in other ports, such as Boston, rather than returning to King's Lynn empty, thus forming a triangular trade route.

Importantly, the one-way flow of goods between these towns, in addition to the lack of diversity in commodities, made for trade links that were particularly fragile. Thus, while King's Lynn was a useful trade link for Hull in the earlier period, the relationship between the two ports collapsed very quickly after 1569, as shown in Figure 2.1 below. As explained by Williams, Hull was an important centre for the distribution of grains during the first half of the sixteenth century, but that trade dramatically diminished after the 1560s, as Selby became the dominant grain port in the Hull region.[27] As the route between Hull and King's Lynn relied almost entirely on the supply of grain, the contraction of that market in Hull severed the link between the two ports, and vessels that previously shipped grain into Hull shifted their view towards Selby, as evidenced by data made available via the Medieval and Tudor Ships Project.[28]

Similarly, trade between Hull and the ports of Great Yarmouth, Dunwich, and Southwold relied entirely on the health of the fishing industry, resulting in trade with those ports expanding significantly after the 1560s and then reducing again after 1575. While Yarmouth had been a port of major commercial significance from at least the fourteenth century, its role in English maritime commerce extended even further after 1560, owing to the rapid rise of Norwich in becoming the 'second city in the kingdom'.[29] By 1570, the expansion of

---

[26] For example, TNA E190/305/1 fol.16r, E190/306/1 fol.15v, E190/306/4 fol.5r, E190/306/17 fol.17r, E190/307/2 fol.10v.

[27] Williams, pp. 69–137, 51, 55–57, 61–82.

[28] To take just one example, the 30-ton *Elizabeth* of Keadby travelled from King's Lynn to Hull on numerous occasions up to 1570, and then after 1570 altered its route such that most of its voyages embarking from King's Lynn landed in Selby or Berwick-upon-Tweed: see Lambert and Baker, www.medievalandtudorships.org.

[29] Robert Tittler, 'The English Fishing Industry in the Sixteenth Century: The Case

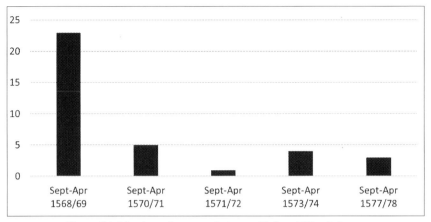

Figure 2.1. Number of voyages between Hull and King's Lynn.

Norwich had gone so far that the authorities considered there to be an excess of ships on the River Yare and feared that boatmen were illicitly conveying 'suspect persons' on their vessels.[30] Great Yarmouth benefited from that expansion through the provision of coal to Norwich and became a more substantial urban and commercial centre, which in turn boosted its established herring industry, explaining the rapid increase in trade with Hull after 1560.

The reduction in trade between East Anglia and Hull after the mid-1570s is more difficult to explain, but several coinciding factors probably had an impact. In the town of Yarmouth itself, the combination of an extraordinary levy placed on Norfolk landowners in 1573/4 that limited cash revenue available among the town's traders and an outbreak of plague in 1576 reduced commercial activity in the town and diminished its broader trading capabilities. In addition, after the 1570s, a shortage of affordable salt had a negative impact on the broader fishing industry, which had a knock-on effect on the output of fish from East Anglia. Therefore, as the trade between Hull and East Anglia hinged entirely on the ability of the East Anglian ports to provide fish, this reduction in overall commercial output almost entirely severed that trade link.[31]

Finally, while the majority of onwards trade in essential goods is missing from the port books, the customs records do provide some clues as to Hull's interaction with ports a little further afield, but still within the general area,

---

of Great Yarmouth', *Albion: A Quarterly Journal Concerned with British Studies*, 9 (1977), 46; Williams, pp. 61–67.

[30] Williams, p. 63.

[31] Tittler, 'The English Fishing Industry in the Sixteenth Century', pp. 55, 57.

such as Boston, Scarborough, Whitby, Grimsby, Bridlington, and Lincoln. The nature of exchange with these places is especially important to note since Hull's relationships with those towns generally echo the relationships Bristol and Southampton had with the ports to which they supplied essential goods, indicating continuity in coastal exchange in three vastly different regions. Like many of the ports local to Bristol and Southampton, those in Yorkshire and Lincolnshire provided Hull with goods easily sourced in their own region and received mixed commodities in return. That largely involved the supply of foodstuffs, wine, and raw materials, but also included miscellaneous products listed under the titles of 'haberdasher wares' and 'upholstery wares', which were received from Boston.

Willan loosely defined haberdasher wares as '[a]rticles of personal apparel comprised largely from hats, gloves, shoes, and stockings' and he categorised upholstery wares as household products, largely consisting of furniture. Willan suggested that these products were shipped coastwise from London into Hull, and there is certainly some evidence of that below.[32] However, they also entered Hull from Boston, suggesting that the commercial landscape was more complex than Willan appreciated and that there was also a thriving local industry based around the transportation of those goods. In return, Hull provided mixed cargoes of similar products, presumably sourced via its strong commercial ties with London. These mixed cargoes again centred on the supply of necessary products such as foodstuffs and wine but were also tailored to the particular needs of the receiving ports. For example, the many shipments of pitch and tar that were transported into Whitby reflect the minor shipbuilding industry in that town, and some proportion of the salt transported into Scarborough was most likely used for the preservation of fish, reflective of the town's substantial fishing industry.[33]

Trade with London and the east – shipbuilding materials, defences and infrastructure

Aside from trade with ports in their local regions, each of the case study towns also had commercial ties with more distant areas and, for Southampton and Hull, that included significant links to London and the east. As Bristol's trade with the eastern regions was extremely limited, those few rare vessels that did

---

[32] Willan, *The English Coasting Trade: 1600–1750*, pp. 102–03, 15–16; Willan, *The Inland Trade: Studies in English Internal Trade in the Sixteenth and Seventeenth Centuries*, pp. 15, 31–32.

[33] Rosalin Barker, *The Rise of an Early Modern Shipping Industry: Whitby's Golden Fleet, 1600–1750* (Woodbridge: Boydell Press, 2011), pp. 1–8; William G. East, 'The Historical Geography of the Town, Port, and Roads of Whitby', *The Geographical Journal*, 80 (1932), 489–91; Nash, pp. 210–12.

venture from Bristol to ports in the east are discussed in the context of 'trade further afield' below and this section will instead focus on Southampton and Hull. Both Southampton and Hull had extensive and well-established trading relationships with various eastern ports, many of which were comparable to the relationships other provincial ports on the southern and eastern coasts experienced during this period, as supported by the work of T. S. Willan.[34] Building on Willan's work, this section will cover two key trends: the flow of goods required for establishing effective infrastructure and defences (such as industrial goods, metal products, and ordnance) from where they were produced in the North East, to London, and then onwards to widespread provincial ports; and the distribution of iron from the Sussex Weald.

Turning first to the North East, London made up around 20% of Hull's coastwise voyages over the sample period and involved the transportation of particularly high-value commodities. In line with the established historiography, which highlights the important role north-eastern ports played in the supply of industrial wares, Hull provided a range of products that were produced in its local region, including lead, iron, ordnance, oil, soap, and pewter, as well as occasional shipments of goods sourced from further afield, such as feathers, wine, and butter.[35] In addition, as with almost every port within reasonable reach of the capital, Hull also provided grains, which were constantly in fierce demand in large urban centres.

Interestingly, although scholarship of the earlier period has demonstrated the importance of the London grain market to its hinterland and beyond, and Ralph Davis has suggested that Hull's ability to expand in the later sixteenth century resulted in part from the supply of foodstuffs to London, the customs records for the 1560s and 1570s show that commodities shipped into London from Hull were extremely varied.[36] Foodstuffs only accounted for a small proportion of goods, with shipments instead containing a variety of finished and unfinished products sourced from the wider region, calling that assessment into question for Hull at this time. In exchange, and drawing a clear parallel with ties between the capital and the periphery elsewhere, Hull received a miscellany of products from London, some of which were overseas imports and some of which were sourced from other English regions. As England's foremost entrepôt, London provided towns across the realm with both essential

---

[34] Willan, *The Inland Trade: Studies in English Internal Trade in the Sixteenth and Seventeenth Centuries*, pp. 26–30.

[35] Willan, *The English Coasting Trade: 1600–1750*, pp. 80–83.

[36] For analysis of notable scholarship on the earlier period, see Margaret Murphy, 'Feeding Medieval Cities: Some Historical Approaches', in *Food and Eating in Medieval Europe*, ed. by M. Carlin and J. Rosenthal (London: Hambledon, 1998), pp. 117–31.

and luxury goods. In Hull, this included iron, almost certainly obtained from Sussex, and overseas goods such as wine and brasil.

From here, it is possible to follow the flow of industrial goods, received in London from Hull, onwards into regions further west, such as Southampton. Throughout the 1560s, 1570s and 1580s, London was consistently the fourth or fifth most popular destination for ships embarking coastwise from Southampton, as Southampton merchants were drawn to the capital to collect materials associated with shipbuilding and port infrastructure. Such goods were required in large volumes along the south coast, and particularly in the naval port of Portsmouth and on the vulnerable Isle of Wight. In exchange, Southampton supplied London with goods to which it had access as a regional distribution centre. This included goods sourced from the local region (such as firewood), overseas commodities imported via Southampton (such as wine or spices), and products obtained from other domestic regions (such as Cornish tin), as shown in Appendix B. Importantly, James Brown has noted that the availability of industrial goods in London, combined with the strong market for a broad range of products in the capital, provided a new commercial opportunity for Southampton merchants after the loss of the Italian trade and, as we shall see in subsequent chapters, trade with London could provide a substantial source of income.[37] As such, the exchange of goods between Southampton and London required fairly sizeable collateral and was largely preserved for the mercantile elite.

Finally, although the North East had a reputation as a key location for the provision of industrial goods, it was not the only region with a substantial foothold in that arena, and the Sussex Weald was also vital in the supply of iron to ports across the realm, including those a substantial distance away (as discussed separately below). This was particularly true of Southampton, and 25% of Southampton's coastwise voyages over the full dataset were undertaken with Sussex ports. Southampton's foremost trading partner in Sussex was Meeching (now called Newhaven), which accounted for around 45% of shipments, followed by Chichester at around 20%, and Rye, Hastings, Shoreham-by-Sea, and Arundel at between 6% and 8% each. As Chichester lay outside of the Weald and was primarily a grain port, it was the only Sussex town with links to Southampton that did not provide Wealdon iron, instead supplying foodstuffs and wine. Nonetheless, every other port in the Sussex region provided large volumes of iron and ordnance to Southampton.

The need for such goods in Southampton was clear; consistently hostile relations with kingdoms in continental Europe meant that cannon, shot, and materials for the provision of land reinforcements were vital to the upkeep of the region, both in Southampton itself as well as in Portsmouth and on the

---

[37] Brown, p. 13; Lamb, pp. 51–54.

Isle of Wight. Thus, the domestic distribution of iron and iron products represented a key element of Southampton's commercial enterprise. These factors, in combination with a broader expansion in the overseas and domestic export of iron from the Weald during the sixteenth century, meant that trade between Southampton and Sussex boomed during the years preceding the Anglo-Spanish war, as evidenced by the significant proportion of Southampton's overall coastal enterprise that was dominated by trade with Sussex.[38] In return, and much like Southampton's relationship with other south coast ports, Southampton provided Sussex with a range of necessary supplies to which it had access as a central trading hub, creating an abundant and fruitful commercial exchange.

Southern trade with Cornwall, Devon and the South West

In the same way that Bristol was largely excluded from trade with London and the eastern markets, Hull was generally absent from the commercial exchange experienced in the South West. While we shall see below that very occasional voyages were made between Hull and ports in Cornwall, Devon, Dorset, Gloucestershire, Hampshire, Wiltshire and Sussex, these journeys were by no means the norm and did not represent a permanent presence in that region. However, for ports further south, Cornwall, Devon and Somerset presented an excellent opportunity for potentially high-value trade. Southampton and Bristol both took full advantage of those markets, with south-western trade representing some 16% of coastal voyages through Southampton and some 21% of coastal voyages through Bristol.[39] Moreover, in all cases, those trade links involved the domestic import of either local goods that were produced in the region in which the port was situated (e.g. Cornish tin from Cornwall) or, more commonly, overseas goods in which those ports specialised (e.g. Irish wool from Minehead). In exchange, as major commercial centres themselves, Bristol and Southampton provided ports in the South West with mixed cargoes of commodities sourced via both their coastal and overseas trade links.

In terms of those ports that provided Southampton and Bristol with goods produced in their local region, the case of Cornish tin is the starkest. Tin was an essential product and both Southampton and Bristol sourced their

[38] Mavis E. Mate, *Trade and Economic Developments, 1450–1550: The Experience of Kent, Surrey and Sussex* (Woodbridge: Boydell Press, 2006), pp. 177–78.

[39] For completeness, the Cornish and Devon ports with which Southampton traded were Dartmouth, Exeter, Falmouth, Fowey, Helston, Helford, Mount's Bay, Mousehole, Plymouth, Salcombe, Topsham, Torquay, and Truro. The twenty-four Cornish, Devon and Somerset ports with which Bristol traded were Barnstaple, Bideford, Bridgwater, Coombe, Dartmouth, Dunster, Exeter, Falmouth, Fowey, Ilfracombe, Luxborough, Minehead, Mount's Bay, Northam, Padstow, Penryn, Penzance, Plymouth, St Davids, St Ives, St Michael's Mount, Topsham, Truro, and Washford.

Table 2.1. Commodities traded between Southampton, Bristol and the South West

	Southampton		
Modern county	**Port(s)**	**Goods shipped into Southampton**	**Goods shipped out from Southampton**
Devon	Dartmouth, Exeter, Plymouth, Topsham, Torquay, and Salcombe	Primarily bay salt, some shipments of Cornish tin, millstones and wine	Mixed cargoes including wheat, malt, bacon, hops, Sussex iron, Normandy glass, canvas, beer, hides, firewood and woad
Cornwall	Truro, Mount's Bay, Helston, Falmouth, Fowey, Helford, and Mousehole	Cornish tin	

	Bristol		
Modern county	**Port(s)**	**Goods shipped into Bristol**	**Goods shipped out from Bristol**
Somerset	Bridgwater	Iron and wine	Cotton, wool, dry wares, iron, oil, soap and wine
	Minehead	Wool	Mostly iron, some salted fish and other miscellaneous goods
Devon	Plymouth	Mostly prunes and oil, some hides	'Smith's coals', grindstones, soap, nails and lead
	Barnstaple	Mixed cargoes, mostly oil and iron, some Spanish wool, luxury goods and wine	Mixed cargoes including grains, calfskins, dry wares, hides, linen, cloth, soap, iron, lead, pewter, wine and cotton
	Bideford	Wine	
Cornwall	Padstow	Cornish tin, salt and salmon	
	St Ives	Mostly iron, some wine and calfskins	

tin from Cornwall, where it was most abundant. However, Bristol received far fewer shipments of tin from Cornwall than Southampton did, owing to Southampton's historic role as the staple of metals, which allowed the port to fulfil an essential role in providing tin to London and the east coast. The importance of the London tin trade to Southampton's overall commercial viability will be discussed below, and we shall see that a great many wealthy and elite merchants engaged in that activity. However, it is important to note here that the Cornish ports were key nodes in the trade networks of the South West, and Cornish tin was a widely sought-after product.

Aside from Cornish tin, most commodities that were domestically imported into Bristol and Southampton from the South West were sourced from overseas. For example, the trade between Southampton and Devon highlights the strong links Devon shippers had with France, especially with the Bay of Bourgneuf, which was a famous salt-producing region. Likewise, although Duncan Taylor has shown that Welsh iron was particularly widespread during this period, the data assessed here suggests that much Spanish iron was shipped into Bristol during the 1570s, travelling coastwise via ports in the south, including Barnstaple, Bridgwater and St Ives.[40] Similarly, Bristol received Irish wool that was imported via Minehead, French wine imported via Bridgwater, and luxury products such as prunes, oil, and wine from the Devon ports, which had strong ties to Spain and the Mediterranean.[41]

In the reverse direction, Southampton and Bristol provided a range of commodities sourced from a broad area. Many of those (such as iron, cloth, leather, grain, and other foodstuffs) were necessary products across the kingdom and were in high demand in most regions, but other shipments were tailored to the ports into which they were transported. For example, Bridgwater had a substantial woollen cloth industry and so raw wool and soap featured heavily in shipments from Bristol to Bridgwater.[42] Likewise, Somerset ports such as Minehead and Bridgwater were at the centre of the trade in fish, accounting for the shipments of salted fish that entered Minehead from Bristol.[43] Similarly, the

---

[40] Philip Ashford, 'The West Somerset Woollen Trade, 1500–1714', *Proceedings of the Somerset Archaeology and Natural History Society*, 151 (2008), 167–70; Chris Evans, Owen Jackson and Göran Rydén, 'Baltic Iron and the British Iron Industry in the Eighteenth Century', *The Economic History Review*, 55 (2002), 649–50; Alison Grant, 'Breaking the Mould: North Devon Maritime Enterprise, 1560–1640', in *Tudor and Stuart Devon: The Common Estate and Government: Essays Presented to Joyce Youings*, ed. by Todd Gray, Margery Rowe and Audrey Erskine (Exeter: University of Exeter Press, 1992), pp. 119–40 (p. 120); Taylor, pp. 54–61, 70–74.

[41] Taylor, pp. 61–64.

[42] Ashford, pp. 165, 67, 69–70; Taylor, pp. 52–54.

[43] Maryanne Kowaleski, 'The Expansion of the South-Western Fisheries in Late Medieval England', *The Economic History Review*, 53 (2000), 435–38.

particularly high proportion of industrial goods transported into Plymouth from Bristol was a result of its vulnerable position on the south coast. Plymouth acted as an embarkation point for various diplomatic and military expeditions during the earlier period and would go on to be pivotal in the Anglo-Spanish war, making it a prime target for foreign attacks. This resulted in a significant shipbuilding industry, as well as creating a need for land reinforcements, making Plymouth an important market for the sale of industrial wares.[44]

Trade further afield

Although it is evident that the majority of coastal trade undertaken through the case study ports remained within a relatively narrow radius (typically extending no more than some 250 nautical miles from the port in question), in all three regions some voyages were made to domestic ports substantially further afield. These longer journeys represented exceptional shipments to collect specific products at times of need, rather than being sustained features of the regions' commercial landscapes, and they were largely made in order to obtain particularly sought-after commodities that were key to the upkeep of any urban centre, namely fuel, industrial wares, and foodstuffs (primarily grain). However, owing to the additional costs and risks associated with longer-distance travel, they deserve brief mention.[45]

Of the commodities for which merchants were willing to travel further afield, coal and grain were by far the most common, suggesting that participation in trade to more distant locations was opportunistic and was largely a response to exceptional demand. Indeed, the markets for grain and coal were highly volatile and both commodities were essential to the survival of any urban centre, resulting in periods of particular need during times of dearth.[46] In Hull, for example, the longest trade links in the entire dataset were

---

[44] Maryanne Kowaleski, *Local Markets and Regional Trade in Medieval Exeter* (Cambridge: Cambridge University Press, 2003), pp. 34–39; Kowaleski, 'The Expansion of the South-Western Fisheries in Late Medieval England', pp. 451–52.

[45] In Southampton, trade with Wales and Newcastle accounted for around 2% of coastal voyages over the full dataset. In Bristol, trade with London, Dover, Crostwick, Millthrop, and Workington accounted for no more than 3% of the total coastal voyages through the port. In Hull, trade with Berwick-upon-Tweed, Cornwall, Devon, Dorset, Hampshire, Wiltshire and Sussex accounted for around 3% of total coastal trade. TNA E190/814/7, E190/814/11, E190/814/12, E190/815/1, E190/815/2, E190/815/8, E190/305/1, E190/305/11, E190/305/12, E190/306/1, E190/306/4, E190/306/16, E190/306/17, E190/307/2, E190/307/3, E190/307/9, E190/307/16, E190/1128/12, E190/1128/13, E190/1128/14, E190/1129/1, E190/1129/18, E190/1129/20, E190/1129/22, E190/1130/2.

[46] John Hatcher, *The History of the British Coal Industry* (New York: Clarendon Press, 1993), pp. 346–76, 572–89; William G. Hoskins, 'Harvest Fluctuations and English Economic History, 1480–1619', *The Agricultural History Review*, 12 (1964).

those on which merchants occasionally either supplied grains to or collected grains from regions significantly far afield, including Berwick-upon-Tweed (which was only around 200 nautical miles from Hull but was high-risk due to its proximity to the Scottish border) and ports in Cornwall, Devon, Dorset, Gloucestershire, Hampshire and Wiltshire (each of which was upwards of 300 nautical miles from Hull and involved the navigation of some complex and difficult coastline).[47]

This was also true in the case of Bristol, a town which was well positioned to take advantage of increased demand for grain owing to its proximity to Gloucestershire (one of England's foremost grain-producing regions) and increased demand for coal owing to its ties to the Welsh coal industry and its own substantial coal deposits (discussed in more detail below).[48] As such, voyages were occasionally made out of Bristol to Dover (some 500 nautical miles away), Crostwick (some 600 nautical miles away), and Workington (some 350 nautical miles away), in order to supply grain and coal during times of particular need. The individuals that participated in the transportation of grain and coal across all three ports are discussed in more detail in Chapter 5, but it is noteworthy that, in the right circumstances, the sale of these low-value goods could be a profitable venture and, on occasion, traders were willing to put up substantial collateral to supply regions considerable distances from their home towns.

The draw of the coal trade is also evident in the case of Southampton. However, in this case, since Southampton did not have a strong link to coal of its own, occasional journeys would be made in order to supply the town with coal sourced from Newcastle or Wales. These journeys are of particular note since they were exceptionally long and risky and they involved an unusual pattern of trade. The seaward journey to Newcastle from Southampton was approximately 440 nautical miles and involved travel around the protruding Norfolk and Suffolk coastline, and the journey to South Wales was around 350 nautical miles and involved navigating the difficult Cornish coastline. Furthermore, such voyages were not undertaken on Southampton ships, but were instead carried out on vessels from either Torquay or London, which would travel north from their home ports to collect coal before travelling south (past their origin) in order to deliver to Southampton.[49] Since Torquay and London were themselves significant markets for the sale of coal, it is unusual that traders from those ports would travel the extra miles rather than selling the cargo in their home town, and suggests that they could obtain a

---

[47] TNA E190/305/1 fol.17r, E190/305/11 fol.3v, 16r, E190/305/12 fol.2r, 3v, 12r, 13r, E190/306/1 fol.15r–17r, 18r, E190/307/2 fol.10r, 11r, E190/307/3 fol.16v, E190/307/9 fol.8r.

[48] Taylor, p. 99.

[49] See, for example, E190/814/7 fol.4v, E190/814/11 fol.2r, 5r, E190/815/1 fol.8v.

higher price in Southampton during those periods, prompting them to make the longer journey. Indeed, given that Southampton's population in 1596 was approximately 4,200, and nearby towns including Winchester, Romsey and Salisbury increased that number significantly, the demand for coal was often high, as further evidenced by the data contained within the Brokage Books that attests to the distribution of coal from Southampton into its wider hinterland.[50]

Interestingly, the high risk and high costs associated with these voyages, combined with the bulky nature and low value of coal, resulted in particular practical approaches that we shall see below were also common in the transportation of coal into Hull, namely taking specific action to minimise costs and maximise quantities of product per shipment. The minimum quantity of coal transported into Southampton from Newcastle was 14 chaldrons and while the customs accounts do not specify whether these were Newcastle, Hull or London measures, even conservative estimates put that at upwards of 23,000 lbs.[51] Likewise, the smallest shipments from Wales carried 8 weys of coal, which, using the Neath, Swansea or Llanelly (rather than the Bristol) measure, puts those at upwards of 26,000 lbs.[52] In addition, on every voyage between Southampton and Newcastle or Southampton and a Welsh port, a single individual acted as both merchant and shipmaster, and carried only their own commodities.[53] This served to reduce outgoings since there was no fee to pay to a shipmaster for commanding, and again allowed for

---

[50] J. B. Blake, ' The Medieval Coal Trade of North East England: Some Fourteenth-Century Evidence', *Northern History*, 2 (1967), 9–11; Coleman; Davis, pp. 13–14; John Hare, 'Miscellaneous Commodities', in *Southampton and Its Region – English Inland Trade 1430–1540*, ed. by Michael Hicks (Oxford: Oxford University Press, 2015), pp. 161–71 (p. 164); Hatcher, pp. 70–96, 129–41, 473–79, 483–504; Tom B. James, 'The Town of Southampton and Its Foreign Trade 1430–1540', in *Southampton and Its Region – English Inland Trade 1430–1540*, ed. by Michael Hicks (Oxford: Oxford University Press, 2015), pp. 11–24 (pp. 13–14); Geoffrey V. Scammell, 'English Merchant Shipping at the End of the Middle Ages: Some East Coast Evidence', *The Economic History Review*, 13 (1961), 329–36; Taylor, pp. 141–52; Willan, *The English Coasting Trade: 1600–1750*, pp. 55–69, 115–28.

[51] Hatcher, pp. 559–69; Charles Hutton, *A Philosophical and Mathematical Dictionary: Containing an Explanation of the Terms, and an Account of the Several Subjects Comprised under the Heads Mathematics, Astronomy, and Philosophy Both Natural and Experimental; with an Historical Account of the Rise, Progress and Present State of These Sciences; Also Memoirs of the Lives and Writings of the Most Eminent Authors Both Ancient and Modern Who by Their Discoveries or Improvement Have Contributed to the Advancement of Them* (London: C. Hutton, 1815), p. 302.

[52] Jones, 'The Bristol Shipping Industry in the Sixteenth Century', p. 146; John U. Nef, *The Rise of the British Coal Industry* (London: Taylor & Francis, 2013), p. 373.

[53] TNA E190/814/11 fol.7r, E190/815/2 fol.2r, E190/815/8 fol.1v, 2r.

maximum quantities to be carried for a single merchant. Merchants and shipmasters were, unsurprisingly, reluctant to trade Welsh or Newcastle coal to Southampton but, given the right demand, they could be tempted and would take steps to maximise profits by transporting large volumes and sacrificing an independent shipmaster.

Aside from grain and coal, industrial goods and other foodstuffs could also occasionally tempt merchants into making longer journeys. In the case of industrial goods, it was again the high value and high demand associated with such products during periods of exceptional need that made them desirable. For example, we shall see below that Bristol had strong links to regions that could supply goods of that kind and was thus well positioned to take advantage of particular demand. As such, occasional journeys were made out of Bristol to London (some 570 nautical miles away) and Milthrop (some 280 nautical miles away), in order to supply lead, wine, train oil, iron, or pitch and tar, as shown in Appendix B.[54] Similarly, as we saw above, Sussex was exceptionally well placed for the provision of iron and thus merchants were occasionally willing to make the journey between Sussex and Hull in order supply iron to the North East. Since only eight vessels travelled between Hull and Sussex over the full dataset, Sussex was by no means a principal commercial market for Hull.[55] However, this link is notable as it highlights that the market for Sussex iron, which was both abundant and of high quality, was extensive and spanned almost the entire kingdom, including regions some 280 nautical miles away around a complex coastline. Iron was a necessary product across the kingdom, and the North East was no exception, not least owing to its close proximity to the Scottish border, creating a need for reliable fortifications.[56]

In terms of other foodstuffs, Hull was again well-equipped to take advantage of periods of high demand. This was especially true of fish and salt, which were both highly desirable and plentiful in the North East, meaning that local traders would occasionally be willing to travel further afield to gather those products and supply them to regions where demand was substantial and a high price could be achieved. Like grain, shipments of fish and salt made their way over 300 nautical miles south from Hull to ports in the South West, journeys that were both high in risk and cost.[57] Moreover, in the opposite direction, merchants were willing to travel the 200 nautical miles to Berwick-upon-Tweed and risk approaching the dangerous Scottish border in order to collect

---

[54] TNA E190/1129/1 fol.9v, 10r, E190/1128/12 fol.9r, E190/1128/13 fol.13r, E190/1129/22 fol.11v.

[55] TNA E190/305/11 fol.1v, E190/305/12 fol.3r, E190/306/1 fol.21r, E190/306/4 fol.2r, 3r.

[56] Steven A. Walton, 'State Building through Building for the State: Foreign and Domestic Expertise in Tudor Fortification', *Osiris*, 25 (2010), 70–72.

[57] For example, TNA E190/305/11 fol.2v.

herring, both for consumption in the local area and for onward transportation elsewhere. Like Great Yarmouth, Berwick was positioned in the centre of a great fishing region, in this case having easy access to abundant salmon fishing.[58] However, despite its important role in the supply of fish, and its strategic position on the Scottish border, Berwick was ill-equipped to take in large vessels and was in a poor state of repair.[59] As a result, Willan noted that between Christmas 1690 and Christmas 1691, only thirteen coastal voyages were undertaken between Berwick-upon-Tweed and any other English port.[60] However, the sources assessed in this volume point to a larger, although still limited, coasting trade between Berwick-upon-Tweed and Hull in the earlier period, and it is logical that the town would have been of greater commercial significance in the years before hostilities with Scotland tempered under James I.[61] Nonetheless, voyages between Hull and Berwick were still relatively uncommon and, as in the case of grain and coal, the substantial distances merchants were willing to travel for fish and salt attest to the selling power that certain commodities could achieve during times of dearth.

Regional specialisms

While there were some commercial trends from which few large provincial ports were immune, there were others that did not transcend geographic boundaries. Indeed, in all three of the regions examined here, certain geographic and political factors led to the formation of specific commercial arrangements that were either unique to the ports themselves or unique to the wider regions in which they were situated. As mentioned at the start of this volume, this highlights a major weakness in the established historiography, resulting from a tendency among maritime scholars to take the findings from a single case study port and apply them to the wider kingdom. While some scholars acknowledge the significant impact that regional differences could have on localised features of the maritime landscape, this is not true across the board, and a large proportion of our inherited knowledge has been based on analysis derived from within very narrow geographic boundaries. While it is unrealistic to expect that a single scholar could examine every port in the kingdom in great detail, study of several case study ports situated within significantly

---

[58] 'Section 4.1: The History of the Salmon and Sea-Trout Net Fisheries of the Tweed and the Eye', in *Tweed & Eye Fisheries District Fisheries Management Plan* (Melrose: The Tweed Foundation, 2014), pp. 1–6 (pp. 1–4).

[59] Albert J. Loomte, 'An Armada Pilot's Survey of the English Coastline, October 1597', *The Mariner's Mirror*, 49 (1963), 300; Willan, *The English Coasting Trade: 1600–1750*, p. 111; to a lesser extent, see Walton, pp. 72–76.

[60] Willan, *The English Coasting Trade: 1600–1750*, p. 112.

[61] Ibid.

different geographic locations highlights the degree of variation and allows for comparative analysis of trends that appear to have been widespread and those that were specific to individual regions. Thus, in the final section of this chapter we will examine those trade links that were specific to particular ports or regions, turning first to the unusual relationship between the port of Southampton and the Channel Islands (primarily Guernsey and Jersey).

Southampton's Channel Islands trade

Broadly speaking, and as seen above, the domestic ports with which Southampton traded can be divided into two categories: those that had strong overseas and coastal trade links and were themselves redistribution centres (e.g. London or Poole); and those that focused on a particular regional product that was sent to Southampton for onwards redistribution (e.g. Sussex or Cornwall). However, owing to their unique political and commercial alliance with the mainland, the Channel Islands fitted into neither of those two groups. An exceptional trade link had existed between the mainland and the islands of Guernsey and Jersey from at least the fourteenth century, whereby specific customs concessions were granted to Islanders. That link remained strong throughout the Tudor period, but the specific nature of the connection shifted over time. In particular, there existed a degree of regional rivalry between the ports of the south coast of England over their island connections.[62] As a result, from the early sixteenth century, Southampton specifically offered Channel Island shippers even more generous concessions in order to draw them away from Poole, a technique that proved highly successful.[63]

Furthermore, the relationship between Southampton, Jersey and Guernsey was strengthened still more in 1560 when a new royal charter was granted that extended Islanders' rights to trade custom-free. That 1560 charter had significant ramifications specifically for Southampton's relationship with the Islands as necessary supplies sourced from Southampton were henceforth exempted from all duty (an even greater concession than previous charters had granted). Aside from the trade impact of that change, there were also important ramifications for the later establishment of the port books, since duty-free goods were typically recorded in the coastal accounts, whereas goods incurring duty

---

[62] Marguerite Syvret and Joan Stevens, *Balleine's History of Jersey* (Gloucestershire: History Press Limited, 2011), pp. 48, 69, 90–92; Tim Thornton, *The Channel Islands, 1370–1640: Between England and Normandy* (Woodbridge: Boydell Press, 2012), pp. 63–64.

[63] Mary A. E. Green, *Calendar of State Papers Domestic: Elizabeth* (London: British History Online, 1869), www.british-history.ac.uk/cal-state-papers/domestic/edw-eliz/1595-7/pp48-68 (accessed 27 August 2019), p. 337; Ruddock, 'London Capitalists and the Decline of Southampton in the Early Tudor Period', p. 137; Thornton, p. 63.

were typically recorded in overseas records. As a result, goods that were not tax-exempt continued to be recorded in Southampton's overseas port books, whereas the tax-exempt essential goods were listed in the coastal port books (despite them travelling to the Islands). As a consequence of this change, we see within Southampton's coastal port books many ships embarking from Southampton carrying tax-exempt goods but no vessels returning from the Channel Islands, since these presumably carried continental products that were subject to customs and were therefore recorded in the overseas accounts.[64]

There was clearly space in this system for smuggling, and it is very possible that some of the shipments recorded in the coastal port books as tax-exempt also included some taxable goods. However, overseas trade is beyond the scope of this volume and the goods that were listed in the coastal port books would have anyway been commonly transported to the Islands from Southampton. Such shipments mostly contained commodities in which Hampshire was rich, namely firewood and beer. Firewood was almost certainly drawn from the New Forest and surrounding woodland and the extent of the brewing industry in Southampton suggests that at least some proportion of the beer was local export.[65] The town did also provide occasional shipments of grain or leather, but these were unusual.

Interestingly, while the nature of the commodities Southampton provided to the mainland remained stable, the levels of trade undertaken to Guernsey and Jersey fluctuated substantially throughout the period under investigation and this can be attributed to socio-political changes on the Islands. Throughout the 1560s and 1570s, Guernsey took the lion's share of Southampton's trade, probably owing to its geographic proximity to the mainland, its lower risk of attack or influence from France, and its greater degree of political integration with England up until the mid-sixteenth century.[66] However, in 1578 the Guernsey Bailiff and Jurats opened negotiations with the Privy Council regarding a variety of matters, including regulation of markets, trade, and taxes. The dispute was not resolved until the late 1580s, during which time the political relationship between Guernsey and the mainland was highly strained, whereas Jersey maintained cordial relations with England. As a result, Jersey was able to seize a larger share of the mainland trade, reducing the stake of Guernsey merchants and shipmasters (as shown in Figures 2.2 and 2.3).[67]

---

[64] John C. Appleby, 'Neutrality, Trade and Privateering, 1500–1689', in *A People of the Sea: The Maritime History of the Channel Islands*, ed. by Alan G. Jamieson (London: Methuen, 1986), pp. 59–105 (pp. 71, 74–75); Wiggs, pp. 126–27.

[65] Judith M. Bennett, *Ale, Beer, and Brewsters in England: Women's Work in a Changing World, 1300–1600* (Oxford: Oxford University Press, 1996), pp. 46–57; Reeves, pp. xii–xv.

[66] Thornton, pp. 92–110.

[67] John R. Dasent, *Acts of the Privy Council of England* (London: British

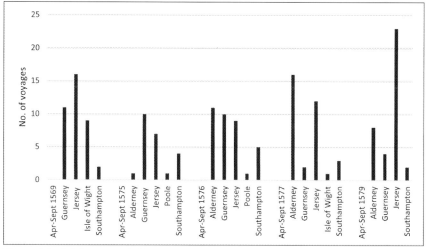

Figure 2.2. Origin ports of ships trading between Southampton and the Channel Islands.

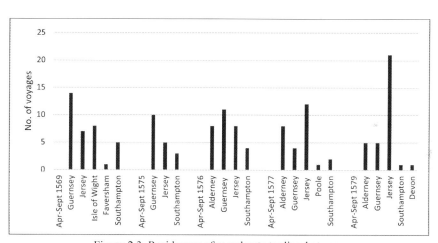

Figure 2.3. Residences of merchants trading between Southampton and the Channel Islands.

Nonetheless, although the commercial relationship between Guernsey and Southampton broke down in the 1570s, the broader trade route between Southampton and the Islands was well established, and the trade in duty-free goods was dominated by a select group of Islanders who regularly engaged in that activity. Moreover, those voyages often included multiple merchants who shared hull space and, unlike the other traders explored here, they often allocated a proportion of that space to the shipmaster. Given that it was common in overseas trade for the shipmaster to be part paid with a space on the vessel, and considering the close relationship between the Islands and continental Europe, it seems very likely that many of these vessels entered England carrying overseas goods.[68] Thus, owing to the unique relationship Southampton had with the Channel Islands, this trade took on a markedly different form from Southampton's commercial activity with other domestic ports, as we shall see in Chapters 4 and 5. This serves to highlight the versatile nature of coastal commerce, which spanned individuals from all regions and involved a range of operational approaches, often dictated by the circumstances in which that trade was undertaken.

Bristol's Welsh trade

Although the Welsh ports had officially come under crown jurisdiction through a series of parliamentary measures introduced in the 1530s and 1540s, the reality of their management was a little more complex than the customs systems in English ports.[69] Therefore, like the Channel Islands, ports in Wales occupied an unusual commercial position within the wider maritime economy of Tudor England, especially with regard to the opportunities available for engagement in illicit trade, as discussed below. Nonetheless, regular trade was undertaken between Bristol and the Welsh ports and, in total, trade with Wales accounted for around 29% of coastal voyages undertaken through the port of Bristol over the full dataset.[70] Trade was undertaken between Bristol and seventeen

---

History Online, 1895), www.british-history.ac.uk/acts-privy-council/vol11 (accessed 16 September 2019), pp. 200–01, 335–36, 60, 78–79; John R. Dasent, *Acts of the Privy Council of England* (London: British History Online, 1896), www.british-history.ac.uk/acts-privy-council/vol12 (accessed 16 September 2019), pp. 16, 130, 56, 266; Thornton, pp. 118–19.

[68] Cheryl A. Fury, 'The Elizabethan Maritime Community', in *The Social History of English Seamen, 1485–1649*, ed. by Cheryl A. Fury (Woodbridge: Boydell Press, 2012), pp. 117–39 (pp. 118–20); Geoffrey V. Scammell, 'Manning the English Merchant Service in the Sixteenth Century', *The Mariner's Mirror*, 56 (1970), 10–11; Robin Ward, *The World of the Medieval Shipmaster: Law, Business and the Sea c.1350–c.1450* (Woodbridge: Boydell Press, 2009), pp. 52–66.

[69] Taylor, pp. 125–29.

[70] TNA E190/1128/12, 13, 14, E190/1129, 1, 18, 20, 22, E190/1130/2.

separate ports in Wales, of which ten accounted for any substantial volume of trade.[71] There were inevitably a number of common threads that ran through all of Bristol's trade with Wales. However, the specific commercial nature of trade with each port sometimes varied fairly significantly and resulted in a somewhat complex commercial landscape. As such, examination in this section will be divided into incoming and outgoing shipments.

As we saw above, the organisation of trade between provincial ports often revolved around the collection of a broad range of products at large provincial ports, sourced from smaller subsidiary ports that specialised in particular goods. Indeed, in this case, the customs records show that Bristol supplied Welsh ports with a mix of domestic and overseas goods obtained from a wide range of regions, in exchange for local specialist products. In particular, the Welsh ports provided a steady supply of frieze cloth and leather, most likely destined for overseas export. Frieze cloth was one of the new draperies, and was more specifically a form of 'coarse woollen cloth, with a nap, usually on one side'.[72] Frieze was generally low-cost, although Welsh, Bristol and Irish frieze differed in price and quality. Evan Jones has observed that Irish frieze was imported into Bristol in substantial quantities and Duncan Taylor has highlighted the importance of Bristol frieze in Bridgwater's export market.[73] However, Welsh frieze has a more turbulent history and Taylor noted that there was a surprising dearth of product entering Bristol from Cardiff during the sixteenth century. Likewise, he traced a decline in the level of frieze exported from Milford Haven by comparing port books from 1565/6 and 1585/6 and substantiating those with civic sources.[74] While the data explored in this volume does not allow for investigation of the period after 1580, the more intensive run of port book data for the earlier period allows us to build on Taylor's assertions.

Figure 2.4 shows the number of shipments that entered Bristol from the Welsh ports carrying frieze cloth between Period 1 and Period 4, broken down into months. Although the precise volumes of cloth have not been assessed, the number of voyages gives a rough indicator of the amount of trade undertaken.

---

[71] Of the seventeen Welsh ports with which Bristol traded, the number of voyages to/from Aberystwyth, Caerleon, Laugharne, Neath, Newport, Newton Nottage, Oxwich, Pembroke, Port Eynon and Swansea was too low to warrant detailed investigation. Those which represented any significant volume of trade were Aberthaw, Carmarthen, Cardiff, Chepstow, Haverfordwest, Milford Haven, and Tenby.

[72] A nap being the rough, unfinished surface that results from the weaving process. See Flavin and Jones, 'A Glossary of Commodities, Weights and Measures Found in the Sixteenth-Century Bristol Customs Account', p. 114.

[73] Jones, 'The Bristol Shipping Industry in the Sixteenth Century', p. 35; Taylor, p. 52.

[74] Taylor, pp. 153–208.

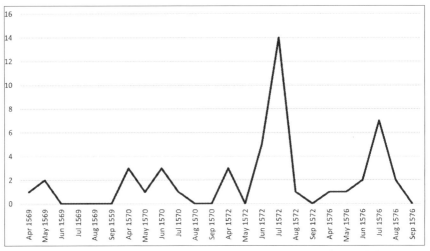

Figure 2.4. Shipments of frieze cloth into Bristol across the five periods.

Likewise, although this data cannot provide a full picture of the cloth traded coastwise from the Welsh ports, it does quantify their relationship with Bristol. It is evident here that the market for Welsh frieze in Bristol was rather volatile. The one consistency was that the months of August and September were generally very poor months for the transportation of frieze into Bristol, but otherwise, the levels of trade were highly unpredictable. Taylor's data certainly shows a general decline in the coastwise export of frieze from Milford Haven between 1565 and 1585 but, at least in terms of trade with Bristol, the broader market for Welsh frieze did not appear to markedly decline until at least 1576. In fact, the Welsh ports formed an important part of Bristol's coastal enterprise throughout the period investigated here, providing sought-after goods like new draperies for overseas export.

This was also true in the case of leather, which was supplied to Bristol for onwards transportation overseas. As noted by Evan Jones and others, the illicit export of leather 'formed an important part of [Bristol's] commerce' during the sixteenth century, and the data assessed in this volume suggests that there was very little domestic redistribution of Welsh leather from Bristol, and certainly not enough to account for the quantities that entered Bristol from the Welsh ports, suggesting that at least some proportion was illegally exported.[75] Interestingly, the Bristol port books can also help to support

---

[75] Jones, 'The Bristol Shipping Industry in the Sixteenth Century', pp. 147–79; Jones, *Inside the Illicit Economy: Reconstructing the Smugglers' Trade of Sixteenth Century*, pp. 47, 71, 207; Stephens, 'The Cloth Exports of the Provincial Ports,

assertions by seventeenth-century antiquarian George Owen that there was a clear commercial divide between the Welsh ports that specialised in the sale of bovine products and those that focused on ovine commodities. In particular, towns in Pembrokeshire specialised in the production and sale of lambskins, whereas most other regions in South West Wales tended to trade in calfskins.[76] Indeed, Welsh ports that were positioned only *slightly* east of Pembrokeshire were still distinctively more focused on bovine products. For example, Carmarthen (outside Pembrokeshire) and Tenby (within Pembrokeshire) were a mere thirty miles apart, but Carmarthen supplied a mix of animal hides, whereas Tenby was more focused on the supply of lambskins.[77]

Finally, although limited in volume, the transportation of wine into Bristol from Chepstow is also indicative of Bristol's overseas trade links. As noted by Taylor, Dimmock, and Jones, Chepstow acted as something akin to a tax haven for the import of foreign products (especially wine) into Bristol.[78] Although the crown made considerable efforts throughout the sixteenth century to quell the tax-free import of wine via Welsh ports, Taylor has noted that this means of tax evasion continued into the 1570s, and the data assessed here shows wine entering Bristol from Chepstow as late as 1577.[79] It is beyond the scope of this volume to explore this illicit trade in detail, and indeed Taylor, Jones, and others have already done so, but it is nonetheless important to note that illicit trading in Bristol was rife and that coastal trade could provide a means through which merchants could evade tax. Moreover, like any other trade route, this resulted in specific operational characteristics in that region and we shall see exactly how those manifested in the Bristol/Chepstow trade in Chapters 3 and 5.

In return, and as anticipated, Bristol provided Welsh ports with mixed commodities from various other domestic regions and from overseas. This trend is unsurprising and aligns with Bristol's broader role as a centre for redistribution. Nonetheless, the specific nature of the goods included in these mixed cargoes brings to light two particular trends that deserve further explanation. First, the data displayed in Appendix B clearly highlights the important role

---

1600–1640', pp. 233–41; Willan, *The Inland Trade: Studies in English Internal Trade in the Sixteenth and Seventeenth Centuries*, p. 38.

[76] Taylor, p. 191.

[77] TNA E190/1128/12 fol.15r-v, E190/1128/13 fol.19r–21r, E190/1128/14 fol.14r–15r, 16r, E190/1129/1 fol.16v–19v, E190/1129/18 fol.12r-v, 16r–17v, 19r, E190/1129/22 fol.12r–14v.

[78] Spencer Dimmock, 'Urban and Commercial Networks in the Later Middle Ages: Chepstow, Severnside, and the Ports of Southern Wales', *Archaeologia Cambrensis*, 152 (2003); Jones, *Inside the Illicit Economy: Reconstructing the Smugglers' Trade of Sixteenth Century*, pp. 47–48; Taylor, pp. 129–30.

[79] TNA E190/1129/22 fol.14r.

Bristol had in providing wine to the surrounding region. Yet while wine was transported coastwise from Bristol to most Welsh ports, Chepstow and Cardiff were notable exceptions. As we have seen, Chepstow continued to act as an entrepôt for wine into Bristol as late as 1577 and, in earlier years, Cardiff had taken up a similar mantle, albeit on a smaller scale. Although the continuing corrosion of power of the marcher lords meant that the import of wine into Bristol via Chepstow and Cardiff was substantially winding down by the 1570s, both ports were well established as entry points for vessels returning home carrying wine. This established commercial position, combined with their favourable geographic position in the Severn estuary meant that these ports had satisfactory overseas connections and did not require the domestic provision of wine.[80] However, all other Welsh ports assessed here received wine from Bristol and, like the small ports inland on the River Severn, the subsidiary ports in the Severn estuary could not compete with Bristol merchants for a role in overseas commerce. Unless local merchants partook in a particular commercial arrangement that was beneficial to Bristol merchants, as was the case in Cardiff and Chepstow, such traders heavily relied on the port to provide necessary overseas goods, such as wine.

Secondly, trade with Aberthaw and Haverfordwest is of particular interest as the flow of traffic to those ports was one-way; they received mixed cargoes from Bristol but sent nothing back in return. In the case of Aberthaw, there is little evidence of a triangular trade route. On some occasions, Newport vessels would remain in the Severn estuary for several weeks, jumping from port to port, and there is evidence in the Cardiff port books of some Aberthaw vessels entering Bristol from Cardiff, but voyages of both kinds were rare. Likewise, a number of vessels transported butter directly into Bristol from Aberthaw, but that did not occur until after 1580, and the vessels that travelled between Bristol and Aberthaw are also absent from any overseas accounts.[81] This suggests that these ships entered Bristol in ballast, purely to collect

---

[80] Dimmock, pp. 53–54, 62–63, 61–67; Taylor, pp. 124, 29–32.

[81] With regard to the activities of Newport vessels in the Severn estuary: between 16 May and 6 November 1576, the 16-ton *Margaret* and the 16-ton *Mary Rose* of Newport travelled extensively between Cardiff, Bristol and Newport. Likewise, between 27 July and 26 September 1580, those same ships travelled with frequency between Bristol, Cardiff, Newport and Aberthaw. However, that mode of operation was limited largely to those vessels and was not representative of broader trade in the area. See TNA E190/1129/18 fol.6v, 11r, 12r, 12v, 17r, 19r, E190/1130/2 fol.18v, 20r. With regard to the trade with Cardiff and the transportation of butter from Aberthaw, see Lambert and Baker, www.medievalandtudorships.org; and Edward A. Lewis, 'The Welsh Port Books (1550–1603): With an Analysis of the Customs Revenue Accounts of Wales for the Same Period', in *Cymmrodorion Record Series* (London: Honourable Society of Cymmrodorion, 1927), pp. 2, 7, 21–22, 30–35.

products to return to Aberthaw.[82] While it is surprising that traders would make the decision to sail empty rather than take any goods at all, Evan Jones has demonstrated that many Bristol vessels travelled overseas in ballast, relying on their return cargoes to secure a profit.[83] Aberthaw was both very close to Bristol and extremely small, suggesting that traders making the journey to Bristol may have been sure of a reasonable return on even a one-way trip, especially if the goods available at Aberthaw were limited.[84]

Conversely, in the case of Haverfordwest, it is possible that this one-way flow of traffic resulted from the port's ties with Milford Haven. The Bristol and Milford Haven port books contain various instances in which vessels travelled from Milford to Bristol and embarked from Bristol to Haverfordwest, and that show various Haverfordwest merchants active within Milford. Therefore, even without consulting any Haverfordwest customs accounts, it is reasonable to assert that this formed a triangular route and is unsurprising given the geographic proximity of the three ports.[85] Given the small size of Aberthaw and Haverfordwest, and given that they were two of several 'subordinate communities within the larger Bristol channel', their lesser commercial role in the region makes economic sense but serves to highlight the range of complex relationships that large commercial centres like Bristol generated.

Hull's trade with Newcastle

Various historians have speculated that Hull played a significant role in the coastwise distribution of Newcastle coal throughout the medieval and early modern periods. However, owing to the earlier particular accounts lacking coastal records, they were only able to substantiate this claim to a limited extent.[86] Furthermore, while T. S. Willan has provided the most detailed exploration of Hull's role in the coastwise transportation of coal to date, the breadth of his work resulted in a fairly shallow exploration and some of his presumptions about the character of Hull's engagement in the coal trade are challenged by the data under examination here. As such, this volume provides the first comprehensive overview of Hull's role in the trade in Newcastle coal,

---

[82] Lambert and Baker, www.medievalandtudorships.org.

[83] Evan T. Jones, 'The Shipping Industry of the Severn Sea', in *The World of the Newport Medieval Ship: Trade, Politics and Shipping in the Mid-Fifteenth Century*, ed. by Evan T. Jones and Richard G. Stone (Melksham: University of Wales Press, 2018), pp. 135–59 (pp. 146–47).

[84] Philip Jenkins, 'Wales', in *The Cambridge Urban History of Britain*, ed. by David M. Palliser (Cambridge: Cambridge University Press, 2000), pp. 133–50 (p. 137).

[85] Lambert and Baker, www.medievalandtudorships.org; Lewis, 'The Welsh Port Books (1550–1603)', pp. 68–69, 84–88, 95–99, 126–29, 35–36, 56, 59, 225–26.

[86] Childs, pp. 6, 41; Davis, pp. 12–15; Kermode, 'The Merchants of York, Beverley and Hull in the Fourteenth and Fifteenth Centuries', pp. 204–09.

finding that Newcastle represented Hull's busiest coastal trade link, accounting for around 60% of the port's coastwise voyages over the sample period.[87]

More specifically, Willan's assessment of Hull's engagement in the Newcastle coal trade concluded that coal entered Hull from Newcastle and was then sent onwards to London, and he suggested that 'to a limited extent […] trade with London was a "one-way" trade, [as] a large proportion of the ships returned in ballast'.[88] However, the data analysed here does not support that assertion and, as we saw above, vessels travelled frequently between Hull and London, carrying mixed commodities in both directions, and rarely transporting coal. The established literature therefore provides a scant basis for our understanding of the relationship between Newcastle, Hull, and London. Indeed, aside from occasional shipments to far-flung domestic ports, such as Southampton or Sussex, very little Newcastle coal was re-exported from Hull coastwise in any direction, and certainly not towards London.[89] Therefore, the final destination of the large volumes of Newcastle coal that were transported into Hull is unclear and is not explained in the existing literature.

Although there are various problems with trying to determine where Newcastle coal transported into Hull ended up, there are four possible explanations, and examination of each of these in turn allows us to make some propositions. First, it is possible that some proportion of Newcastle coal that entered Hull was exported overseas. Unfortunately, there are significant limitations in the availability of overseas port books for the region for this period: an extremely low number of overseas customs accounts for Hull survive and none survive for Newcastle. Furthermore, the few records that do exist for Hull are primarily searcher accounts, which in this case did not record the commodities transported but merely noted whether a relevant cocket was obtained.[90] As a result, we can see that various ships embarked from Hull destined for foreign ports (principally La Rochelle, Antwerp, Bordeaux, Gdansk, or Norway), but it is not possible to ascertain whether these ships carried coal. We can only surmise that some quantity of coal may have been transported overseas, and

---

[87] Literature on the establishment and growth of Newcastle in becoming England's foremost coal-producing region is extensive and does not require reiteration here, however Hatcher's 1993 volume provides a good introduction to the importance of the Newcastle Hostmen in the national context: see Hatcher, pp. 31–96, 508–46.

[88] Willan, *The English Coasting Trade: 1600–1750*, p. 111.

[89] TNA E190/305/1 fol.17r, E190/814/11 fol.7r, E190/815/8 fol.1v, 2r.

[90] The surviving overseas port books for Hull for the period between 1565 and 1590 are catalogued under TNA E190/304/2, E190/307/12, E190/308/1 and E190/308/4. For some entries, the customs officials did record the commodities transported, but this information is largely missing.

indeed Jennifer Kermode has made this assertion for the earlier period, albeit accounting for only small quantities.[91]

Secondly, it is very likely that some proportion of Newcastle coal was retained for use in the town of Hull. Although population figures for this period are notoriously unreliable, Hull almost certainly had upwards of 1,500 inhabitants throughout the sixteenth century, and probably had a great number more.[92] Moreover, Hull's port facilities and its position on the mouth of the River Humber made it an important commercial town, and a Spanish 'spy' noted in 1597 that the area was capable of taking in 'five hundred ships'.[93] As a result, the port inevitably required a supply of fuel. However, even taking these factors into consideration, it is highly unlikely that Hull could have absorbed the extensive volumes of coal that entered the port from Newcastle.

Thirdly, while it is likely that a small proportion of coal was transported overland into the broader hinterland, this is again unlikely to have accounted for a large proportion of the product Hull received from Newcastle. While the region does not benefit from the survival of any Brokage Books, as Michael Hicks was able to utilise for Southampton, John Hare and others have shown that, for the most part, coal was transported by water rather than by land due to its exceptionally low value and bulky nature. Land transportation of coal was typically reserved for areas with restricted access and which lacked sufficient river systems.[94] While it is therefore likely that some small quantities of coal were transported inland by cart, it seems improbable that this accounted for a significant quantity and, thus, we are left with the possibility that coal was fed into the surrounding area by river.

In theory, ships leaving Hull by river should have been recorded in the coastal port books, however, the reality of the situation was more complex. Commissioners undertaking a survey of the port in 1565 noted that Hull and York benefited from a special relationship in which goods were 'brought frome yorke to hull in lyghters & there laded' and, in return, 'merchandise was [...] unladed at hull & carried up [the rivers Humber and Ouse] by lyghters' to York.[95] Moreover, the commissioners noted that the creeks surrounding Hull were 'playne countrey lacking [in] fewelle', and that, as a result, coal was routinely deposited at other ports and creeks along the Ouse, on the condition

---

[91] Kermode, 'The Merchants of York, Beverley and Hull in the Fourteenth and Fifteenth Centuries', p. 183.

[92] 'Hull in the 16th and 17th Centuries', in *A History of the County of York East Riding*, ed. by Keith J. Allison (London: Victoria County History, 1969), pp. 90–171.

[93] Loomte, p. 300.

[94] Hare, pp. 163–66; Willan, *The English Coasting Trade: 1600–1750*, pp. xii–xiii. See also Masschaele.

[95] TNA E159/350 fol.151r.

that it was only used for local consumption.[96] Thus, it seems that the customs officials would record the large incoming shipments of coal from Newcastle, but would not then record the dividing up and transporting of that coal by lighters to regions further inland. Not only would such an exercise have been time- and labour-intensive, but customs officials may have considered failure to record these voyages as quasi-legal, owing to the specific local political arrangements in place, and especially given that Hull was excluded from various crown customs policies, such as the establishment of a Legal Quay.[97] Moreover, similar perceived exemptions from the recording of local trade (in cases where no crown custom was due) also existed in other domestic ports, as noted by Evan Jones and Duncan Taylor.[98] Therefore, the most likely explanation is that most Newcastle coal travelled onwards on the Humber, the Ouse and the Trent to the various inland markets accessible via river.[99] Coal shippers made use of that extensive river system in order to sustain a healthy local trade in coal, independent of any engagement with London.

Aside from coal, Hull did also receive small quantities of 'white salt' from Newcastle, which was again a key product of the Newcastle region.[100] However, unlike coal, white salt was transported onwards by coast from Hull to diverse ports, rather than being shipped inland by river.[101] This primarily owed to the fact that white salt was of relatively poor quality and was deemed inappropriate for use in the fishing industry, which was particularly prevalent in the North East. Yet it was a much-needed household product, and was therefore saleable across the kingdom, particularly in wealthier urban centres.[102] In the case of both the coal trade and the salt trade, Hull acted as a central meeting point for the collection and redistribution of desirable products, and we shall see below that many local traders took advantage of those opportunities. Finally, in the reverse direction, although small quantities of grain were occasionally transported into Newcastle from Hull, significantly more ships entered Hull from Newcastle than in the reverse direction.[103] This suggests that the coal

[96] TNA E159/350 fol.152d.

[97] East, 'The Port of Kingston-upon-Hull during the Industrial Revolution', pp. 191–92.

[98] Jones, *Inside the Illicit Economy: Reconstructing the Smugglers' Trade of Sixteenth Century*, pp. 39–40; Taylor, pp. 67–68, 73–74.

[99] Evan Jones, 'River Navigation in Medieval England', *Journal of Historical Geography*, 26:1 (January 2000), 67–68.

[100] Scammell, 'English Merchant Shipping at the End of the Middle Ages: Some East Coast Evidence', p. 329; Nash, pp. 213–15.

[101] TNA E190/305/11 fol.2v.

[102] Williams, p. 83.

[103] Over the full dataset, around 690 ships entered Hull from Newcastle, whereas only 44 embarked from Hull carrying commodities destined for Newcastle.

trade was by far the more significant attraction and, thus, while some ships left Hull carrying grain, most travelled to Newcastle in ballast.

Conclusions

We have seen in this chapter that there were some commonalities in the coastal trade routes that extended out from Bristol, Southampton, and Hull. First, all three ports acted as vital suppliers of essential goods to the lesser ports in their regions. Large shipments of essential goods sourced both from overseas and from other domestic ports made their way to the head port before being broken down into smaller shipments for onwards redistribution to towns in the region. As this form of trade was key to ensuring the survival of local towns, it made up a large proportion of coastal shipments in all three regions and, as we shall see in Chapter 3, it was largely dominated by local traders. While this form of trade may not have been the most lucrative option for an Elizabethan merchant or mariner, it was vital to the upkeep of the kingdom's towns and villages and offered a potential revenue stream for those with limited resources to invest or with limited experience in maritime enterprise.

Conversely, the trade in north-eastern industrial wares required much greater initial investment but also offered more opportunity for high profits. While this trade largely excluded ports as far west as Bristol, those on the southern and eastern coasts were well-integrated into the flow of such goods from the north, into London, and then onwards to other provincial ports. In Southampton, for example, trade with London and Sussex, both of which involved the provision of industrial wares, ordnance, and materials for shipbuilding and infrastructure, accounted for the lion's share of coastal voyages through the port. Likewise, in Hull, trade with London was second only to trade with Newcastle, and it likely provided a much more substantial source of income.

Similar trends were also evident in the west, where the ports of Devon, Cornwall, and the South West provided Bristol and Southampton with industrial wares, as well as luxury goods sourced from overseas; a trade from which Hull was largely excluded. For example, the Devon ports exhibited their Spanish and Mediterranean connections by providing iron, wool, and luxury goods, and Minehead's strong ties with Ireland were utilised in the supply of Irish wool. In exchange, Bristol and Southampton supplied towns across the kingdom with products obtained both from overseas and from other domestic ports, often in mixed cargoes that were tailored to the specific needs of the port receiving the goods. These were both major commercial centres and were pivotal in the supply of products to a wide geographic region. Again, this link provided much opportunity for potentially high-value trade and made up a significant proportion of Southampton and Bristol's overall coastal activity.

Finally, in all three ports, merchants and mariners were occasionally willing to make more expensive journeys to domestic ports further afield. However, these shipments were unusual and did not represent a permanent presence in those regions. Instead, they were made sporadically, and usually in response to particular demand for highly sought-after products, namely grain, foodstuff, and coal. During times of particular need, the supply of such commodities could be a potentially profitable endeavour, and also carried a degree of social kudos, owing to the often-detrimental implications of grain shortages during times of dearth. Thus, when the pull was especially strong, some individuals were willing to absorb the higher risk, put up the extra collateral, and make the journey to more distant parts.

In addition to these common trends, the data examined here also reveals a number of commercial trends that were specific to each of the case study ports, usually resulting from the specific geographic, social and political context in which they were situated. For example, the unique political relationship Southampton enjoyed with the Channel Island ports of Guernsey and Jersey created opportunity for the supply of essential goods to a region somewhat further afield and with extensive trade links to France. It is highly likely that this resulted in some degree of illicit trading, although that is beyond the scope of this volume, but it was nonetheless a welcome potential revenue stream for traders seeking a market for their goods and fruitful ties to Europe.

The same can be said for Bristol's trade with Wales, through which local merchants found a market for their goods, and especially for wine. Again, the unusual political situation in which those trade routes existed resulted in some degree of illicit trading, but nonetheless provided a potentially lucrative outlet for domestic trade, as well as a highly beneficial source of textile products, some of which were absorbed into the town itself, some of which were destined for riverine or overland transportation, and some of which were destined for sale overseas.

Further north, in Hull, it was proximity to Newcastle that created a specific form of coastal exchange, and the trade in Newcastle coal accounted for over 60% of the port's total coastwise activity. However, coal obtained from Newcastle was not transported into London, as early historians suggested, but instead made its way inland on the rivers Humber and Ouse in order to supply the Yorkshire region. In this respect, Hull's geographic position allowed it to monopolise trade destined for ports further inland on the river system, acting as something of a gateway to Yorkshire and beyond.

As discussed above, and in line with a general consensus that the sixteenth century saw widespread economic hardship, the early historiography of all three ports has tended to paint a gloomy image of these towns, being empty of trade and falling into disrepair. In all cases, more recent scholarship has challenged this view, but has not explored in detail the role that coastal commerce played in the upkeep of these ports during such a period of stagnation. The data assessed here shows that a bias towards overseas trade has produced an excessively negative image of maritime commercial activity in Elizabethan England's provincial ports. In fact, evidence from the coastal port books suggests that a steady stream of trade flowed through Bristol, Southampton, and Hull to ports across the kingdom, and the beneficial position of these towns allowed them to act as central meeting points for commodities sourced from both overseas and other domestic ports.

To take just one example, the sources assessed in this volume indicate that, contrary to this historiographic narrative, Hull's trade with London did not depend on the supply of a single commodity (e.g. coal or foodstuffs) but rather involved a mutual exchange of mixed cargoes, often including high-value and sought-after commodities, which, as we shall see below, drew in members of the mercantile elite, many of whom gained substantial wealth through trade with the capital and who took steps to prevent London traders encroaching on that route.

The purpose of this chapter is not to dispute the strong economic evidence that confirms that these ports suffered some degree of economic stagnation during this period, but to highlight that, when you look beyond overseas trade, ports across the realm were still bustling hubs of maritime activity. Moreover, as we shall see in Chapter 5, this trade was in some cases highly valuable and could offer the shrewd Elizabethan trader opportunity to build an extensive and lucrative maritime career.

3

The dynamics of the coastal trade

In Chapter 2 we saw that England's provincial ports benefited from a mix of markets, including some that were common in ports across the realm and some that were specific to the particular port and its region. These markets were determined to some extent by the practical needs of the towns, but social and political factors also had an impact on commercial activity. For example, we saw that the specific legal and political relationship between Southampton and the Channel Islands led to the formation of a very particular trade link, which, in turn, impacted the commodities exchanged and the distribution of trade between islands. Such regional differences were commonplace and the practical character of the trade undertaken through each port cannot be separated from its social, political, and commercial characteristics.

The same can be said of the elements of trade explored in this chapter, which were impacted too by the wider context of the port in question. In each case, the degree to which local traders dominated particular routes, the means through which merchants and mariners elected to engage in that trade (for example, the methods used to reduce risk), and the vessels utilised on those routes were determined to some degree by the nature of the trade link and the commodities transported, which were, in turn, impacted by the wider regional context. We shall see that the practical nature of the coasting trade varied considerably between trade routes, determined by the geographic features of the region, the commodities traded, and the social and political context in which the route was situated. In combination with Chapter 2, this will provide a vital backdrop for analysis of the merchants and mariners themselves, as we progress to a more detailed exploration of the individuals who made up the coastal workforce.

The extent of the coastal workforce

Before moving on to look at the specific features of particular routes, there are a number of broad trends that can be determined through overarching analysis of the data extracted from the coastal port books. First, it is evident from the data analysed here that each of the three ports under investigation benefited from a fairly large coastal ship fleet. Although a crude way of analysing ships and merchants, a simple tally of the total data can provide an initial indication of the number and geographic distribution of the ships and traders in each case study port over the years 1568–1580.[1] For example, in Southampton, forty unique Southampton vessels have been identified across the period, in Bristol forty-one, and in Hull around 100. However, these vessels only accounted for a small proportion of the total ships that travelled through each port over time. For example, although forty Southampton vessels were involved in coastal trade through Southampton over these twelve years, those only accounted for some 5% of the total vessels that traded coastwise through the port, with the other 95% coming from diverse regions across the kingdom. Likewise, the forty-one Bristol vessels that traded through Bristol in that same period only accounted for 8% of the total ships that flowed coastwise through the port. Hull was a slightly different story and of the 480 separate vessels that engaged in Hull's coastal commercial activity across this period, 24% were Hull ships. The reasons for this difference are discussed in more detail below.

Nonetheless, much the same can be said of the merchants that engaged in coastal trade in the three ports. Of the 544 merchants that traded coastwise via Southampton during this period, only seventy-two (or 13%) were Southampton residents. Similarly, in Bristol, only 188 (32%) of the 589 merchants that traded through the port were Bristol residents. As Southampton and Bristol were particularly well-connected ports and were central hubs for the redistribution of domestic and overseas commodities, trade in those regions attracted merchants and shipmasters from across the kingdom who were keen to take advantage of the ports' vibrant and diverse markets. Moreover, the extensive overseas trade links in those ports meant that many local merchants were tied up in overseas trade and only engaged in coasting to a limited extent. Equivalent statistics are difficult to determine for Hull, owing to deficiencies in the port book data, but analysis in Chapters 4 and 5 suggests that the proportion of traders that were from the port itself was somewhat higher, owing to the importance of the coastal trade to the region. As hinted in the historiography, coastal commerce played a particularly important role in the maritime trade of the North East and, thus, while a large number of Bristol and Southampton vessels were mostly involved in overseas trade, many of Hull's mercantile elite (and the ships they utilised) were substantially involved in coastal commerce. Moreover, owing to the prevalence of coal in the North East, these ships tended to be much larger than those that routinely engaged in coastal trade in Southampton or Bristol. Therefore, at least in terms of tonnage, Hull's coastal fleet was significantly greater than that of either of the other case study ports.

[1] As discussed in the Introduction and shown in Appendix A, this includes forty port books over a span of twelve years (eleven port books for Southampton, eleven for Bristol and eighteen for Hull). TNA E190/1128/12, 13, 14, E190/1129/1, 18, 20, 22, E190/1130/2, E190/814/5, 6, 7, 11, 12, E190/815/1, 2, 8, E190/305/1, 11, 12, E190/306/1, 4, 16, 17, E190/307/2, 3, 9, 16.

Although trade through the case study ports was not undertaken in the large by individuals from the ports themselves, it was near-exclusively undertaken by English traders on English vessels. In Bristol, no foreign vessels appear in the sample at all, in Southampton only one foreign vessel appears, and in Hull only three were listed. Moreover, all three of the foreign vessels that traded through Hull came from the Netherlands and appeared over two months in 1568.[2] This is no surprise given that legislation required all native shipping to be undertaken on English vessels, but it does highlight the important role coastal shipping played in boosting the English maritime industry.[3] Furthermore, frequent markings of 'ind[igenous]' throughout the records suggest that the merchants were almost exclusively Englishmen. As a result, coastal activity was largely free from foreign competition and remained firmly in English hands. Englishmen dominated coastal commerce in all three of the case study ports, but local control over coastal trade routes was especially important in Hull, owing to the importance of the coastal trade to the broader commercial health of the port, and the comparative difficulty for local traders in Hull to reap the financial rewards of overseas commerce.[4]

Merchants, mariners, and vessels

Aside from overarching trends pertaining to the practical nature of the merchants and vessels engaged in coasting, various trends were specific to certain types of trade route and commodity. These differences can be broadly divided into the practical features of activity undertaken between large trading centres and activity undertaken between large trading centres and their subsidiary ports, as examined below. However, before we move into the substantive analysis, it is important to note that the size of each shipment varied substantially per voyage, and even within the confines of the maximum tonnage available on each vessel, the quantities and values of the cargoes that were carried varied significantly. As such, the overall value of the shipments that flowed through the ports is particularly difficult to determine and is, anyway, beyond the scope of this volume. Nonetheless, examination of indicative shipments, combined with a general sense of the types of goods traded on particular

---

[2] Those were the *George* of Vlissingen (40 tons), the *Lyngbande* of Haarlem (30 tons), and the *Sea Rider* of Antwerp (40 tons): see E190/305/1 fol.10r, 16r-v.

[3] Gary Paul Baker, 'Domestic Maritime Trade in Late Tudor England c. 1565–1585: A Case Study of King's Lynn and Plymouth', in *The Routledge Companion to Marine and Maritime Worlds, 1400–1800*, ed. by Claire Jowitt, Craig Lambert and Steve Mentz (London: Routledge, 2020), p. 101.

[4] Childs, pp. 6, 41; Alan Dyer, pp. 12–16; East, 'The Port of Kingston-upon-Hull during the Industrial Revolution', pp. 199–200; Kermode, 'The Merchants of York, Beverley and Hull in the Fourteenth and Fifteenth Centuries', p. 55.

routes, can indicate which routes were of particularly high value and which were dominated by shipments of a lower value. Thus, we can determine whether local merchants and mariners favoured high-value or low-value trade links, laying a vital foundation for closer analysis of the individuals involved in coastal trade in the chapters that follow.

Trade between large commercial centres

Perhaps the most notable characteristic of the merchants and vessels that travelled between large commercial centres was their tendency to be drawn from the local community. In other words, unlike trade between the case study ports and their subsidiaries, which was primarily undertaken by individuals linked to the subsidiary, trade between case study ports and other large commercial centres tended to be dominated by vessels and traders sourced from the case study town itself. For example, some of Southampton's most established merchants were willing to make the journey to Poole or to the ports of the Isle of Wight to trade. This likely resulted from the fact that those ports were themselves regional trading hubs that benefited from their own supply of desirable overseas products, such as Azores woad or French wine. Likewise, merchants engaged on the Southampton/London route resided in Southampton and were mostly members of the local mercantile elite, who were themselves engaged in overseas activity.[5] While in earlier periods Southampton's trade with London was partially controlled by Italian merchants, by the 1570s and 1580s, with the exception of one individual from Ireland, English traders dominated all coastal shipping.[6] Control over such a key domestic trade route was important to Southampton merchants and demonstrates the extent to which coastwise activity could draw in individuals beyond small-scale, low-status traders, as we shall see in Chapters 4 and 5.

This was also true in Bristol, where trade with London drew in a particularly large proportion of ships and merchants originating from the town itself, including members of Bristol's mercantile elite. As shown in Chapter 2, Bristol was less substantially involved in trade with London than Southampton or Hull. However, given the right circumstances, even merchants situated on the other side of the kingdom could be drawn into trade with the capital.

---

[5] For example, Richard Biston, Bernard Courtney, John Crook and Richard Goddard Junior all traded on the route between Southampton and London, and we shall see in Chapter 5 were all substantially involved in overseas trade out of Southampton, with Crook and Goddard later becoming privateers. TNA E190/814/5 fol.5v, 7r-v, E190/814/6 fol.3v, 8r, E190/814/7 fol.1v, 5v, E190/814/11 fol.6r, 7v–8r, E190/814/12 fol.1r, 3r, 4v–5r, 6v, 9r, 12v, E190/815/1 fol.6v, 8v, E190/815/2 fol.2v, 5r, E190/815/8 fol.2r-v.

[6] TNA E190/814/5 fol.12r; Ruddock, 'Alien Merchants in Southampton in the Later Middle Ages', pp. 1–17; Ruddock, 'London Capitalists and the Decline of Southampton in the Early Tudor Period', pp. 138–39.

Likewise, Bridgwater, Plymouth, Padstow, and St Ives all offered highly desirable overseas commodities, and therefore pulled in local elite merchants and local ships. As we shall see below, both Bristol and Southampton could rely on traders from smaller specialist ports to provide a steady stream of their products into the town, but in larger ports of a similar nature, where merchants were able to engage actively in overseas commerce of their own, there was less need or desire to engage in coastal commerce and local traders thus had to make the effort to travel to collect necessary goods themselves.

As a result, trade links of this kind tended to attract some particularly large vessels, which were either owned by or largely used by members of the mercantile elite. The historiographical consensus has been that coastal trade was undertaken on particularly small ships and, while this was certainly true in many cases (as we shall see below), some ports attracted much larger vessels. For example, the *William* of Plymouth appeared in Bristol's coastal port books on three occasions, always travelling between Bristol and Plymouth, always commanded by shipmaster Owen Raymond, and being listed as between 80 and 140 tons. The *William* carried mixed shipments of coal, lead, honey, and black soap from Bristol to Plymouth, returning with Toulouse woad and wine, and was likely owned by famed mariner William Hawkins, who appeared as merchant on all of its coastal voyages through Bristol.[7] The involvement of this vessel is especially indicative of the strong overseas trade links present in Plymouth and, indeed, the *William* also undertook various shipments to La Rochelle, also commanded by Owen Raymond.[8] The Bristol market was hungry for luxury goods and this could attract established merchants who were willing and able to make the long journey around the Cornish coastline in order to sell high-value wares.

Likewise, Southampton's trade links with other key commercial centres also attracted a number of vessels of substantial size. Ships measuring upwards of 90 tons were particularly common in the trade with Poole and Portsmouth, where the average tonnage of ships was also high, at 17 and 25 tons, respectively. Likewise, the 19-ton average of ships trading between Southampton and the Isle of Wight suggests that a fair number of larger vessels were involved on those routes. Equally, the vessels utilised in the trade between Southampton and London were especially large, ranging from 6 to 60 tons, with a 22-ton average. For London, Poole and the ports of the Isle of Wight, the utilisation of larger ships can be credited to the fact that those towns also acted as collection hubs for overseas commodities and for goods transported from other domestic ports. Indeed, the majority of ships that appeared on the Southampton/London

---

[7] TNA E190/1128/13 fol.15r, 20v, E190/1128/14 fol.6v; and see Craig Lambert, 'Tudor Shipmasters and Maritime Communities, 1550–1600', in *Routledge Companion to Marine and Maritime Worlds, 1400–1800*, ed. by Claire Jowitt, Craig Lambert and Steve Mentz (London: Routledge, 2020).

[8] Lambert and Baker, www.medievalandtudorships.org.

trade route originated from ports heavily involved in overseas trade, namely Southampton (27%), the Isle of Wight (17%), Poole (8%) and London (7%). Many of the ships deployed from those areas also engaged in overseas trade and were, in many cases, relatively large.[9] For example, the largest ship to trade between Southampton and Poole was the 100-ton *Primrose* of Poole that provided imported goods to Southampton, including wine and Spanish salt, and also undertook overseas voyages to Bayonne in France.[10]

However, the case of Portsmouth was a little different, and here the larger size of the vessels can be attributed to the bulky and varied nature of the provisions required. For example, the 25-ton *Grace of God* carried minions, falcons, iron and other miscellaneous goods, and the 50-ton *Diamond* carried, among other products, hops, nails, shovels and hemp.[11] Conversely, the 9-ton *Edward* carried just a small quantity of wheat.[12] Interestingly, the specific character of the trade between Southampton and Portsmouth also impacted the type of individuals involved and, unlike the other ports in this chapter, did not attract ships or merchants from a prominent single origin. This was very likely a result of the fact that Portsmouth was principally a naval town and had very little in the way of a standing mercantile fleet so, instead, ships came from across the south to provide Portsmouth with necessary defensive supplies, resulting in the mix of individuals and vessels sourced from a broad geographic area.[13]

Similarly, the unique commercial character of the ports of Devon and Cornwall also accounted for differences in their links with Southampton, namely that the ships used in Southampton's Cornish trade were fairly small, whereas those that travelled between Southampton and Devon were somewhat larger, although both routes attracted local elite merchants who were also engaged in overseas trade. This regional difference resulted from the fact that commercial exchange with Devon involved vessels that were also engaged in overseas trade, and involved the provision of mixed overseas commodities, drawing in vessels of a larger size.[14] However, tin shipped into Southampton

---

[9] This is confirmed through a study of the Medieval and Tudor Ships Project: see ibid.

[10] TNA E190/815/2 fol.7r-v; and see ibid.

[11] TNA E190/814/11 fol.1r, 7r and E190/815/8 fol.2r.

[12] TNA E190/814/7 fol. 3v.

[13] Estimates of merchant ship fleets in individual ports are notoriously difficult to verify and crown ship surveys dramatically under-recorded the vessels belonging to each town. However, analysis of data provided in the Medieval and Tudor Ships Project suggests that Portsmouth may have been home to around 40 separate vessels during the second half of the sixteenth century, compared to some 190 in Southampton, perhaps as many as 600 in Hull, and in the region of 280 in Bristol. Lambert and Baker, www.medievalandtudorships.org.

[14] For example, the 40-ton *Dragon* of Plymouth often travelled between Plymouth and La Rochelle, and the 16-ton *Sparrowhawk* of Dartmouth routinely voyaged between

for overseas export was largely freighted on Italian vessels, whereas merchants who transported tin across the south coast utilised smaller ships that were a better fit for the route, being more suited to sailing the treacherous waters of the Cornish coast and more able to navigate the county's small creeks and havens.[15]

This was also true of Southampton's trade in Sussex iron, which likewise involved a significant number of merchants from Southampton and the surrounding area, who largely utilised small ships (ranging from 2 to 40 tons, with a 12-ton average). Many of those vessels were of Sussex origin (25% from Meeching, 14% from Brighton, 13% from Hastings, and 8% from other Sussex ports), and the rest were Hampshire ships (18% from the Isle of Wight, and the remainder scattered across Hampshire ports such as Portsmouth and Lepe, with Southampton vessels accounting for less than 1%). That the ships involved would be small is unsurprising given the short distance they travelled and considering the nature of the goods they transported. Iron and ordnance were bulky commodities but were also of relatively high value and therefore it was a logical approach to run frequent voyages freighting smaller loads as a way to reduce the collateral required.[16] Only six ships over 30 tons sailed between Southampton and Sussex, most of which were involved in the transportation of wine and foodstuffs into Rye or Chichester, and do not appear to have been involved in the iron trade.[17]

However, that these voyages largely involved Hampshire merchants freighting goods on Sussex (rather than Hampshire) ships is more unusual.

Dartmouth and various French ports, both of which also appear in the coastal accounts for Southampton. Likewise, we can trace the 35-ton *Michael* of Salcombe through the customs accounts and observe it undertaking numerous trips between Southampton and Dartmouth throughout 1576 before departing for Spain on 17 February 1576 and returning to Dartmouth from La Rochelle on 25 March 1577. See TNA E190/814/5 fol.1v, 8v, E190/814/7 fol.2v, E190/814/11 fol.2r, E190/814/12, E190/815/1 fol.1r, 4r, 6r, 7v; Lambert and Baker, www.medievalandtudorships.org.

[15] Lambert and Baker, www.medievalandtudorships.org; Wiggs, p. 72.

[16] Iron was valued at around 4s per C in the 1582 Book of Rates. It is unclear exactly what fell under the title of 'ordnance', but gunpowder was valued at 33s 4d per C in the 1594/5 Book of Rates, hand guns cost from 6s to 9s, and a small ship-gun may have cost around 20s, whereas a 'great gun of copper with two chambers' may have fetched a price of £35, with many other types of gun sitting between those extremes and some naval guns fetching even more. See Flavin and Jones, 'A Glossary of Commodities, Weights and Measures Found in the Sixteenth-Century Bristol Customs Account', p. 43; L. G. Carr Laughton and Michael Lewis, 'Early Tudor Ship-Guns', *The Mariner's Mirror*, 46 (1960), 245, 57–58, 65.

[17] Those were the 40-ton *James* of Meeching, *John* of Plymouth, *Peter* of Chichester, and *Parrot* of Rye, and the 30-ton *Bonaventure* of Newport and *Lion* of Southampton. See TNA E190/814/11 fol.2v, 8r, E190/814/12 fol.1r–2r, 6r.

As we shall see in Chapter 4, this can be attributed to the fact that many Southampton traders engaged in this commercial activity were wealthy and politically active, but employed the services of local Sussex shipmasters in order to access trade into the Weald, most of whom specialised in the transportation of iron and likely owned or part-owned small ships suited to the freighting of iron products. That being said, the relatively frequent involvement of Isle of Wight vessels is notable and reflects the particular need for defences on the island. As these vessels were primarily very small (<10 tons), they may have been used for coastal shipments in the main, with short journeys across the channel also being likely, as demonstrated in research by Lambert and Baker, and Blackmore[18].

Similar practical differences are more difficult to ascertain in the case of Hull, owing to deficiencies in the primary sources regarding the residential affiliation of Hull's merchants and shipmasters. However, some notable features can be determined. As noted above, the average size of the ships involved in coastal commerce in Hull was much higher than those engaged in coastwise trade in Bristol or Southampton, and that owed in large part to the substantial size of the colliers that transported Newcastle coal. Although the Hull port books do show a few very small vessels (including five under 10 tons) and a range of medium-sized ships (around 140 between 11 and 30 tons) engaged in trade between Hull and Newcastle, 159 vessels engaged on that route measured over 30 tons, and 96 of those were upwards of 50 tons. As a result, the average tonnage of the vessels that traded coastwise between Hull and Newcastle was 38 tons, an average figure substantially higher than on any other trade route examined in this volume. This operational trait resulted from the fact that coal and salt were both low-value but particularly bulky, meaning that large vessels were required in order to maximise profits. Indeed, Willan has proposed that purpose-built colliers were developed specifically to accommodate the transportation of coal, being specially adapted to maximise volumes transported per shipment.[19]

Interestingly, however, the ships utilised in the trade between Hull and London were similarly sized to those that travelled between Hull and Newcastle, in spite of the higher-value goods they freighted. The smallest vessels on this route measured 12 tons and the largest 100, with an average tonnage of 36. This can be partially explained by the fact that the journey

---

[18] Craig Lambert and Gary Paul Baker, 'An Investigation of the Size and Geographical Distribution of the English, Welsh, and Channel Islands Merchant Fleet: A Case Study of 1571–72', in *The Maritime World of Early Modern Britain*, ed. by Richard Blakemore and James Davey (London: Amsterdam University Press, 2020), pp. 98–99; Robert Blackmore, 'Keep Calm and Ignore the Armada', *BBC History Magazine* (September 2023).

[19] Willan, *The English Coasting Trade: 1600–1750*, pp. 11–12.

was long, the range of goods was extensive, and the opportunities to sell in London were great. Thus, traders utilised large ships to make the most of those opportunities. However, in a number of cases, the large size of these vessels resulted from the fact that they served the dual purpose of trading to London and trading in Newcastle coal, and indeed 85% of voyages between Hull and Newcastle were undertaken on ships from Hull, Newcastle, or other Humber ports, with London vessels accounting for only 3%. For example, between 1568 and 1578, the 50-ton *Mary Fortune* of Hull undertook numerous voyages to Newcastle (at least three or four a year) and occasional trips to London (usually annually).[20] Likewise, over the same period, the 60-ton *Trinity* of Hull divided its voyages equally between Newcastle and the capital.[21] Furthermore, as we shall see in Chapter 5, various merchants that traded between Hull and London also traded overseas, and so it is likely that some of these vessels also made voyages to foreign ports.

Conversely, the ships utilised in the trade with East Anglia were substantially smaller than those used in the Newcastle trade, although those ports too were regional trading hubs, and that again owed to the nature of the commodities traded, being focused almost entirely on the provision of grain. Interestingly, while Williams has demonstrated that the majority of grain transported out of King's Lynn was carried in King's Lynn bottoms, that was not the case in the trade with Hull. Indeed, on the King's Lynn/Hull route, King's Lynn ships accounted for only 17% of voyages, second to Keadby (at 19%), and not much more dominant than ships from Wells-next-the-Sea (at 14%), or Burnham, Hull, and York (each at 7%).[22] The dominance of ships from Keadby is surprising, given the very small size of the village and its lack of mention in the historiography.[23] Although somewhat beyond the scope of this volume, the sources evaluated here suggest that Keadby was an important port town during this period. It had a fairly substantial ship fleet that was engaged in a significant volume of trade, and a review of the data available via the Medieval and Tudor Ships Project reveals several hundred voyages undertaken on Keadby vessels, travelling across diverse trade routes including Hull, Berwick-upon-Tweed, London, Newcastle, and various Lincolnshire ports.[24]

---

[20] TNA E190/305/1 fol.1v–2r, 3r, E190/305/12 fol.3v–5r, 13r, E190/306/1 fol.10v–11r, 12v, 20v, E190/306/17 fol.17r, E190/307/2 fol.1v, 2r, 3r, 10r, E190/307/9 fol.2v.

[21] TNA E190/305/1 fol.10v, 16r, E190/305/11 fol.4v, 13r, 16v, E190/305/12 fol.5r, E190/306/1 fol.11r, E190/306/4 fol.4r, E190/307/3 fol.1v.

[22] Williams, pp. 156–57.

[23] Very little has been written on Keadby before the nineteenth century, beyond a brief mention of the Isle of Axholme in Gerald A. J. Hodgett, *Tudor Lincolnshire* (Lincoln: History of Lincolnshire Committee, 1975), pp. 2, 5, 71, 78, 80, 160–61.

[24] Lambert and Baker, www.medievalandtudorships.org.

Trade between head ports and the lesser ports in their regions

As mentioned, trade routes between large commercial centres and lesser ports in their regions tended to involve fewer merchants and vessels that originated from the large port in question. For example, we saw above that Southampton ships and merchants accounted for a large proportion of shipments on the routes between Southampton and Poole/the Isle of Wight/London. However, Southampton ships were negligible on the routes between Southampton and Weymouth/Lyme Regis. Likewise, the vast majority of merchants involved in Bristol's trade with Gloucestershire and Worcestershire were local to those two counties and their vessels accounted for over 80% of the ships on those routes. The one exception to this trend was trade with Tewkesbury, which involved a large number of Bristol brewers, for reasons discussed in more detail in Chapters 4 and 5. This was also true of the vessels utilised on the trade routes between Hull and the ports of Yorkshire and Lincolnshire, which mostly originated from local lesser ports in the region.

As Southampton, Bristol and Hull were central meeting points for a broad range of commodities, many traders situated in the lesser ports in the region were willing to make the journey to those key commercial centres to take advantage of their extensive markets. However, as those towns could offer little in return beyond goods produced in the local region, merchants situated in larger ports had scarce need to travel to those regions. Instead, they relied on small-scale traders from those lesser ports to supply their specialist products in exchange for the wide range of commodities available in the principal ports. Thus, while trade between large commercial centres was fairly balanced, such that traders from both ports on the route engaged in the commercial exchange, trade between large commercial centres and their subsidiary ports was more uneven. This meant that local traders in the smaller ports dominated the routes on which there was limited scope for large-scale exchange of high-value overseas goods, and were given space within the commercial environment only insofar as they were able to provide local goods for sale in those larger markets. As we shall see in Chapters 4 and 5, individuals of this kind tended to be smaller-scale in their commercial endeavours and were largely absent from the overseas trade in their regions.

This was also reflected in the nature of the vessels used on such routes, with much smaller ships being particularly commonplace. For example, ships trading between Southampton and Weymouth/Lyme Regis averaged around just 15 tons. In the case of Weymouth, this can be partially credited to the fact that the harbour was unsuitable for large vessels. Yet Lyme Regis could cater for ships of up to 100 tons and, in that case, the use of smaller vessels may have been somewhat influenced by a desire to reduce risk, resulting from the high-value and high-risk nature of the primary commodity transported on that route, Lyme Regis green glass, as discussed in more detail below.[25] As we have seen, some practical characteristics of the trade undertaken were determined by the specific commercial nature of the region, and some were determined by broader overarching themes that applied more widely to all ports of certain kinds.

Indeed, this also applied to the operational characteristics of the trade between Bristol and Hull and their respective lesser ports. For example, trade on the River Severn rarely extended beyond the estuary and involved travel on a narrow river system that traversed significantly inland. Moreover, as we saw above, the Severn trade largely involved the transportation of lightweight and low-bulk products. As a result, the ships utilised were very small, averaging just 13 or 14 tons, including at least five vessels under 3 tons, and none over 30, making them the smallest ships in the dataset. Conversely, in the North East, the smallest vessels that appeared were those that travelled between Hull and Yorkshire/Lincolnshire, which ranged from 10 to 50 tons in size, with a 30-ton average. However, while this was a little higher than those vessels engaged in local trade through Bristol or Southampton, it represents a much lower average than those engaged in trade with London or Newcastle, and the slightly larger size resulted from their occasional engagement in the coal trade in the region.

Finally, the ships involved in trade between Bristol and the Welsh ports were generally unremarkable; they ranged from 4 to 60 tons with a 15-ton average, they traded between Bristol and Wales somewhat regularly, they generally originated from the Welsh ports with which Bristol traded, and they centred on the provision of cloth and leather. However, some larger ships did sporadically travel between Bristol, Cardiff and Milford Haven, possibly owing to the overseas trade links in those three ports.[26] Likewise, whereas the vessels that were utilised in both coastal and overseas commerce carried the goods of Bristol's occupational merchants, the smaller and middling ships tended to be commanded by Welsh shipmasters and usually carried the goods of Welsh merchants, many of whom specialised on those routes. Interestingly, aside from a few tanners and shoemakers, these routes were primarily dominated by

---

[25] Loomte, p. 297; Willan, *The English Coasting Trade: 1600–1750*, pp. 157–58.

[26] For example, the 20-ton *Clement* of Mumbles travelled between various Welsh, Gloucestershire and French ports, and several of the ships that traded between Bristol and Milford Haven also travelled with some frequency to Ireland, most notably the 16-ton *Anthony* of Milford Haven and the 10-ton *Castle* of Milford Haven. See TNA E190/1128/12 fol.15r-v, E190/1128/13 fol.16r, E190/1128/14 fol.4r, 8v, 12v, 14r, E190/1129/1 fol.13r, E190/1129/18 fol.11r, 15r, 19r-v, E190/1129/22 fol.13v–14r; Lambert and Baker, www.medievalandtudorships.org; Lewis, 'The Welsh Port Books (1550–1603), pp. xix–xxviii.

individuals listed as occupational mariners and merchants. This resulted from the fact that many of these voyages involved the transportation of somewhat valuable and highly desirable products on particularly busy shipping routes. Thus, Welsh merchants and mariners could build up a steady and lucrative trade on the routes between Bristol and the Welsh ports, as we shall see in more detail in Chapters 4 and 5.

Repeat engagement and risk management

Aside from the origin and size of the ships utilised and the residential affiliations of the merchants and mariners involved, analysis of the port book data can also tell us much about the practical choices made by coastal traders in the day-to-day running of their maritime businesses. Many of these features are examined in detail in Chapters 4 and 5 within the context of particular individuals and commercial/social groups. However, analysis of the raw numerical data can help us to determine some practical characteristics within the context of specific trade routes. In particular, determining the average number of voyages undertaken per shipmaster or merchant on particular routes can give us an idea of whether trade was undertaken by a small pool of the same individuals or whether it was spread thinly across a diverse group of different shipmasters and merchants.[27] Likewise, statistics pertaining to the frequency with which multiple merchants shared space in the same vessel, or with which the merchant carrying goods aboard the vessel also acted in the capacity of shipmaster, can reveal much about the methods of risk management deployed by traders in connection with particular trade routes or commercial activities.

Repeat interaction and degree of specialism

The average number of voyages undertaken per merchant and shipmaster varied substantially between individuals, reflective of the broad range of ways in which they engaged in coastal commerce. Some traders repeated voyages frequently, covering the same trade routes with regularity, whereas others engaged on an *ad hoc* basis. In particular, as a result of the symbiotic nature of the relationship between overseas and domestic commerce, a ship returning

---

[27] For simplicity, the average figures for voyages undertaken per shipmaster or merchant that are given throughout this chapter are calculated as the average across five comparable six-month periods (rather than per year or per month). Furthermore, the figures relating to merchants do not include instances where multiple merchants appear on a single ship. Multi-merchant voyages represent approximately 6% of shipments across all three ports over the full period and are explained in more detail in subsequent chapters.

from overseas with a large cargo of goods sent ripples across the coastal trade systems as those imported goods were re-shipped internally, prompting some traders who rarely engaged in coastal enterprise to partake. For instance, in the North East, Hull's trade with ports in East Anglia, Yorkshire, and Lincolnshire was undertaken by a mix of individuals that repeated trade on those routes with regularity and individuals that dabbled in coastal commerce only occasionally. Many of those traders had commercial interests elsewhere and their participation in coastal trading was largely reactionary, with individuals responding to both incoming overseas vessels and broader commercial trends in the region. For example, Robert Tidman frequently traded between Hull and Boston, primarily transporting haberdasher wares, whereas George Anderson ran sporadic trips between Hull and Whitby carrying miscellaneous commodities.[28]

Importantly, much the same can be said of Hull's trade with London, in which a small selection of individuals participated frequently, with others taking part only occasionally. This is consistent with most trading activity investigated in this chapter, but is particularly significant for two reasons. First, it suggests that this practical characteristic applied as much to Hull's trade with London as it did to much shorter (and cheaper) trips to towns in the port's immediate surrounding area, demonstrating the breadth of participation on even long-distance and high-value coastal voyages. Secondly, the level of repeat trade among shipmasters was substantially higher than that of merchants, and we shall see in Chapters 4 and 5 that a dedicated body of occupational mariners built long and fruitful businesses based on Hull's trade with London, forming business ties with members of Hull's mercantile elite.

Hull's trade with Newcastle likewise attracted a mix of specialist and *ad hoc* traders. In this case, whereas those who occasionally dabbled in Newcastle coal travelled to Hull from a broad region, those involved in more regular trade between the two ports largely resided in the local area. As the most abundant trading opportunity in the region, it is hardly surprising that Hull and Newcastle traders would be keen to dominate, and indeed John Hatcher has explored the 'colossal' hold the Newcastle Hostmen had over the northern coal trade throughout the period, as discussed in more detail in Chapters 4 and 5.[29] Yet, this route was also very well established, and the commodity in question (Newcastle coal) was both cheap and abundant, making for a low threshold for participation and making it an appealing trade in which to occasionally partake.

Nonetheless, while it is fair to surmise that coastal trade was generally undertaken by a mix of specialist and *ad hoc* traders, there were also regional

[28] TNA E190/306/1 fol.13r, E190/306/4 fol.5r, 8r, E190/306/17 fol.13r, E190/307/3 fol.10r.
[29] Hatcher, pp. 508–46.

differences, as well as differences stemming from particular trade routes and commodities. For instance, in Southampton, trade with ports that mainly consisted of overseas commodities involved many individuals who awaited large overseas shipments and reacted accordingly to redistribute those goods coastwise. For example, John Crook ran upwards of nine coastal voyages per year carrying overseas commodities, but there was little consistency in the ports to which he travelled, with his routes extending to a broad range of locations, including London, the Isle of Wight, Poole, Sussex and Plymouth.[30] Conversely, trade in local products was less directly impacted by the arrival of an overseas shipment, and thus involved more individuals who specialised on particular trade routes. William Water of Dartford regularly ran three or four voyages per year between Southampton and Sussex, often making use of the same shipmaster and always carrying Sussex iron, reflective of the commonality of repeat engagement on that route owing to the specialist nature of the iron trade and its lack of vulnerability to trends in foreign trade.[31]

Likewise, we also see a high rate of repetition among merchants on the trade route between Southampton and Cornwall, and we shall see in Chapter 4 that a number of specific traders formed charter parties with the same, or similar, groups every few years, often involving merchants from across the kingdom in order to transport a high-value local product: Cornish tin. Such specialisms were also commonplace in Bristol's trade in local produce, and those who traded into Bristol from Worcestershire and Gloucestershire repeated voyages with unusual frequency. In no other trade explored in this volume did the average number of voyages per merchant or shipmaster exceed three and the vast majority did not exceed two over the full dataset. However, the average number of voyages for shipmasters and merchants on the River Severn was sometimes as high as six or seven, and often exceeded three. This highlights the extent to which this trade was dominated by a small number of exceptionally active traders. These individuals plied the same short-distance routes, using the same ships and running the same goods repeatedly. They rarely left the river system and many frequently acted as both shipmaster and merchant.

Interestingly, a large proportion of the individuals that traded on the Severn were identified by the customs officials as 'trowmen', which may help to further substantiate the operational characteristics that were evident in Bristol's inland trade. Severn trowmen were a distinctive occupational group specific

---

[30] TNA E190/814/5 fol.1r, 4r, 5v–6r, 7r-v, 8r, 11v, 12v–13r, E190/814/6 fol.3v–5r, 6v, 7v–8r, E190/814/7 fol.1v, 3v, 5v, 6r, E190/814/11 fol.1r–2v, 7r-v, E190/814/12 fol.1r, 2r, 3v–6v, 8v, 10r, E190/815/1 fol.3r, 6v, 8v, E190/815/2 fol.5r, 7r, E190/815/8 fol.2r-v, 5v, 6v–7r.

[31] TNA E190/814/6 fol.8v, E190/814/11 fol.5v, E190/814/12 fol.2v, 5r, 6v, 7v, 8v, E190/815/1 fol.6r-v, 7v, 8v, 9r, E190/815/2 fol.1r, 2r, E190/815/8 fol.2r.

to the River Severn and were named after the vessels they sailed. The 'trow' was a type of flat-bottom barge with a highly adaptive mast that allowed for travel under bridges and easy stowage on the quayside.[32] Although trows could be adapted for sea travel with the addition of a temporary keel, they were designed primarily for use on river networks, and a review of the data made available via the Medieval and Tudor Ships Project suggests that they rarely travelled further than Bristol.[33] We shall see in Chapter 5 that trowmen did not exclusively sail trow barges, but they did occupy a distinctive social space separate from other Gloucestershire and Worcestershire traders, and they were the lifeblood of the River Severn, dominating trade in the region and rarely extending beyond their established trade routes. Of the 819 merchants who were given an occupational title in the Bristol customs records, fifty-seven were listed as trowmen, making them the second largest occupational group in the accounts.[34]

That being said, some regional trade routes were immune from the dominance of the trowmen, such as the route between Bristol and Tewkesbury, on which Bristol traders (rather than Gloucestershire/Worcestershire traders) were unusually prevalent, accounting for some 18% of merchants. Almost all of those Bristol merchants were recorded as brewers and utilised Tewkesbury vessels to domestically import grain into Bristol. This was generally a one-way flow of traffic, with Bristol brewers only appearing as merchants on ships travelling from Tewkesbury to Bristol, and those vessels often making the reverse journey in ballast. However, in some cases, those ships returned to Tewkesbury several days later carrying wine purchased by the shipmaster in Bristol. The fact that individuals from Tewkesbury occupied dual roles as merchant/shipmaster, and that Bristol brewers appear in the port books as merchants, highlights again the broad skillsets from which coastal traders benefited and the flexible nature of coastal commercial activity, which allowed individuals from a broad social spectrum to engage in maritime trade with varying degrees of frequency and specialisation suited to their wider business models.

---

[32] Grahame Farr, 'Severn Navigation and the Trow', *The Mariner's Mirror*, 32 (1946), 79–80; Basil Greenhill, 'The Story of the Severn Trow', *The Mariner's Mirror*, 26 (1940), 286.

[33] Farr, p. 93; Lambert and Baker, www.medievalandtudorships.org.

[34] The largest group were those listed as merchants, who appeared most often in trade with Wales and Cornwall, but also likely included those who did not specifically fit into a particular craft group. This is discussed in more detail in Chapter 5.

Risk management

Finally, we briefly turn to the methods utilised by early modern merchants and mariners to reduce risk. While such action was perhaps more crucial in overseas travel (where the voyage was often long, the landscape of travel and trade unpredictable, and the cargoes were usually of high value), coastal traders also sought to increase the chances of turning a profit on their voyages. Indeed, while coasting typically involved smaller investments, was largely undertaken in a political and commercial landscape to which traders were already accustomed, and often required less extensive practical sailing ability, there were particular factors that increased the precariousness of specific coastal trade routes. In particular, the need to navigate an especially complex part of the coast, or the transportation of a particularly high-value cargo, often led to coastal traders seeking means to reduce the risk of financial loss.

In overseas trade, the methods through which merchants reduced risk were diverse, but in coastal commerce, this typically meant hiring a separate shipmaster to command the vessel and/or collaborating with other merchants to split the space in the hull. In this way, the shipmaster and merchant(s) shared legal responsibility for the voyage, and merchants could reduce their investment by dividing the costs among a number of individuals that wished to trade on the same route and fill the vessel to capacity without individually shipping a large quantity of product.[35] Importantly, both of these operational approaches also decreased the capacity for profit on a particular voyage (either owing to the extra outlay required to hire a separate shipmaster or because individual merchants were then carrying less of their own product to sell), meaning that it was a delicate balance in the business models of early modern merchants between maximising profit and reducing risk. By looking at the degree to which traders implemented these two operational approaches on particular trade routes or when carrying particular commodities, we can assess not just the means of reducing risk on coastal voyages, but also the impetus for taking (or not taking) such action.

For example, in the case of Southampton's trade with the ports of Dorset and Hampshire, the journeys to which were particularly short and required very little navigational or sailing skill, we see that there was generally a very low tendency for merchants to share hull space, reflective of the low level of risk associated with those routes. The one exception, however, was the trade route with Lyme Regis, on which merchants operated in one of two ways: either they pooled their resources to hire a larger ship (>10 tons), or singularly utilised a smaller vessel (<10 tons).[36] This difference in operational approach

---

[35] Ward, pp. 97–123.
[36] TNA E190/814/5 fol.3r, 10v, E190/814/6 fol.6r, E190/814/11 fol.1r, 5v, 6r,

can be attributed to the high value, fragile nature and low weight/bulkiness of Lyme Regis' primary export, green glass, meaning that it was desirable to transport low quantities in a single shipment to reduce the extent of potential loss in the event of wreckage or attack from pirates.[37] This could be achieved by utilising a small vessel and transporting small quantities belonging to a single merchant, or by filling a larger ship with small quantities of goods belonging to multiple individuals.

Moreover, this latter approach was also applied with particular regularity to Southampton's trade with Cornwall and London, with twenty-six of the seventy-seven voyages between Southampton and Cornwall involving more than one merchant (a higher proportion of multi-merchant voyages than in trade with any other region), and seventeen of the 104 voyages between Southampton and London involving multiple merchants. In Cornwall, this operational approach can be attributed to the risky nature of travelling in Cornish waters, combined with the high value of tin, providing a particular need to reduce individual investment and provide protection against a potential loss.[38] In London, however, the voyages on which multiple merchants carried cargo were only those travelling outbound from Southampton towards London (not those travelling in the reverse direction), which mostly involved the transportation of a single high-value commodity, such as Cornish tin, wine, or spices, in this case providing incentive to reduce risk on only a single leg of the journey, demonstrating the very specific application of particular practical approaches to specific trade routes and commodities.

In terms of the practice of hiring an independent shipmaster, this was generally the norm in coastal trading across all three regions (especially in the case of merchants who also engaged in overseas trade, for whom this was a typical operational approach), except in cases where exceptionally low-value goods were involved. Thus, in the Hampshire and Dorset region, the only route that frequently saw vessels commanded by a merchant on board was that between Southampton and Weymouth. Despite assertions by a Spanish

---

E190/814/12 fol.2r–3v, 5v, 6v, 9r, E190/815/2 fol.1r–2r, 5v, 6v, E190/815/8 fol.1r-v, 3v.

[37] Green glasses were valued at around 1s 6d per dozen, making them significantly more costly than unspecified drinking glasses, which were usually around 13d per dozen, or 'brace' glasses, which had a value of around 17d per dozen; see Flavin and Jones, 'A Glossary of Commodities, Weights and Measures Found in the Sixteenth-Century Bristol Customs Account', p. 41.

[38] The work of Jones and Flavin puts tin at 30s per C, compared to 15s per C for white lead, or 10s per C for copperas: see ibid., pp. 23, 50, 54, 102. For discussions on the dangers of navigating Cornish waters, see Kenneth R. Andrews, 'The Elizabethan Seaman', *The Mariner's Mirror*, 68 (1982), 250; Loomte, p. 294; Cathryn Pearce, *Cornish Wrecking, 1700–1860: Reality and Popular Myth* (Woodbridge: Boydell Press, 2010), pp. 21–31.

'spy' in 1597 that Weymouth was nothing more than 'a port ... for small ships which rest[ed] on dry land at low water', Weymouth represented an important region for coastal trading in Southampton.[39] Yet that trade almost exclusively focused on shipping firewood, making it both a short-distance and low-value venture, involving only very small vessels, as noted above. It was therefore both practical and cost-efficient to minimise the crew required and undertake such trips without an independent shipmaster.

This approach can also be seen particularly starkly in the case of Hull's trade with Newcastle, which centred on the provision of an especially low-value commodity (Newcastle coal), which was largely undertaken with the merchant also acting in the capacity of shipmaster, and which was exclusively undertaken with the goods of only a single merchant on board. All 734 voyages between Hull and Newcastle that are analysed here carried the goods of only a single merchant, and only thirty-one involved the hiring of a shipmaster independently from the merchant on board. Notably, this also applied to those rare voyages on which Southampton merchants transported coal, for which they typically acted in both the capacity of shipmaster and merchant and carried a large quantity of only their own product in order to increase profits.[40]

Likewise, many merchants who participated in Southampton's trade with Devon often also commanded the vessels on which they sailed. This is inconsistent with the typical mode of operation for merchants that were substantially involved in overseas activity, who more often hired a separate shipmaster. However, this particularly high figure resulted from the low value of some of the cargoes carried, such as beer or firewood, which encouraged merchants to maximise profits by also taking command of the ship. Of course, not all merchants had the practical skills to sail a ship, but it is notable that lower-value goods prompted an increased tendency to do so, even on slightly longer voyages. Moreover, some merchants who engaged in coastal commerce certainly were also accomplished shipmasters, and this will be explored in more detail in Chapter 5.

Interestingly, this operational approach was less common on the routes between Bristol and the Devon ports. While there were some instances in the trade with Bideford and Barnstaple where the merchant also acted as shipmaster, those were largely undertaken by Barnstaple mariners Robert Bennett and John Simons, and their activities were not representative of wider trading practices in the region.[41] In Southampton, the high merchant/shipmaster figure resulted from the transportation of low-value commodities,

[39] Loomte, p. 297.
[40] For example, TNA E190/814/7 fol.4v, E190/814/11 fol.2r, 5r, 7r, E190/815/1 fol.8v, E190/815/2 fol.1v–2r, E190/815/8 fol.1v–2r.
[41] TNA E190/1128/12 fol.10r, 13r, 15r, E190/1128/13 fol.7v, 16r, E190/1128/14 fol.4r, 14v, 15r, E190/1129/1 fol.1v, 11r-v, 16r, 17r-v, 18v, E190/1129/18 fol.6r, 7r, 8r, 16v.

which caused individuals to alter their operational approach in order to reduce costs. However, Bristol's trade with Devon usually involved the transportation of high-value commodities such as wine, oil and luxury goods, in which case the need to reduce costs was less pressing and the desire to protect investments was increased.

The same can be said of the merchants involved in Southampton's trade with Cornwall or London, who were unlikely to command the vessels on which they transported goods, reflective of the commodities carried and the individuals involved. Aside from the fact that these voyages involved the transportation of high-value goods, high-status merchants more generally tended to hire occupational shipmasters on a voyage-by-voyage basis, rather than forming long-term business partnerships with specific mariners or acting in the capacity of shipmaster themselves, as we shall see in Chapter 4. Indeed, and much like the decision to divide shipments between multiple merchants, this operational approach was particularly common among merchants that also traded overseas, who were more likely to trade in high-value commodities, who very likely operated within charter parties routinely in their foreign trade, and who were accustomed to hiring separate shipmasters on a voyage-by-voyage basis, suggesting this was, at least to some degree, a continuation of their routine forms of commercial activity.

Aside from these broad trends, there were a number of instances in which the shipmaster and merchant were one and the same for regionally specific reasons. For example, in Bristol's trade with the Welsh ports there were a number of instances where the shipmaster carried only their own cargo. This type of voyage was particularly common in trade with Carmarthen and Haverfordwest, and usually involved individuals identified as occupational mariners, who otherwise routinely undertook voyages carrying the goods of occupational merchants.[42] Notably, there was little variation in the commodities transported by these individuals when they acted solely in the capacity of shipmaster compared to when they acted as shipmaster/merchant. This suggests that they were career seafarers, who occasionally dabbled in the transportation and sale of products that were most common on their typical trade routes, again showing the diversity of skill and knowledge present in the maritime community. We shall see in subsequent chapters that these shipmasters forged successful maritime careers shuttling between Bristol and South Wales, and they evidently also had sufficient knowledge and equity to occasionally invest in their own product on those routes with which they were well acquainted, taking advantage of their maritime expertise to participate in the capacity of merchant.

On the other hand, as Bristol's trade with Plymouth involved the transportation of coal, we would expect a higher proportion of individuals on

---

[42] See throughout TNA E190/1128/12, E190/1128/13, E190/1128/14, E190/1129/1, E190/1129/18, E190/1129/22, E190/1130/2.

that route to act as both shipmaster and merchant, as was the case in the coal trade in both Southampton and Hull. However, unlike in Southampton and Hull, where coal was transported on its own in large quantities in order to maximise potential profits, in Bristol coal was freighted alongside other goods in mixed shipments, usually among high-value commodities such as lead, soap, and wine. Therefore, in the Bristol coal trade, the impetus to reduce risk was increased and a separate shipmaster was usually hired.[43] Most research on the pre-1700 coal industry has been largely focused on the east coast, but can provide some explanation for this difference in regional trade practices. Nef has shown that not only did the South West burn substantially less coal than the east, but the cost of coal, including its transportation, was substantially lower in the South West than in other parts of the kingdom. The geographic proximity of the major south-western ports to the coal-producing regions of South Wales allowed safe and relatively low-cost access to coal, and Bristol also benefited from access to its own coalfield, albeit one of limited output. Moreover, distance from London lessened the demand for coal and shielded Bristol and the surrounding region from political manoeuvring in the capital that often had a dramatic impact on pricing.[44] Hatcher described Bristol as having an 'enviable reputation of enjoying abundant cheap fuel' and noted that Daniel Defoe 'marvelled at the low price of coal there'.[45] As the demand for coal and cost of transportation in the South West was much lower than elsewhere, very different operational characteristics took form. Rather than maximising volumes of coal to make a voyage worthwhile, traders from the South West would transport small quantities alongside higher-value products. This stark contrast between Hull and Bristol might be expected, given the geographic distance between the ports and their many socio-political differences, but the dramatic difference between Southampton and Bristol is more surprising and supports Nef's theory that a clear dividing line existed somewhere along the Devon coast.[46]

Conclusions

We saw in Chapter 2 that a healthy stream of coastal trade flowed through the three case study ports and that a bias towards overseas trade has painted a needlessly gloomy image of these ports during this period. In this chapter we

---

[43] Lead was valued at £8 per ton in 1594/5, Castile soap at 15s per C, and wine was usually worth between £5 and £7 per ton, compared to 6s 8d per wey for coal. See Flavin and Jones, 'A Glossary of Commodities, Weights and Measures Found in the Sixteenth-Century Bristol Customs Account', pp. 22, 54, 92; Jones, 'The Bristol Shipping Industry in the Sixteenth Century', p. 22.

[44] Nef, pp. 52–56, 87–90; Hatcher, pp. 135–41, 78–84.

[45] Hatcher, pp. 178–81.

[46] Nef, pp. 88–90.

have expanded on that conclusion to show that each port under investigation here benefited from a significant coastal ship fleet, much of which has been generally overlooked in the historiography. In particular, Hull's coastal ship fleet was vast in terms of both the number of individual vessels and the tonnage of those ships. Indeed, it is likely that Hull challenged even the largest and richest southern ports in terms of availability of tonnage, and the town almost certainly played a larger role in the economic health of the North East than has been previously acknowledged.

Moreover, as a result of legislation aimed to bolster the English maritime industry, English vessels and English merchants controlled coastal trade routes, and the majority of those vessels and merchants were drawn from the broad region in which each port was situated. For example, although Lillian Wiggs suggested that Southampton's London trade was under the control of foreign merchants, the sources assessed here indicate that almost all of Southampton's coastal commercial activity was in English hands, and mostly in the hands of local traders from the region.[47] Due to legislative intervention, domestic trade was largely free from foreign competition, enabling local traders access to often fruitful trades, many of which benefited from a low threshold for participation in terms of financial investment, commercial contacts, and practical sailing ability. As we shall see in Chapter 5, many individuals engaged in coastal enterprise brought fortune and prosperity to their towns, in addition to paying local customs and quay fees to the corporation.

It has also been possible in this chapter to examine the operational nature of the coasting trade in some detail, providing a more nuanced understanding of the ships and traders that plied those routes. For example, we have seen that the way large commercial centres engaged in trade with other large commercial centres was rather different from their engagement in trade with lesser ports in their area. Commercial exchange with ports that were themselves regional trading hubs typically involved the mutual provision of mixed redistributed cargoes and was usually undertaken on relatively large vessels, including a significant proportion of ships from the ports at both ends of the voyage. However, the relationship between large centres and their subsidiaries was more uneven, and vessels from the larger port usually played a lesser role in trade, with those ships from the smaller port providing specialist goods tending to dominate.

Furthermore, even beyond that level of regional variation, individual coastal traders also adjusted the operational nature of their engagement in coastal commerce dependent on the commodities transported and the trade route plied. Some individuals engaged consistently with a specific trade route or commodity over a long period, whereas others dipped into coastal trading

---

[47] Wiggs, p. 2.

for just a few voyages a year as an aside to a primary career. For example, a number of the ships that were most common on the Severn River network were, to a certain extent, restricted to inland trade. As a result, the average tonnage of the vessels involved in trade with Gloucestershire, Worcestershire and the West Midlands was exceptionally low, and individuals on those routes traded with an unusually high level of repetition.

Likewise, commercial activity on other routes where smaller ports supplied Bristol with goods produced in their local region was also dominated by local individuals who engaged in the same trade with a high rate of repetition. However, trade on routes between Bristol and other major commercial centres involved more Bristol merchants, who travelled on much larger ships and were often also involved in overseas trade. These individuals did not tend to specialise in coastal commerce but instead engaged sporadically as an aside to their overseas activities. Coastal commercial activity attracted individuals from a broad spectrum of occupational backgrounds with varying degrees of wealth and social stature, many of whom adapted their operational approach to suit the trade in which they wished to engage.

Finally, this adaptation of operational approaches to suit particular trade routes and commodities was especially evident in the efforts traders took to reduce risk on particular voyages. While coastal merchants rarely collaborated with other traders to share hull space, they would make an exception for voyages on which they were transporting particularly high-value or high-risk products. Such action reduced the profitability of the voyage by reducing the volume of product transported but also reduced losses in the event the vessel foundered or was attacked by pirates. Conversely, when the goods transported were particularly low-value, they would revert to their standing position of carrying only their own goods, but would also often change their approach from acting only in the capacity of merchant to also commanding the vessel, in order to cut costs and maximise profits. This was most obvious in the case of the Newcastle coal trade, where we have evidence of over 700 coastal shipments, all of which utilised particularly large ships, the vast majority of which involved one individual acting in the capacity of both shipmaster and merchant, and carried the goods of that single individual.

This sat in stark contrast to the trade between Hull and London, where the ships utilised were also large, but they more often carried the goods of multiple merchants and were usually commanded by a separate shipmaster. As the goods transported on that route were of higher value and lower bulk than Newcastle coal, acceptable profit margins could be achieved by transporting smaller quantities, even with the costs of hiring a separate shipmaster. Each of these practical features of coastal commercial activity points to a diverse and adaptive community of traders, many of whom were guided by their knowledge of the trade in which they were engaging, and who made practical decisions based on the needs of the specific voyage. As a result, clear trends emerge in the port books regarding the dynamics of the coastal trade during the Elizabethan period that emphasise the vibrant nature of the maritime workforce, many of whom were sufficiently knowledgeable and adequately willing to adjust their practical approaches to forge successful careers from engagement in coastal enterprise, as will become clearer still in Chapters 4 and 5.

4

Business networks, seafaring communities and commercial models

Having laid out some vital context, we turn now to examine the commercial and social characteristics of the individuals that exploited the coastal trade routes described above. The research underpinning this chapter relies on the use of Social Network Analysis in order to visualise and analyse the business networks of individuals involved in coastal trading, particularly focusing on interactions between shipmasters and merchants. The specific methods utilised in this research are described in an accompanying article.[1] However, it is important to briefly describe the scholarly background to the application of Social Network Analysis to historical research (i.e. Historical Network Research) and to explain how the findings presented here were extracted from the port book data. The term 'Historical Network Research' (HNR) is relatively new, taken up by historians in recent decades in an attempt to unite an academic community that was divided over the legitimacy of applying sociological principles (particularly Social Network Analysis (SNA)) to historical research.

Although SNA has been an interdisciplinary venture from its inception, involving sociologists, citation analysts, and archaeologists, its traditional reliance on mathematical and statistical frameworks disrupted the status quo of traditional historical research, and it long remained marginalised by historians unwilling to reinvent traditional historical practices.[2] In an attempt to find a middle ground, researchers sought a solution that would allow them to reap the

---

[1] Leanna T P Brinkley, 'Understanding the Early Modern English Coastal Trading Community: A Case Study of Network Prosopography', *Journal of Historical Network Research* (2021).

[2] There are many notable researchers that could be mentioned here but, in particular, see: Geoffrey Irwin, 'Pots and Entrepots: A Study of Settlement, Trade and the Development of Economic Specialization in Papuan Prehistory', *World Archaeology*, 9 (1978); Peter V. Marsden and Nan Lin, eds, *Social Structure and Network Analysis* (London: Sage Publishing, 1982); Douglas R. White and H. Gilman McCann, 'Cites and Fights', in *Social Structures: A Network Approach*, ed. by Barry Wellman and Steven Berkowitz (Cambridge: Cambridge University Press, 1998), pp. 380–400.

benefits of SNA while maintaining methodological integrity in their historical studies. The solutions they developed allowed for some degree of quantification of historical places, people, and events, but also incorporated traditional historical methods. The application of HNR has proven a fruitful endeavour and has caught the attention of academics from a broad range of subjects. Research in this field has ranged from broad discussions regarding the concept and categorisation of social class, to geographically and culturally specific studies of subjects such as the networks of the Medici family.[3] Of course, the question of whether HNR is possible, or indeed appropriate, in a specific field of study relies heavily on the available sources. Without reliable data, there can be no data analysis. Yet the types of sources used by historians who have successfully implemented HNR are extremely varied.[4] By applying stringent historical research methods alongside methods of SNA, such historians have found an effective and elegant way of understanding the structural elements that defined our past.

However, while this is undoubtedly a change to be celebrated, the explosion of interest in networks in recent years has come with a variety of problems. Without the proper tools available, many historians have gone on to claim networks in their research without adhering to even the most basic concepts of SNA. Indeed, a number of HNR scholars have berated the over-use and under-consideration of the term 'network'. Mike Burkhardt has been especially critical, accusing historians of turning the concept into nothing more than 'a trendy term to attract potential readers'. So damaged is the idea of network theories in historical analysis, claims Burkhardt, that it 'is no longer useful in all fields of historical research'.[5] There is little need to relay the details of these criticisms, and indeed many skilled analysts have already pinpointed

---

[3] Many examples could be drawn on to demonstrate this point, but to list just a few, see: Peter S. Bearman, *Relations into Rhetorics: Local Elite Social Structure in Norfolk, England, 1540–1640* (New Brunswick, NJ: Rutgers University Press, 1993); Lilyan A. Brudner and Douglas R. White, 'Class, Property, and Structural Endogamy: Visualizing Networked Histories', *Theory and Society*, 26 (1997); John F. Padgett and Christopher K. Ansell, 'Robust Action and the Rise of the Medici', *American Journal of Sociology*, 98 (1993); John F. Padgett and Paul D. McLean, 'Organizational Invention and Elite Transformation: The Birth of Partnership Systems in Renaissance Florence', *American Journal of Sociology*, 111 (2006).

[4] Charles van den Heuvel and others, 'Circles of Confidence in Correspondence', *Nuncius*, 31 (2016); Naomi Rosenthal and others, 'Social Movements and Network Analysis: A Case Study of Nineteenth-Century Women's Reform in New York State', *American Journal of Sociology*, 90 (1985).

[5] Mike Burkhardt, 'Networks as Social Structures in Late Medieval and Early Modern Towns: A Theoretical Approach to Historical Network Analysis', in *Commercial Networks and European Cities, 1400–1800*, ed. by Andrea Caracausi and Christof Jeggle (London: Pickering and Chatto Publishers, 2014), pp. 13–44 (p. 13).

the problems and offered satisfactory solutions.[6] Nonetheless, it should be noted that any historian wishing to engage in such analysis must ensure that they understand the core theories that underlie SNA before embarking on an exploration of networks.

Therefore, before embarking on the research underpinning this chapter, it was necessary to form a robust methodological framework within which to examine the business relationships forged by coastal traders. Fortunately, many of the surviving sources pertaining to the early modern seafaring community provide much scope for the application of network theory. The data available in the early modern customs records alone provides a plethora of information regarding the commercial ties between merchants and mariners who operated in English (and in some cases Welsh) ports. By extracting shipmasters and merchants from the customs records as nodes and linking them by their involvement in the same voyages, it was thus possible to determine the nature of their business connections.[7] Through this chapter we will examine the relationships forged between shipmasters and merchants, analysing the characteristics (occupations, preferred cargoes, preferred trade routes, residencies) of individuals that elected to work together, the frequency of repeat interaction, the ways in which relationships were formed, the motivations for collaboration, and the role of propinquity (physical proximity) in the forging of business ties. Using analysis software *Gephi*, it was possible to examine in detail the groups that worked together on a regular basis, as well as those who were drawn

[6] See, for example, ibid.; Claire Lemercier, 'Formal Network Methods in History: Why and How?', in *Social Networks, Political Institutions, and Rural Societies*, ed. by Georg Fertig (Turnhout, Belgium: Brepols, 2015), pp. 281–310.

[7] For the purposes of this analysis, there is no distinction made between a shipmaster/merchant tie and a merchant/merchant tie, and both are undirected. Arguably, in some cases, a shipmaster/merchant tie could have been directed, for example if the shipmaster was hired directly by a merchant (or merchants) for a single voyage. However, in reality, the relationships were more complex and a straightforward hire was not always the form of business connection. For example, instances in which a shipmaster and merchant had a long-term business arrangement created a more equal partnership than a contract where a number of shipmasters might vie for a single job, and a directed tie would not be a reasonable representation of this type of relationship, and would likely create a false impression of the way in which merchants and shipmasters interacted. Fury, Ward, and Lambert have offered detailed assessments of the career paths and business approaches taken by seafarers: see Fury, 'The Elizabethan Maritime Community'; Cheryl A. Fury, 'Training and Education in the Elizabethan Maritime Community, 1585–1603', *The Mariner's Mirror*, 85 (1999); Lambert, 'Tudor Shipmasters and Maritime Communities, 1550–1600'; Ward. For an explanation of the differences between directed and undirected ties, see Scott B. Weingart, 'Introduction to Networks and Network Analysis for Humanists', *Computer Technologies for the Historical Research of Intellectual Networks Study Day* (2013).

together by particular economic trends and local/regional/national events, and to examine the specific business models of particular traders.

The nodes in the graphs were allocated certain attributes, which were exhibited according to various colour-coding systems, the details of which are displayed and explained throughout the succeeding chapter. This method allowed for detailed assessment of the characteristics of the individuals between whom business connections were formed, and for an overarching view of the networks that formed around particular commodities, trade routes, regions, and social groups. Of course, in instances where an individual acted in both the capacity of the shipmaster and the merchant, these ties are not visible, and since 98% of Hull's trade with Newcastle was undertaken in that way, analysis of the business networks forged in Hull focuses on trade outside of the Newcastle coal industry. For simplicity, relationships beyond engagement in specific voyages identified in the customs records (such as familial, residential, or personal relationships) were not visualised in the network graphs that were generated, but are nonetheless discussed in some detail within the chapter for individuals or groups of particular interest. Owing to the complexity of the networks around which coastal trading revolved, this chapter is divided into three parts, looking in turn at the networks of Southampton, Bristol, and Hull.

Coastal networks in Southampton

As we saw in Chapter 2, Southampton's commercial ties during this period were far-reaching. In the most extreme cases, merchants and mariners travelled to Southampton from regions as far east as Hull and as far west as South Wales, on voyages spanning many hundreds of nautical miles. However, while it is important to acknowledge the extensive reach of the town's coastal trade routes, such ports were by no means Southampton's foremost commercial partners, and most voyages to regions further afield were undertaken *ad hoc* by individual merchants in response to particular demand. Conversely, activity between Southampton and its primary trading ports was undertaken with regularity and consistency and, as we shall see below, was often carried out by established networks of merchants and mariners, who forged network ties with individuals who shared their commercial interests in order to engage with particular trade routes and markets. Indeed, we shall see that the networks that formed around Southampton's Cornish tin trade were markedly separate from those that formed around Southampton's iron trade with Sussex or those that formed around small-scale local trade within the Hampshire and Dorset region. That being said, there were particular individuals that crossed between those networks and tied together otherwise disparate groups, such as elite merchant John Crook, and there was also scope for mobility among lesser traders to transition from small-scale local networks into larger and more lucrative networks that engaged in high-end trade such as commercial exchange with London. In this section, we will look in turn at a number of the core groups within the context of their primary trading activities, and then finally examine the impact that regional changes had on the degree to which individuals from separate towns engaged with one another through the port of Southampton (a concept termed here as 'cross-county integration').

Cornish tin and the London connection

We turn first to the networks surrounding one of Southampton's most important commercial enterprises: the trade in Cornish tin. It has been well established that the tin trade played a significant role in Southampton's economic successes during the early modern period, and we saw in Chapter 2 that Cornish trade made up some 8% of total coastwise activity through the port during the late sixteenth century. Southampton was established as the staple of metals in 1492 and, although trade with Cornwall was by no means the most extensive of Southampton's coastal activity, the high value of Cornish tin meant that it represented a particularly important trade for the town. As a result, Alwyn Ruddock has observed that London merchants had a strong presence in Southampton during the earlier period, and the evidence presented in this chapter suggests that Londoners still played a significant role on that trade route in the late sixteenth century. Moreover, we shall see that London merchants were able to forge partnerships with traders from a broad range of locations, forming extensive network ties with merchants and seafarers from across the region and beyond.[8]

The network graphs generated from the port book data pertaining to the Cornish tin trade reveal a number of notable characteristics of that commercial activity, including both the practical characteristics of the trade and the individuals engaged in it, the most immediately noticeable of which was the tendency for merchants to share hull space. As discussed in Chapter 3, merchants were particularly keen to share hull space in the case of the transportation of Cornish tin due to its high value and the dangers of navigating the Cornish coast, which resulted in a desire to reduce the level of risk on each voyage. In network terms, this resulted in the formation of a high number of merchant-to-merchant ties and particularly dense network graphs. Importantly, in most cases, individuals principally undertook single-merchant voyages when engaging in the trade in other commodities, but changed their

[8] Ruddock, 'London Capitalists and the Decline of Southampton in the Early Tudor Period', pp. 144–49.

operational approach to collaborate with other merchants in order to transport high-value cargoes like tin.[9]

For example, important Southampton merchant Robert Eire undertook nineteen voyages through Southampton across the full dataset. Six of those involved the transportation of Cornish tin, on which he shared hull space with other high-level Hampshire and London merchants, and thirteen involved the transportation of other commodities, on which only Eire's cargo was carried.[10] This was also true of the merchants that formed the star-shaped cluster involving John Venard, William Davies, Thomas Eire and John Goddard visible in Figure 4.2 below, which also represents a single multi-merchant voyage carrying Cornish tin. Once more, most of the merchants on that voyage more typically carried other commodities in single-merchant shipments, but came together in order to form a charter party to split the cost of a consignment of tin. Similarly, London merchants Thomas Davies and John White engaged in varied trade through Southampton, interestingly including a rare trip to Newcastle by White in 1569 in order to collect coal, but only shared hull space when trading in Cornish tin, adapting their operations and network ties to suit the commodity transported.[11]

However, this was not the case for all merchants, and others, such as Southampton merchants Hugh Devart and Gerald Demarest and Channel Island merchants William Davies and John Vernard, appear to have specialised their coastal enterprises in Southampton, only ever trading in Cornish tin and resultingly always sharing hull space with other merchants, creating dense network clusters.[12] This was also true of individuals engaged in other high-value cargoes and the network graphs generated from the data pertaining to shipmaster Roger Limbery, who usually ran two or three voyages per year between Southampton and Lyme Regis carrying the high-value cargo of green glass, also contained numerous merchant-to-merchant ties, reflective of his preference for collaborating with other merchants.[13] Interestingly, while William Davies and Hugh Devart appeared on the same tin voyage in 1575, they were markedly separate in the network graphs extracted from the 1577

---

[9] For example, see TNA E190/814/5 fol.1v–2v, 6v, 8r, 12r E190/814/6 fol.1v, 2v, 4v, 6v, 7r, E190/814/7 fol.2v, 5v, E190/814/11 fol.2v, 4v, 6v, E190/814/12 fol.1r, E190/815/8 fol.5v.

[10] TNA E190/814/5 fol.2v, 4v–5r, 6r-v, 8r, 12r, E190/814/6 fol.1r, 2r-v, 4v, 6v–7r, E190/814/7 fol.4r, 5v, 7r. 8r.

[11] TNA E190/814/5 fol.3v, E190/814/7 fol.2r, 4v, E190/814/11 fol.6v, E190/814/12 fol.3v, 9r, E190/815/1 fol.8v, E190/815/2 fol.2v, 3r, 5r, 6v, E190/815/8 fol.2v–3r, 6v.

[12] TNA E190/814/5 fol.4v, 7v, E190/814/6 fol.4r, 6r, E190/814/7 fol.7r, E190/814/11 fol.4r, 5r, 6v, E190/814/12 fol.3v, 7v–8v, E190/815/1 fol.5r, 8r-v, E190/815/2 fol.2v, 3r, E190/815/8 fol.1r, 2v–3r.

[13] TNA E190/814/6 fol.4r, E190/814/7 fol.7r, E190/814/11 fol.6v, E190/814/12 fol.7v, 8r, E190/815/1 fol.8r, E190/815/2 fol.3r, E190/815/8 fol.1r, 2v.

data. There is little evidence in the port books that explains this divide, and it may simply have been a matter of practicality. However, civic sources suggest that, while Devart was an important member of the Southampton community, he struggled to maintain business relationships, often appearing in local records as the instigator of trouble. He frequently fell out with other merchants, was regularly accused of violence, and was stripped of his burgess status on more than one occasion, perhaps explaining his inconsistent interaction with members of the Southampton mercantile elite.[14]

Aside from the practical approach these merchants took to the transportation of Cornish tin, the individuals with whom they elected to form charter parties reveal much about the commercial nature of the tin trade in Southampton. It is clear that the Cornish tin trade attracted particularly large groups of affluent and high-status elite merchants. For example, if we turn back to Robert Eire, we see that in 1569 he appeared among a cluster of three Southampton merchants running a shipment of tin from Helston in Cornwall into Southampton, at least two of whom were members of the Southampton mercantile elite.[15] Eire himself was a member of the gentry family of Eyre, who had long-established ties to the Wiltshire region. Eire served as both mayor and MP for Salisbury before moving to Southampton in 1565, and he was appointed Captain of Southampton in 1570, being tasked with protecting the town following Elizabeth I's excommunication by Pope Pius V. Likewise, John Caplein was from a prosperous mercantile family, his father (John Caplein senior) being a burgess of Cornwall and servant to the Receiver-General there.[16] Interestingly, John Caplein actually engaged in two multi-merchant Cornish tin voyages through Southampton in that year, each of which involved separate groups of merchants but both of which involved Robert Eire, and it is quite possible that his Cornish connection enabled those men to trade into that region, especially given the specific role of the Receiver-General in overseeing the transportation of tin into Southampton from Cornwall.[17]

---

[14] Butler, 'Hugh Durvall (1541–1587)', http://www.tudorrevels.co.uk/records.php (accessed 27 August 2019). Note that the spelling of Devart's surname is particularly inconsistent across records, and in the port books he is listed variously as Dirvatt, Duvatt and Durval: for example, see E190/814/6 fol.6r, E190/814/11 fol.4r, 5r, 6v, E190/814/12 fol.3v, 8r-v, E190/815/1 fol.8r, E190/815/2 fol.2v, E190/815/8 fol.3r.

[15] TNA E190/814/7 fol.7r.

[16] Butler, 'John Capelyn (1516–1570)', 'John Capelyn (1548–1605)', 'Robert Eire (1562–1584)', http://www.tudorrevels.co.uk/records.php; Ruddock, 'London Capitalists and the Decline of Southampton in the Early Tudor Period', p. 149; John Martin, 'Appendix 2 – the Eyres of Newhouse, Brickworth, Landford and Bramshaw', in *A History of Landford in Wiltshire* (History of Landford, 2019), p. 11.

[17] Ruddock, 'London Capitalists and the Decline of Southampton in the Early Tudor Period', pp. 141–49.

Similarly, many other core members of the mercantile elite in Southampton elected to occasionally engage in the coastal transportation of Cornish tin alongside their other businesses. This included wealthy overseas trader and twice mayor Richard Biston, affluent local merchant and extensive landowner Hugh Devart, and prolific overseas trader and privateer John Crook, whose networks are discussed at more length separately below.[18] That each of these members of the mercantile elite elected to invest in Cornish tin is reflective of the high value and prestigious nature of that trade.

Moreover, in many cases, the networks of such individuals were tied together via London merchants who travelled to Southampton in order to provide a supply of tin to the capital. For example, the broad network connections forged by London merchant John White demonstrate the exceptional networking power Londoners could hold within the port. White tied together several separate multi-merchant tin-carrying voyages throughout this period and engaged with a broad variety of individual merchants and shipmasters from across the kingdom. Before 1575, White appeared only once in Southampton's coastal port books, on a ship freighting coal on which he also acted in the capacity of shipmaster. Then, in 1575, as shown in Figure 4.1, he shared a voyage with a range of men including London merchant Thomas Davies, who had existing south coast contacts.[19] That 1575 voyage allowed White broader access to individuals from across the region and he was able to trade extensively through 1577 when the tin trade boomed, tying to a broad range of Hampshire merchants and tying together various mercantile clusters, as shown in Figure 4.2.

Thereafter, John White held a privileged position among coastal traders in Southampton, and this was particularly evident in 1579 when, in spite of especially low overall levels of trade through Southampton, White continued to engage in the transportation of tin alongside merchants from Hampshire, Dorset, Devon, Cornwall and the Channel Islands, as shown in Figure 4.3 below.[20] White's presence in Southampton allowed him to forge ties with individuals from a broad range of locations that persisted and expanded over a number of years, accounting to some degree for the surprisingly high level of cross-county integration in Southampton in 1579, which is discussed in more detail below. The specifics of John White's maritime activities are somewhat beyond the scope of this volume; however, it is clear that White was a sought-after trading partner who was able to forge particularly extensive networks, very likely as a result of his high status as a London merchant.

---

[18] Butler, 'Richard Biston (1558–1603)', 'John Crooke (1563–1600)', 'Hugh Durvall (1541–1587)', http://www.tudorrevels.co.uk/records.php.

[19] TNA E190/814/7 fol.2r, E190/814/11 fol.6v, E190/814/12 fol.9r, E190/814/7 fol.2r, E190/815/2 fol.2v.

[20] TNA E190/815/1 fol.8v, E190/815/2 fol.2v–3r, 5r, E190/815/8 fol.2v–3r, 6v.

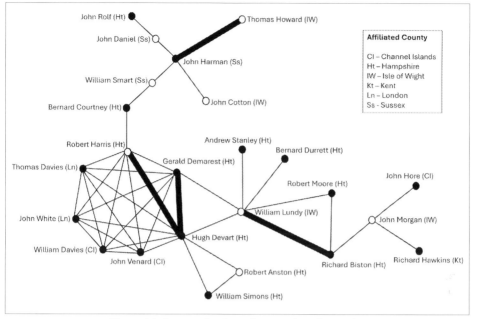

Figure 4.1. A network of merchants and mariners who traded through Southampton in 1575.

Interestingly, this degree of local integration did not apply to all London merchants and some charter parties that traded Cornish tin through Southampton excluded local traders completely. For example, in August 1577, the 12-ton *George* of Helford embarked from Helston, passed through Southampton, and then finally docked in London carrying 105 pieces of tin belonging to four London merchants.[21] As noted above, Southampton was critical in the supply of tin to London in earlier decades, and the sources examined here suggest that many Londoners were still engaged in that activity during the latter half of the sixteenth century.[22] For the most part, the London merchants that came into Southampton to trade engaged directly with Hampshire traders. However, this particular group involved only London merchants and one Cornish shipmaster, bypassing Hampshire traders entirely. While one of those merchants, Laurence Palmer, engaged with at least two Hampshire merchants on other voyages, and Londoners were often well integrated into Hampshire's mercantile community,

---

[21] TNA E190/815/1 fol.8v–9r.
[22] For more in-depth exploration of the role of London merchants in the transportation of tin between Cornwall and Southampton, see Ruddock, 'London Capitalists and the Decline of Southampton in the Early Tudor Period', pp. 144–49.

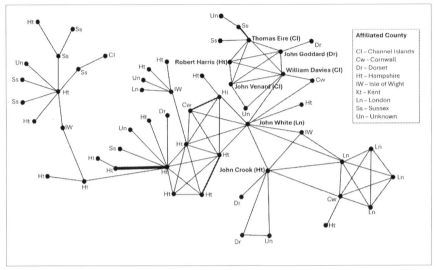

Figure 4.2. A network of merchants and mariners who traded through Southampton in 1577.

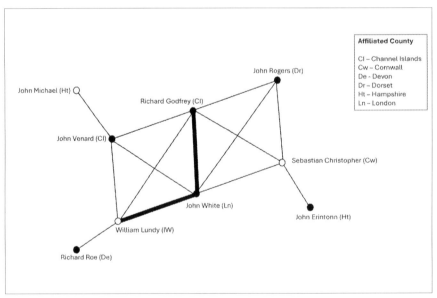

Figure 4.3. A network of merchants and mariners who traded through Southampton in 1579.

this cluster suggests that there was scope for London merchants to engage in the tin trade without the support of Hampshire shipmasters and merchants.

John Crook

Aside from their engagement in the Cornish tin trade, the core members of Southampton's mercantile elite also routinely interacted via other coastal trade routes, collaborating in voyages, exploiting the same vessels, and utilising the same shipmasters, as evident from Figures 4.1 and 4.2 above. However, one Southampton merchant, John Crook, appears to have been an outlier to this generally well-established elite trading network, and there is much evidence to suggest that his personal relationships with other members of the mercantile elite had a direct bearing on his inability to sustain commercial network ties. We shall see in Chapter 5 that John Crook was a wealthy member of the political elite in Southampton, and it is well documented that he had significant overseas trade interests. By 1585 he had expanded his business to include privateering, and he had close personal ties to many of Southampton's most important merchants. Indeed, even within the coastal customs accounts there is evidence of his prestige as his signatures attest to the fact that he often used an agent to transport his goods, a mark of status that was unusual among coastal traders.[23] Moreover, he had familial ties to the leading Southampton merchant family, the Capleins, being married to the widow of John Caplein senior, father-in-law to Edmund Caplein, stepfather to John Caplein Jnr, and fathering eight children of his own with John Caplein's widow.[24] He also had links to important Southampton merchant Bernard Courtney, and his daughter was married to Richard Biston.[25] However, unlike many of Southampton's

---

[23] While it is difficult to determine from the Bristol or Hull port books how many coastal traders dispatched their goods into the care of an agent, servant, apprentice or customer, the Southampton port books give some insight into the frequency of such transactions. Indeed, of the 782 visible signatures in the Southampton books sampled, at least 235 can be positively identified as belonging to the merchant himself, while only 38 were clearly the mark of a servant, apprentice or agent. The remaining 509 were either merchants' marks that could not be clearly tied to a specific merchant or were illegible. See TNA E190/814/5, E190/814/6, E190/814/7, E190/814/11, E190/814/12, E190/815/1, E190/815/2, E190/815/8. For examples of the signatures of Crook and his agents, see TNA E190/814/4 fol.11v, E190/814/5 fol.1r, E190/814/6 fol.6v, E190/814/11 fol.1r, E190/814/12 fol.4r, 8v, 9r. See also Butler, 'John Crooke (1563–1600)', http://www.tudorrevels.co.uk/records.php.

[24] Cheryl Butler, *The Remembrance Books of Richard Goddard 1583, John Crook 1584 and Andrew Studeley 1586* (Southampton: Southampton Record Series, 2021).

[25] Bernard Courtney (or Courtmill) was appointed captain alongside Robert Eire in 1570, and then in the later 1570s was heavily involved in privateering. He traded extensively, owned several vessels and served as mayor. Butler, 'Bernard Courtmill

elite merchants, John Crook rarely shared hull space with other merchants, and there is a clear pattern evident in the network data that suggests Crook was excluded from the broader community within the context of coastal commerce, a divide that deepened substantially over the period under investigation.

While Crook collaborated with esteemed local merchant Bernard Courtney to freight a high-value cargo of lead to London in 1569, that relationship rapidly broke down thereafter. Both men continued to operate along the coast with frequency but they did so independently of one another and their coastal networks expanded entirely separately throughout the 1570s.[26] This was also true of Crook's relationship with other key Southampton merchants and in 1576 he was notably disconnected from such men as John Holford and Richard Etrier, instead electing to engage with Hampshire shipmasters of lesser status who also operated separately from the mercantile elite.[27] This theme continued throughout the period and while 1577 saw the formation of a particularly large and dense network of local elite merchants operating in the town of Southampton, Crook remained very much on the periphery, as shown in Figure 4.2. Crook did appear on one multi-merchant voyage alongside John White and Laurence Palmer in 1577, but given his socio-economic stature, his position in the wider network suggests that he was markedly far removed from the core group, remaining disconnected and being notably absent from those voyages involving the Hampshire merchants with whom he had close personal relationships.

Clearly then, in terms of his coastal trade, John Crook was substantially disconnected from the core network of high-level traders with whom he interacted in his personal life, and his personal history with those families may hold the key to explaining this apparent separation. Indeed, civic records from the town of Southampton are littered with disputes and disagreements between Crook and various other high-level merchants. As Crook was landlord of *The Dolphin* public house, he should have held a privileged position in the town. *The Dolphin* was the second of the two Southampton public houses identified by James Brown as 'prestige High Street inns' and the business was valued in a 1624 probate inventory as having movable goods exceeding £230.[28] Such an establishment would have catered to the civic elite and Crook should have held a venerated position in the town for his landlordship alone. Yet by 1591, he was imprisoned and penniless, having lost his wealth in privateering and having fallen out with his son-in-law Richard Biston. This

---

(1556–1591)', 'Richard Biston (1558–1603)', 'John Crooke (1563–1600)', http://www.tudorrevels.co.uk/records.php.

[26] TNA E190/814/7 fol.1v.

[27] Butler, 'John Holford (1566–1588)', 'Richard Etuer (1565–1604)', http://www.tudorrevels.co.uk/records.php.

[28] Brown, pp. 81–83.

estrangement, according to Cheryl Butler, resulted from his repeated financial mismanagement, which caused a fracture in his personal and familial relationships. In fact, it was his son-in-law himself who eventually had Crook sent to prison.[29] His final downfall in 1591 marked the end of a string of volatile and unsuccessful collaborations, and his gradual detachment from Southampton's mercantile elite in the context of his coastal commercial activity seems to be representative of his broader conflict with those individuals in his personal life and overseas career.[30] Given that Crook should have been well positioned to form substantial business networks and to continue a long and lucrative career, this case study supports Robert Brenner's assertion that the agency of merchants in their endeavours could have a significant impact on their ability to run their businesses.[31]

Nonetheless, while Crook's personal relationships with Southampton's prestige merchants were strained, he still had significant wealth and social standing. As a result, he was able to continue to engage with a range of shipmasters via his agents and could continue to undertake a steady flow of coastal trade through the port. Throughout this period of personal turmoil, John Crook continued to interact with individuals from a range of residential affiliations, highlighting his ability to forge network ties across a broad geographic area in spite of his broader separation from the core Hampshire trading community. Crook was able to form ties with shipmasters *ad hoc*, which in turn facilitated his extensive coastwise commercial activity in spite of his difficulties with sustaining personal and professional relationships.

The Sussex connection

We look now to the east to examine the networks that formed around another of Southampton's key domestic trading partners: the Sussex Weald. As we saw in Chapter 2, journeys between Southampton and Sussex accounted for around a quarter of all voyages through the port, making Sussex the most frequent destination for ships departing coastwise from Southampton. The regularity of trade between the two regions in combination with the fact that the route was dominated by the transportation of a high-value commodity (iron) meant that trade with Sussex also attracted the attention of many of Southampton's elite merchants. However, the somewhat specialist nature of

---

[29] Butler, *Remembrance Books*, pp. xxxviii–xxxvix.

[30] Kenneth R. Andrews, *Elizabethan Privateering: English Privateering during the Spanish War, 1585–1603* (Cambridge: Cambridge University Press, 1964), p. 141; Brown, pp. 81–83; Butler, 'John Crooke (1563–1600)', http://www.tudorrevels.co.uk/records.php.

[31] Robert Brenner, 'The Social Basis of English Commercial Expansion, 1550–1650', *The Journal of Economic History*, 32 (1972), 361–62, 80–84.

the trade in Sussex iron meant that a number of individuals from elsewhere also specialised in the route between Southampton and Sussex. Moreover, we shall see that such individuals were often gatekeepers to engagement in Sussex trade and local merchants often elected to utilise Sussex shipmasters in order to trade into the Weald, resulting in the linking together of otherwise separate trading networks via particularly desirable Sussex shipmasters.

This was certainly true in the case of Robert Eire, who we saw above was an esteemed Southampton merchant who often engaged in the transportation of Cornish tin alongside other members of the Hampshire elite. However, in order to trade into the Weald, Eire expanded his network beyond individuals from the Hampshire region and sought the assistance of shipmaster Reginald Barber.[32] Barber originated from Sussex and almost certainly owned a Sussex vessel during the 1560s, but he moved to Southampton sometime before 1570 and purchased a share in a Southampton ship. Nonetheless, he retained strong ties to his home county and was able to act in the capacity of Eire's Sussex contact, facilitating Eire's trade into a region outside of his typical commercial interests.[33] Notably, this did not only apply to Robert, but also to another merchant by the same surname: a certain Thomas Eyre of Guernsey. It has been difficult to determine whether Thomas and Robert were related, but it is possible that Thomas was Robert's son, who was born in 1535 and owned lands and property throughout Dorset and Wiltshire. Although there is no evidence that Robert's son Thomas ever moved to Guernsey, it is feasible given the breadth of his land ownership and wealth that he had lands there and may have occasionally invested in coastal shipments of iron, especially since each shipment listed in the customs records as belonging to Thomas Eire was signed for on his behalf by an agent.[34] Regardless, like Robert, Thomas typically interacted with shipmasters and merchants from the Hampshire region but looked to Sussex shipmasters in order to accommodate his trade into Meeching, forming a specific Sussex branch of his business networks.[35]

---

[32] For example, in TNA E190/814/7 fol.4r, 8r.

[33] Judging from the frequency and consistency with which Barber utilised the same ships, and considering the small size of those vessels, it is very likely that he had a share in the 10-ton *New Year* of Meeching until around 1570 and the 14-ton *Megg* of Southampton thereafter. For example, see TNA E190/814/5 fol.14r, E190/814/6 fol.2v, E190/814/7 fol.4r-v, 8r; and see also Maryanne Kowaleski, 'The Shipmaster as Entrepreneur in Medieval England', in *Commercial Activity, Markets and Entrepreneurs in the Middle Ages: Essays in Honour of Richard Britnell*, ed. by Ben Dodds and Christian D. Liddy (Woodbridge: Boydell Press, 2011), pp. 165–82 (pp. 168–70); Lambert and Baker, www.medievalandtudorships.org.

[34] Martin, pp. 11–12.

[35] For example, see TNA E190/815/1 fol.8r, E190/815/2 fol.1v, 3r.

Furthermore, if we turn to other members of the Southampton mercantile elite, we see similar operational approaches emerge. For example, Bernard Courtney, who we saw above was a wealthy and well-established Southampton merchant, primarily operated within the large networks of the Hampshire elite but turned to Sussex shipmaster William Smart in order to travel east. Courtney typically engaged in westerly trade from Southampton, mainly trading into Guernsey or Devon, and only very occasionally ventured onto the east coast. Interestingly, Courtney utilised Smart as his shipmaster not only to travel into Sussex but also on a rare trip to London in 1569, on which he freighted oranges, suggesting that he altered his network ties not only to access trade into Sussex, but also to participate in more general easterly activity.[36] This was also true of merchant William Courtney, who likewise primarily traded into Devon and the Channel Islands, but in 1569 entered Southampton from Sussex carrying malt, a voyage for which he hired Sussex shipmaster Noel Kent and utilised the 5-ton *Anthony* of Worthing (Sussex).[37] Like the Eires, Bernard and William had established networks of traders with whom they typically elected to interact within the confines of their routine activity (in this case being trade with Devon and the Channel Islands), but forged connections with Sussex shipmasters in order to facilitate their trade into Sussex and sometimes other eastern ports. Given that Bernard and William both had ties to the Southampton ward of St Michael/St John, both operated on the same trade routes, and both lived in the same house throughout 1568, it is highly likely that they were members of the same family. The fact that their operational approach was very similar suggests that, in some cases, practical modes of engagement in coastal enterprise were dictated by the activities of the broader family unit, as may also have been true in the case of the Eires.[38]

Aside from members of the Southampton mercantile elite, merchants from Sussex also regularly engaged in the supply of iron to Southampton, in some cases forging successful maritime careers from that activity, as we shall see in Chapter 5. Like merchants from Southampton, Sussex traders typically forged networks among other individuals from their region. Thus, we see the formation of dense Hampshire clusters and dense Sussex clusters tied together by a single Sussex shipmaster, as evident from Figures 4.1 and 4.2 above. Within those Sussex clusters, merchants that were particularly prolific on the Southampton-Meeching trade route tended to sit in the centre, surrounded by the nodes of the various shipmasters that they utilised for their Southampton

[36] TNA E190/814/6 fol.2v, E190/814/7 fol.1v, E190/814/11 fol.5r, 6r, E190/814/12 fol.1r, 2v–3v, 5r, E190/815/1 fol.2r, 3v, E190/815/8 fol.5r.

[37] TNA E190/814/7 fol.1v.

[38] TNA E190/814/7 fol.1v, 7v, E190/814/6 fol.2v, E190/814/11 fol.5r, 6r, E190/814/12 fol.1r, 2v, 3r-v, 5r, 9v, E190/815/1 fol.2r, 3v, E190/815/2 fol.7v, E190/815/8 fol.5r; Butler, 'Bernard Courtmill (1556–1591)', http://www.tudorrevels.co.uk/records.php.

voyages, and sometimes indirectly connected to other Sussex merchants who engaged with less consistency via ties to particularly prolific shipmasters. This was particularly true in the case of Sussex merchant John Harman, who was a dedicated iron merchant who transported numerous shipments per year from Meeching into Southampton, and who typically engaged with shipmasters from Sussex that specialised in the transportation of Sussex iron. However, we shall see below that Harman gradually increased his interaction with individuals from outside of the Sussex region throughout the period, in line with a broader trend of increased cross-county integration caused by a combination of heightened levels of overall trade through the port and an increased interest among Hampshire traders in specialising in the iron trade. For example, while Harman almost exclusively utilised Sussex vessels throughout 1569 and largely interacted with Sussex shipmasters, by 1575 he had begun to frequently engage with shipmasters from the Isle of Wight, many of whom had themselves begun to specialise in the Sussex iron trade.[39]

This was also true of highly successful iron merchant John Knight, who we shall see in Chapter 5 forged an eminent political career and gained substantial wealth through his engagement in the coastal transportation of Sussex iron. Although Knight was in fact a Southampton man, he clearly had very strong ties to the Sussex region; his maritime career centred exclusively on trade between Southampton and Meeching and his commercial networks suggest that he had close ties to many Sussex traders. As such, his operational approaches aligned much more closely to those of Sussex merchants than to those of members of the Hampshire mercantile elite, who tended to engage in the iron trade very differently from iron specialists like Knight. Through the early 1570s, Knight almost exclusively engaged with Sussex shipmasters, just occasionally utilising the services of Isle of Wight shipmaster William Lundy, who we shall see below was a prolific local shipmaster who was highly flexible in his business model and would cater to almost any merchant on any route.[40] However, by 1577, Knight had extended his network to include individuals from across the region, rather than just those from Sussex.[41] As in the case of John Harman, this increased level of cross-county integration resulted from a general increase in the levels of Sussex iron trade through Southampton and the fact that more individuals from outside of Sussex began to specialise in

[39] TNA E190/814/7 fol.4v, E190/814/11 fol.3r-v, 4v, 5v, 6v, 8r.
[40] See, for example, TNA E190/814/7 fol.7v, 9r.
[41] Of the shipmasters used by Knight in April–September 1577, Griston, Search, Spriggs, Hudson and Brabant all appear frequently throughout the customs accounts, almost exclusively transporting iron. While these individuals may have had secondary occupations or additional routes through other ports, they certainly focused their trade into Southampton on the iron trade. See throughout TNA E190/814/5, E190/814/11, E190/814/12, E190/815/1, E190/815/2, E190/815/8.

the transportation of iron. The career progression of John Knight is discussed in more detail in Chapter 5, but it is important to note that despite running many voyages, serving as mayor, and being a central part of the Southampton community, he was generally disconnected from the town's merchant elite, indicative of his very different approach to the maritime industry.[42] Others from the mercantile community occasionally signed for Knight's goods, but he generally worked alone.[43] He took a 'hands-on' approach to business and, in spite of being a merchant of some stature, did not employ agents, being physically present on the vessel himself for most voyages, evident from his personal signature under most of his entries.[44] He was a career coastal merchant with a well-established business and he contentedly continued that trade without an apparent desire to expand or to look towards potentially more lucrative overseas ventures, largely confining his network ties to those with a particular interest in iron and having no need to extend his circle.

Other small-scale Hampshire traders

In addition to Hampshire's wealthy and powerful core of elite merchants, a number of smaller-scale merchants and mariners from the region also routinely engaged in coastal commercial activity through the port of Southampton. Like other traders, the approaches these men took to their business and to network formation varied between individuals, with some forming long-term partnerships within particular commercial networks and others trading on an *ad hoc* basis. Likewise, the degree to which particular individuals sought to develop their maritime businesses into more substantial and profitable ventures varied from person to person. Brief examination of a few of Hampshire's key small-scale traders demonstrates again the degree of operational variation between individuals who engaged in coastal enterprise and supports the assertion that personal choice played as much of a role in economic and commercial decision making as broader political and economic factors beyond the control of the individual. Placed in similar situations and faced with many of the same opportunities, individual traders would make varied choices as to how they chose to run their businesses, the routes on which they chose to operate, the commodities they elected to carry, and the degree to which they gambled with higher risk in order to reach for potentially more lucrative and high-status trade.

That being said, certain situational changes did facilitate personal career decisions and this can be seen particularly clearly in the case of Isle of Wight

---

[42] Butler, 'John Knight (1555–1603)', http://www.tudorrevels.co.uk/records.php.

[43] TNA E190/814/5 fol.3v, E190/814/7 fol.7v, E190/814/11 fol.2v, 7r, E190/814/12 fol.1v, 10r, E190/815/1 fol.7r–8r, E190/815/2 fol.1r.

[44] See, for example, TNA E190/814/5 fol.3v, E190/814/11 fol.2v, 7r, E190/814/12 fol.10r.

traders, many of whom took advantage of increased opportunities offered in Southampton during periods of heightened trade. Indeed, while Isle of Wight shippers operated distinctively within networks of other Islanders during the early years of the period under investigation, there was much greater integration with Southampton traders during the later period, reflective of the broader trends of increased cross-county integration that are discussed in more detail below. However, while many Isle of Wight traders became more strongly embedded in the Hampshire community over the period, there was also a general reduction in the number of Isle of Wight traders involved in Southampton's coastal commerce after 1569. This decreased engagement coincided with heightened integration of the remaining Isle of Wight traders into both Southampton networks and networks of individuals from the broader region, suggesting that the disappearance of key Islanders from Southampton's coastal trade may have compelled the remaining individuals to interact more widely and to expand their circles to include individuals from further afield.

This was certainly true in the case of shipmaster William Lundy, who adjusted his network ties from catering only to Isle of Wight traders in the early years of the period to working with individuals from the broader Hampshire region over the succeeding two decades. While this was a trend seen among many Isle of Wight shipmasters, Lundy's personal career trajectory points to him being a particularly desirable shipmaster and he was able to successfully improve his personal circumstances over the 1560s and 1570s, expanding his maritime business and corresponding networks over a fairly short time. Lundy was a prolific shipmaster who catered primarily for merchants from Hampshire on a voyage-by-voyage basis and, like many coastal shipmasters, probably had some form of interest in at least one vessel.[45] Lundy's popularity as a shipmaster was almost certainly influenced in part by the fact that he owned or part-owned his own ship, and his shift towards catering to a broader span of the merchant elite also coincided with him switching from commanding the 10-ton *Mary* of Newport to the 16-ton *Hare* of Newport, supporting this idea further. As the volume of trade through Southampton increased, more individuals were drawn into coastal commerce and this created increased opportunities for individuals who could offer direct access to their own ship. In this case, that privileged position allowed Lundy to engage with members of the mercantile elite such as Richard Biston, John

---

[45] Analysis of the port book data suggests that Lundy likely had an interest in the 10-ton *Mary* of Newport, and then upgraded to the 16-ton *Hare* of Newport in around 1570: see TNA E190/814/5 fol.1v, 2v–4r, 6v, 7v, E190/814/6 fol.1r, 2v, 6v, 7v, E190/814/7 fol.4r, 6r-v, 7v, 9v, E190/814/11 fol.1r, 2r, 6v, 7v, E190/814/12 fol.1r, 4r-v, 6v, E190/815/8 fol.2r-v, 6v.

Crook and Robert Eire, and enabled him to forge a long-term, sustained relationship with Sussex iron merchant John Knight.[46]

Similar trends can be seen in the case of another Isle of Wight shipmaster, John Cotton, who again demonstrates the impact that ship ownership could have on the formation of network ties. Throughout the 1560s, Cotton's engagement in coastal commercial activity was extremely sporadic (although he did undertake some voyages to La Rochelle), but by 1575 he had established a strong presence in Southampton, catering for various merchants from a broad region (especially for Londoners) and within a wide range of industries.[47] His activity had increased even further by 1577, most likely as a result of his investment in a share of the 28-ton *Mayflower* of Southampton. After purchasing the *Mayflower*, Cotton honed his business to focus on the lucrative trade route between Southampton and London, and shortly thereafter undertook overseas voyages for the same merchants for whom he commanded coastal journeys, including important local traders like Nicholas Caplein.[48] Prior to 1577, Cotton's network was limited but, like Lundy, his ownership of a vessel seems to have had an immediate impact on his ability to form network ties.

Conversely, the business networks of Southampton shipmaster John Holford were also impacted by increased levels of trade through the port, but Holford made very different choices regarding his career trajectory. Like Cotton and Lundy, Holford was a very prolific local shipmaster, but unlike those other men he preferred to remain within very close proximity of Southampton waters, typically remained within fifty nautical miles of the port. This restricted geographic reach likely owed to the fact that Holford's main occupation was as a fisherman and the vessel he took charge of, the 4-ton *Jesus* of Hythe, was probably the boat he used for his fishing activities.[49] His engagement in coastal commerce was sporadic and he only took part during periods of increased activity through Southampton, when he almost exclusively freighted

---

[46] Richard Biston was substantially involved in overseas trade, leased various properties within the town, and served as mayor on at least one occasion. See, Butler, 'Richard Biston (1558–1603)', http://www.tudorrevels.co.uk/records.php.

[47] TNA E190/814/11 fol.2r, 4r, 8r, E190/815/2 fol.1r, 2r–3r, 4v, 6r; Lambert and Baker, www.medievalandtudorships.org.

[48] Butler, 'John Cotton (1570–1617)', 'John Hooper (1575–1577)', 'Nicholas Capelyn (1532–1590)', http://www.tudorrevels.co.uk/records.php.

[49] As noted by Maryanne Kowaleski, fishermen were especially likely to own the vessels they commanded and, given that Holford commanded the 4-ton *Jesus* of Hythe for twenty-seven coastwise voyages between 1565 and 1575, it would be surprising if that ship was not his own fishing vessel. See TNA E190/814/5 fol.3v, 5v–6r, E190/814/6 fol.2r, 4r, E190/814/7 fol.1v, 6v, E190/814/11 fol.3v, 7r, E190/814/12 fol.2r, 4r, 5v, 7r, 9r, E190/815/1 fol.1r, 2r, 7r, E190/815/2 fol.2v–3r, 4r–5r, 7r, E190/815/8 fol.7r; Kowaleski, 'The Shipmaster as Entrepreneur in Medieval England', p. 166.

wine, suggesting that he interacted with overseas merchants who used him to redistribute incoming goods.[50] This was certainly true of Richard Etrier, with whom Holford interacted more frequently, and who was a member of the Estur family of Jersey with links to France.[51] Etrier was a highly successful merchant and would go on to become a citizen of London.[52] Nonetheless, when he wished to undertake short-distance voyages close to home he sought the services of an individual well versed on those routes, only utilising a shipmaster other than Holford when trading into London or Poole and forming an especially strong business partnership with Holford in the context of his various journeys to and from Chichester.[53]

The arrival of a large overseas shipment into a port often had a knock-on effect on the coastal trading community, and this particularly applied to individuals like Holford who only engaged in coasting as a secondary occupation. Holford would have been well known in the port and when overseas traders increased the frequency of their coastal activity, they turned to Holford for assistance. While Cotton and Lundy were actively progressing through the maritime hierarchy, John Holford undertook a little coastal work alongside his regular occupation and merely responded to demand. Yet while these shipmasters had very different ways of operating, they all established ties with numerous merchants, including members of Southampton's mercantile elite, and their direct access to suitable vessels combined with their deep familiarity with the local region almost certainly contributed to that privileged position.

Finally, aside from local shipmasters, local Hampshire individuals also engaged in coastal commerce in the capacity of merchant, such as in the case of Paul Elliott. In terms of his networking power, Elliott is of note owing to his role in tying together a large number of Hampshire merchants and shipmasters, including individuals like Isle of Wight shipmaster John Cotton. Elliott himself only appeared in the coastal port books during 1577 and, like John Holford, had a primary career outside of coastal commerce,

[50] We have a record of Holford's fishing career until at least the 1580s: see Butler, 'John Holford (1566–1588)', http://www.tudorrevels.co.uk/records.php.

[51] TNA E190/814/12 fol.2r, 4r, 7r, 9r, E190/815/1 fol.1r, 2r, 7r, E190/815/2 fol.4r, 7r.

[52] Richard Etrier entered into the French church in 1568 and was godparent to three French nationals, Jacques le Clerc, Elisabeth de la Pommail and Daniel Fere. While he originated from a Jersey family, it seems he was born in England and was a core member of the Southampton mercantile elite, but also had substantial ties to France, placing him in a strong position for network formation and engagement in overseas trade. Alan G. Jamieson, ed., *A People of the Sea: The Maritime History of the Channel Islands* (London: Methuen, 1986), p. 79; Butler, 'Richard Etuer (1565–1604)', http://www.tudorrevels.co.uk/records.php.

[53] TNA E190/814/11 fol.7v, E190/814/12 fol.2r, 4r, 7r, 9r, 10v, E190/815/1 fol.1r, 2r, 7r-v, E190/815/2 fol.4r, 7r.

in this case as the town's tallow chandler. Elliott's involvement in coastal trading directly coincided with him being banned from acting in the capacity of tallow chandler after he broke the terms of his licence, and he turned to the coast to take advantage of the prospering market in Cornish tin. Yet, in spite of his fleeting involvement, he had broad connections, including many individuals that were well-known and important figures in the Hampshire maritime community.[54] His position as town mayor and his societal role as tallow chandler almost certainly enabled him to form those broad ties and to partake in coastal commerce on a temporary basis, even in a high-value trade like tin.

Moreover, aside from the fact that Elliott tied together many key Hampshire traders, he also appears to have influenced other individuals to shift their operational approaches. For example, as noted above, John Holford typically commanded the 4-ton *Jesus* of Hythe. However, on the one occasion on which he commanded for Paul Elliott he instead took charge of the 28-ton *Mayflower* of Southampton in order to facilitate his engagement in a multi-merchant tin-carrying voyage. Likewise, most of the merchants that collaborated with Paul Elliott in order to transport tin more typically engaged in the transportation of products other than tin on single-merchant voyages, but were willing to pool resources with other traders to engage in commercial activity in Cornwall.[55] As noted, the trade in tin could be a highly lucrative business venture and, given the right circumstances, many shipmasters and merchants would alter their typical operational approach in order to participate, in this case seemingly brought together by a man with significant local commercial influence.

Changing levels of cross-county integration

Although the individuals discussed above represent the most active members of the Hampshire trading community, local merchants and shipmasters did not exist in isolation; people from across the kingdom entered Southampton to trade, and their periodic involvement affected the nature of the town's commercial activity and the corresponding formation of business networks. In particular, as shown in Figure 4.4, individuals were more likely to interact with people from outside their own affiliated county during periods of increased trade through the port.[56] Thus, in 1569 and 1576, when the number of voyages

[54] Butler, 'Paul Elliott (1550–1613)', http://www.tudorrevels.co.uk/records.php.
[55] TNA E190/814/6 fol.6r, E190/814/11 fol.4r, 5r, 6v, E190/814/12 fol.3v, 8r-v, E190/815/1 fol.8r, E190/815/2 fol.2v, E190/815/8 fol.3r.
[56] The graphs in Figures 4.4 and 4.10 illustrate the correlation between levels of trade and levels of cross-county integration. Levels of cross-county integration have been calculated by determining the percentage of nodes that have an individual from

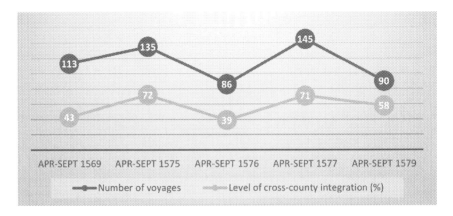

Figure 4.4. Levels of trade and cross-country integration in Southampton.

through Southampton was relatively low, networks were clearly defined by regional affiliation. However, during 1575 and 1577, when the number of voyages through Southampton was higher, there was a much greater degree of interaction between individuals affiliated with different regions. Furthermore, although levels of trade through Southampton were again low in 1579, the corresponding decrease in level of integration was less stark. We shall see below that this resulted from the fact that a number of non-Hampshire traders that entered into Southampton during periods of increased opportunity were able to integrate well into the coastal trading community and maintain their engagement in Southampton even when overall levels of trade decreased. This suggests that increased commercial opportunities did not only allow for the formation of short-term opportunistic network ties, but also for the formation of longer-term business partnerships, as we saw, for example, in the case of John White's engagement in the Cornish tin trade discussed above.

These trends are particularly evident in the case of the engagement of Sussex traders. During 1569 and 1576, when overall levels of trade through Southampton were low, the few Sussex traders that appeared in the customs records were mostly tied to a particular Southampton trader, for whom they fulfilled a role as the 'Sussex branch' of that individual's trading operations.

---

outside their own regional affiliation within their 'first order zone'. Note that the data for Bristol for 1580 is highly influenced by the necessary reliance on searcher records, which has resulted in an unrealistically low level of trade through Bristol during this period. For an explanation of the concept of order zones, see Charles Kadushin, *Understanding Social Networks: Theories, Concepts, and Findings* (Oxford: Oxford University Press, 2012), pp. 33–34.

For example, and as discussed in more detail below, Hampshire merchant Robert Eire typically interacted with a number of Hampshire merchants and shipmasters, but linked with Sussex shipmaster Reginald Barber in order to trade east.[57] However, in 1575 and 1577, when trade with Sussex rose from around 15% of Southampton voyages to around 32% (see Figures 4.5 and 4.6 below), there was an influx of Sussex traders into Southampton and more Hampshire residents began participating in the transportation of Sussex iron, creating greater opportunity for collaboration. For example, while Sussex iron merchant John Harman engaged only with Sussex shipmasters in 1569, by 1575 he had extended his network to include shipmasters from Hampshire and the Isle of Wight, who sought to take advantage of the increased trade in Wealdon iron.[58] Furthermore, although levels of trade were down slightly in 1579, Sussex traders like Harman continued to engage in coastal commercial activity in Southampton and remained well integrated with individuals from other regions, supporting the assertion that periods of increased trade could have a long-term impact on network formation.

However, while there was an overarching correlation between levels of trade and levels of cross-county integration, this did not apply to individuals from all regions, and the ways in which Channel Island traders engaged in commerce in Southampton provide a stark contrast. As discussed in Chapter 2, the relationship between Southampton and the Channel Islands was highly unusual and, as a result, the operational nature of the trade undertaken and the networks that formed were of a different character. Unlike Sussex traders, individuals from the Channel Islands were especially likely to remain within networks of people from their own regions, and this was the case across the whole period, suggesting that changing levels of trade had very little impact on Channel Island commerce.

This may have resulted in part from the desire among Channel Island traders to retain their image as a neutral party, since France and England both theoretically granted Islanders free passage across the Channel during hostile periods in exchange for their neutrality within the broader political landscape. However, in reality, they were in a rather vulnerable position and they pushed hard to maintain an image of neutrality in spite of increased political integration with England.[59] One way in which to maintain an image of impartiality was to refrain from expanding their commercial circles beyond Channel Island traders. Interestingly, while the individuals involved and the islands from which they originated changed from year to year (see Figures 2.4 and 2.5

---

[57] TNA E190/814/5 fol.2v, 4v–5r, 6r-v, 8r, 12r, E190/814/6 fol.1r, 2r-v, 4v, 6v–7r, E190/814/7 fol.4r, 5v, 7r, 8r.

[58] TNA E190/814/7 fol.4v, E190/814/11 fol.3r-v, 4v, 5v, 6v, 8r.

[59] For a more detailed discussion on the neutral status upheld by the Islands, see Appleby, pp. 59–105.

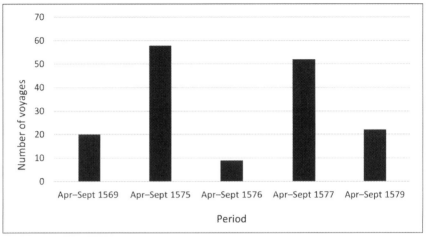

Figure 4.5. Number of voyages undertaken between Southampton and Sussex by period.

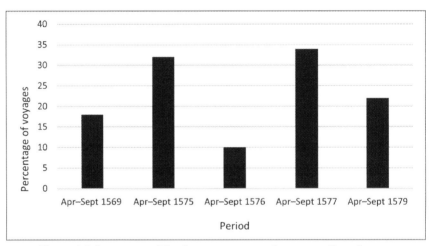

Figure 4.6. Percentage of Southampton voyages that went to/from Sussex.

in Chapter 2), the formation of almost exclusively Channel Island networks spanned all communities, including those from both Jersey and Guernsey.

This is particularly evident in the case of Peter Janverin, who originated from Jersey but moved to Southampton in 1559 to forge a (largely unsuccessful) career as a merchant.[60] In 1563, Janverin was stripped of his burgess status for the colouring of goods, although he was reinstated as a burgess in 1565. By

[60] Brown, pp. 81–82.

1566 he had become owner of an important Southampton pub, *The Star*, which attracted the top tier of the local elite (as both patrons and successive owners), and has been described by James Brown as one of Southampton's two 'Prestige High Street inns'. By the end of the seventeenth century, probate valuations put the movable goods held at *The Star* at upwards of £500, and after taking ownership of the public house, Janverin disengaged from coastal commerce.[61] Janverin demonstrates the exceptional strength of ties between Islanders. Even ten years after moving to Southampton, being made a Southampton burgess, and engaging with Southampton traders in the context of his overseas activity, his contacts as a shipmaster remained focused on the Islands. This highlights the commercial distance Islanders maintained from the mainland, in spite of their increased political integration with Southampton by the mid-1570s.[62]

Coastal networks in Bristol

Turning now to the west and, unlike in Southampton or Hull, the Bristol customs officials elected to record additional data in the port books regarding the occupational titles allocated to merchants that traded through the port. This means that we are able to trace the networks of shipmasters and merchants in Bristol not just by their affiliation with particular commodities and trade routes but also by the occupational groups into which they fit. As such, in this part will explore in turn the networks forged by trowmen, maltmakers and brewers; other craftsmen and small-scale traders; and Bristol's mercantile elite. We will then finish with a brief comparison of the changing levels of cross-county integration in Bristol compared to Southampton.

Trowmen, maltmakers and brewers

As we saw in Chapter 2, the waterways of the River Severn represented the busiest coastal shipping routes extending out of Bristol, with 40% of coastal voyages in the Bristol port books beginning or ending at a Severn port. As a result, and as shown in Chapter 3, a large number of local merchants and mariners forged sustained careers on the basis of the transportation of goods between Bristol and the ports of Gloucestershire, Worcestershire and the West Midlands. Moreover, the vast majority of those individuals were local Gloucestershire or Worcestershire traders, with only Tewksbury experiencing a significant influx of Bristol merchants and mariners. In this section we will examine the network ties forged between those individuals who undertook long-term regular trade on the River Severn and explore the role that occupational groupings played in network formation in this particular scenario.

---

[61] Ibid., pp. 81–94.
[62] Appleby, pp. 77–79; Thornton, pp. 92–125.

Trowmen and maltmakers

As noted in Chapter 3, trowmen occupied a distinct occupational group that was specific to the River Severn, being the sailors of flat-bottom barges named 'trows', which were specially engineered for use on Gloucestershire's tight and winding inland waterways.[63] We shall see in Chapter 5 that trowmen did not in fact exclusively sail trow barges, but they did nonetheless operate within a commercial grouping that was markedly separate from other Gloucestershire and Worcestershire traders. In particular, while trowmen carried the same goods on the same routes as Gloucestershire and Worcestershire maltmen (freighting grains into Bristol from Gloucestershire or Worcestershire and returning with overseas goods), they operated almost entirely separately, suggesting that this was a social division by craft rather than simply a commercial division by commodity. That being said, economic and social changes in the region over time did impact the network formation of both of these groups, as explored in the short case studies that follow.

If we turn first to the early years of the period under investigation, we can see from Figure 4.7 that a distinctive group of trowmen were operating in the port of Bristol in 1569. Indeed, apart from brewer Simon Habert and baker James Benbow, customs officials identified every individual in the trowman network displayed in Figure 4.7 as a trowman. Each of these individuals operated on the same routes, freighting grains into Bristol from Gloucestershire or Worcestershire, many resided in the same small towns, and they mostly utilised the same selection of vessels.[64] This suggests that these individuals were part of a tight-knit community of traders, operating within established networks and rarely deviating from their set business operations. While a number of these traders formed stronger network ties with specific individuals (most notably Tristan Palmer/Hugh Sallarwaye and Thomas Brown/James Chamberlain), we shall see throughout this chapter that trowmen had a general tendency to look inwards towards their community, working within the confines of the river system to forge stable careers in coastal trading. Moreover, while the maltmaker networks of Figure 4.7 were less clearly defined, those with stronger ties (Thomas Cocks/George Moore and Thomas Lowe/Thomas Richard) were all maltmakers and we shall see that maltmakers did typically forge ties with a range of individuals from within their own occupational community.[65]

---

[63] Farr, pp. 79–80; Greenhill, p. 286.

[64] TNA E190/1128/12 fol.2v–3r, 4r, 5r, 7r-v, 8r, 9r, 11r, 13r, 15r, E190/1128/13 fol.3v, 6r, 12v, 13v–14r, 15r-v, E190/1128/14 fol.1v, 2v, 5v, 7r, 8r, 9r, 10r, E190/1129/1 fol.1r, 10v, 11v, E190/1129/22 fol.14v.

[65] TNA E190/1128/12 fol.2r–4v, 6v, 8r, 9r, 12v–13r, E190/1128/13 fol.3v, 6r-v, 7v, 11v–12r, 13v, 14r, 17r, E190/1128/14 fol.5v, 7r–8v, 9v, 10r-v, 12r, E190/1129/1 fol.4r-v,

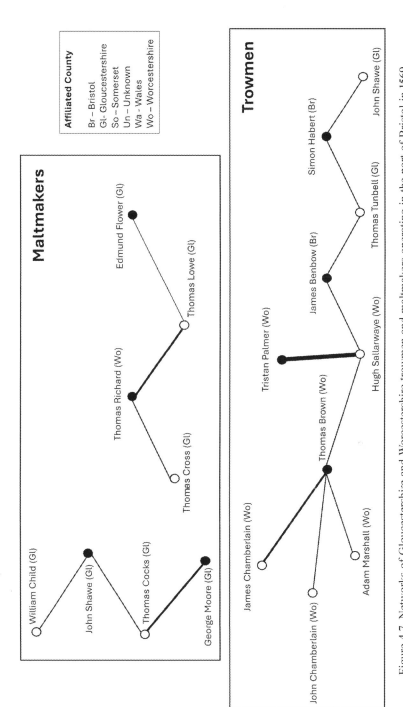

Figure 4.7. Networks of Gloucestershire and Worcestershire trowmen and maltmakers operating in the port of Bristol in 1569.

Indeed, if we jump forward a year to the summer of 1570, it is evident that a number of networks that involved traders of the River Severn remained relatively stable. For example, the strong business partnership between trowmen Tristan Palmer and Hugh Sallarwaye that is evident in Figure 4.7 persisted and strengthened during 1570. Likewise, a number of maltmaker networks (for example, a network containing prolific maltmakers Richard Pert and Richard Ball) continued to operate in the port of Bristol, made up almost entirely of men listed as maltmakers in the port books.[66] However, Gloucestershire, Worcestershire and West Midlands networks were also susceptible to the changes that resulted from increased overall activity through the port, and many merchants and mariners took a flexible approach to their maritime businesses, opportunistically undertaking trade on routes outside of their established business models when particular opportunity arose.

For example, between the summer of 1569 and the summer of 1570, the volume of trade undertaken between Bristol and the Severn ports increased substantially and a number of network ties were formed as a result of increased trade through the port. In particular, several maltmakers and trowmen opportunistically engaged with merchants from other groups during this period, most notably occupational merchants and clothiers. For example, while Hugh Sallarwaye, James Chamberlain, Adam Marshall, John Saddler and William Child typically commanded voyages for trowmen, their networks in 1570 all contained at least one occupational merchant or clothier.[67] Likewise, shipmaster Thomas Lowe typically preferred to command voyages for maltmakers such as Richard Stone and Robert Davies. Yet, by 1570, he was tied to a mixed-residency network via Bristol draper and merchant Thomas Pitt, suggesting that he was willing to shift his approach and cater to Bristol merchants during periods of increased activity.[68] We shall see in Chapter 5 that Pitt was an established overseas trader and, like many of Bristol's mercantile elite, only occasionally participated in coastal commerce. Lowe's interaction with Pitt is indicative of the networking power that Bristol merchants had in the port, such that they could compel shipmasters like Lowe to stray from their typical business approaches.

However, by 1576 the volume of trade through Bristol had generally decreased (as shown in Figure 4.10), and the routes between Bristol and the Severn ports were particularly hard-hit, likely resulting from poor

---

5r–6v, 7v, 8v–9r, 10v, 14v, 15v, 19r, E190/1129/18 fol.5r, E190/1129/20 fol.1v, E190/1129/22 fol.10v.

[66] TNA E190/1128/13 fol.3r-v, 5r, E190/1128/14 fol.2r, 4r–5v, 6v–7r, 8v–9v, 10r, 11v, 12r–13r.

[67] TNA E190/1128/13 fol.1v, 3v, 5r, E190/1128/14 fol.1v–2v, 4v–5v, 7r, 8r–9v, 10r–11v, 13r.

[68] TNA E190/1128/14 fol.10r–11r, E190/1130/2 fol.4r, 8v.

grain harvests in 1575 and 1576. As a result, several key Gloucestershire, Worcestershire and West Midlands traders were absent from the commercial networks of that year. In this case, the most notable absences were trowmen Hugh Sallarwaye, Tristan Palmer and Adam Marshall, and the maltmaker networks that had appeared with consistency in earlier periods. Nonetheless, as shown in Figure 4.8, in spite of those core members retreating from coastwise trade through Bristol, the Severn networks that remained were still occupationally defined, and there is much evidence that these individuals were part of the same tight-knit community.

For example, Roger Brook and John Saddler had appeared within the same network in earlier years and, while they operated separately in 1576, they were both able to forge network ties with a range of other trowmen, suggesting they had extensive contacts within that community. Likewise, trowmen Adam Marshall, John Aware, John Brook and Roger Brook all utilised the same vessel over an extended period, suggesting that they may have each had a share in that ship.[69] Furthermore, given that Roger and John Brook shared a surname and occupational title, both lived in Worcestershire (no more than perhaps twenty miles apart), and utilised the same vessel, it seems likely that they were related, although this is difficult to substantiate.[70]

Similar trends continued in Bristol throughout the late 1570s, with the number of trowmen and maltmakers operating in the port being consistently lower than in the late 1560s. However, a limited number of Worcestershire trowmen networks did continue to trade south and, as before, they continued to look inwards into their own occupational groups in order to forge network ties, such as in the case of trowmen (and likely relatives) John and Richard Caper.[71] Nonetheless, as we have seen throughout this chapter, operational business decisions and commercial ties were not always consistent across groups with similar characteristics, and trowman Samuel Hooper exemplifies this fact nicely. Like many small-scale coastal traders, Hooper typically acted

---

[69] All four traders appeared on the *Peter* of Bewdley that was recorded at between 10 and 20 tons across the port books. TNA E190/1128/12 fol.11r, 13r, E190/1128/13 fol.1v, 6v, E190/1128/14 fol.2r-v, 5r, 7v, 11r, E190/1129/1 fol.5r, E190/1129/18 fol.6v, E190/1129/20 fol.3r, 6r, 7v, E190/1129/22 fol.1v, 3v, 5r–7r, 9r, 10r.

[70] Roger Brook is listed in the customs records as residing in Worcester and John Brook is usually recorded as residing in Bewdley, although he is sometimes just listed as residing in Worcestershire. See, for example, E190/1128/13 fol.16v, 17v, E190/1129/1 fol.5r, 6r, 7r, E190/1129/20 fol.5r, E190/1129/22 fol.1v, 5v, 9r, E190/1130/2 fol.14r–16v.

[71] Aside from sharing a surname, John and Richard Caper were both trowmen, both resided in the small town of Bridgnorth in Shropshire, traded on the same routes, and utilised the same vessel (the 15-ton *Matthew* of Bridgnorth). TNA E190/1128/13 fol.14r, 15r, E190/1129/20 fol.8r, E190/1129/22 fol.6r–7r, 8r, 10r, E190/1130/2 fol.16v, 17v–18r, 19r.

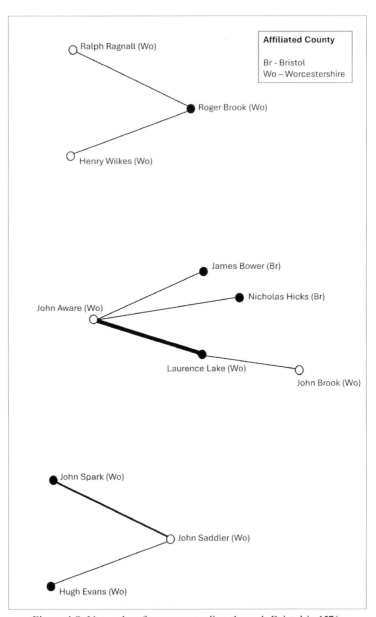

Figure 4.8. Networks of trowmen trading through Bristol in 1576.

as both merchant and shipmaster on voyages between Worcester and Bristol, commanding his own ship and carrying only his own goods. However, Hooper would occasionally command for other merchants and, on such occasions, his network formation was very different from those trowmen discussed above, with his business ties being far less skewed towards other members of his occupational group.

Indeed, he commanded voyages for merchants from a broad range of occupational backgrounds, including maltmaker Edward Baston, vintner John Wilson and occupational merchant John Edward.[72] His engagement with a maltmaker is especially notable since maltmakers and trowmen rarely overlapped, and this suggests that Hooper had a wider reach within the region than the trowmen discussed above. Owing to Hooper's limited involvement in Bristol's coastwise commerce, it is difficult to determine how he was able to forge such extensive network ties, but his broad participation demonstrates the range of forms that coastwise commercial activity could take, even within clearly defined occupational groups. Moreover, like many trowmen and maltmakers, Hooper frequently switched between operating as shipmaster and as merchant, suggesting that such men often had dual skillsets. This likely increased their ability to look inwards to their community for maritime collaboration, but also meant that they could be flexible in their approach, occupying different positions on the vessel for different voyages depending on the needs of the particular journey.

Brewers

Like trowmen and maltmakers, Bristol brewers too made their living transporting grains into Bristol from ports inland on the Severn. However, this group again operated largely separately from other traders on those routes and, in this case, the ships they utilised were not commanded by other brewers but were instead typically commanded by members of the Swanley mariner family. The Swanley family were based in Gloucestershire, were particularly prolific on the trade routes north of Bristol and were of significant local influence, as we shall see in Chapter 5. Craig Lambert has noted that the Swanleys ran a stable and fruitful business in the South West, involving trade between various Gloucestershire, Bristol and North Devon ports, and stemming from the commercial activities of Richard Swanley. However, by the period under investigation here, Richard was coming to the end of his career. He sailed his last voyages in the early 1570s and passed his business to his sons Thomas, George and William. Lambert has highlighted that Thomas was the only son to make a rare overseas voyage to Ireland before 1595 (by which time it is likely that Richard Swanley had died) and the data analysed here

[72] TNA E190/1130/2 fol.14v–15v, 16v, 17v–18r, 19r-v.

suggests that Thomas may have taken control of the business after his father's departure. Of the sixty voyages in the dataset that involved a Swanley, Thomas commanded thirty-six and this resulted in him forming the largest and most integrated networks.[73] Interestingly, unlike the shipmasters in the maltmaker and trowman networks who were usually allocated the same occupational titles as the merchants for whom they commanded, the customs officials defined the Swanleys as occupational mariners. The reasons for this difference are unclear, and we will see in Chapter 5 that occupational titles were often vague and poorly defined, but it is notable as it highlights the extent to which Severn traders were divided by occupational grouping.

In terms of their networks, like those discussed above, these often shifted and changed in line with broader commercial trends in the port. Between 1569 and 1570, the networks of the Swanley family were fairly stable and they continued to cater primarily to the Bristol brewing community. In particular, Thomas Swanley forged strong and consistent business relationships with brewers William Blast and Thomas Balding, running various shipments for those men per year. Thereafter, however, the Swanleys briefly managed to extend their business networks further and in 1572 Thomas Swanley tied to Bristol traders William Shynge (Shining?) and Robert Kitching, who were both occupational merchants who engaged in coastal commerce only during periods of increased activity. As above, such men looked to established mariners during their brief forays into the coastal trade and Thomas seems to have taken advantage of these opportunities keenly. Nonetheless, while the Swanleys did extend their networks in 1572, many of the men with whom Thomas interacted in that year were the same Bristol brewers with whom he had already established strong relationships, namely William Blast, William Watford, Anthony Cade, Richard Walwine and Anthony Hodge.[74] Such individuals were at the core of the Swanleys' commercial model and they retained their ties to those principal trading partners even when also seeking to extend their business dealings to a broader spectrum of local traders.

Moreover, while the Swanley networks were typically disconnected from the networks centred on trowmen and maltmakers, 1572 saw a rare coming together of those otherwise disconnected groups, with trowman Richard Watson acting in the capacity of shipmaster for one of the Swanleys' most common mercantile partners, Bristol brewer William Watson, as shown in Figure 4.9 below. Watson typically undertook voyages on which he was both shipmaster and merchant but, like Swanley and others, would shift

---

[73] Lambert, 'Tudor Shipmasters and Maritime Communities, 1550–1600', pp. 330–34.

[74] TNA E190/1128/13 fol.13v, 15r, 16r, E190/1129/1 fol.1r, 3r, 4r, 6v–7v, 9r, 13r–14v.

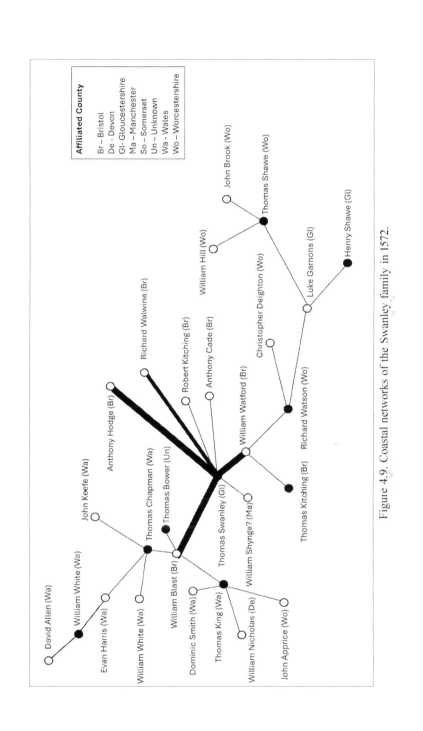

Figure 4.9. Coastal networks of the Swanley family in 1572.

his operational approach during periods of increased trade.[75] In this case, Watson commanded for both Bristol brewer William Watford and draper Luke Garnons, who we shall see in Chapter 5 was a member of the mercantile elite and principally traded in grains. Like many Bristol merchants, Garnons only appears briefly in the coastal customs records and William Watford's engagement was also fleeting. During their forays into coastal commerce through Bristol, both men sought out well-established shipmasters to command their voyages and thus the most prolific coastal traders of the Severn region were tied into larger and better-connected regional networks.

This was also true of William Blast who extended his network in 1572 to include Welshmen Thomas Chapman and Thomas King. While Swanley retained his position as favoured shipmaster for Blast's Gloucestershire trade, Blast also diversified his network in order to take advantage of increased opportunities to trade into Wales. Moreover, the two Welshmen he selected to facilitate his Welsh trade were shipmasters who specialised in the route on which he wished to trade (i.e. Bristol to Tenby).[76] Much as we saw in the case of the Sussex trade with Southampton, Blast established a Welsh branch of his coastal trading network in order to participate in commercial activity that was a deviation from his typical interests. It is beyond the scope of this volume to explore the intricacies of maritime activity within Tenby, but it is of note that many of the shipmasters involved in Tenby trade utilised the same selection of vessels and routinely appeared within the same networks, suggesting that Tenby also benefited from a community of tight-knit mariners.[77] Much like Richard Watford, Blast's decision to extend his network brought together two groups that were typically somewhat insular and that more commonly engaged with only one another.

Finally, 1572 also saw the formation of several smaller networks that involved Bristol traders, one of which brought other members of the Swanley family into focus. Richard Swanley did appear in earlier networks, but those were

---

[75] TNA E190/1128/12 fol.3v, 5r-v, 6v, 7v, 9v, 12v, E190/1128/13 fol.12v, 15r, 17v, E190/1128/14 fol.1v, 8r, E190/1129/1 fol.1v, 3r, 3v, 14r, E190/1129/20 fol.1v, 7v, 11r, 6r-v.

[76] More specifically, Thomas King only traded on the Tenby/Bristol route throughout the full dataset and only commanded Tenby vessels. While Chapman travelled more widely, he still only travelled between Bristol and Welsh ports, and he likewise only commanded Tenby vessels, suggesting that he too had ties to that port. TNA E190/1128/12 fol.4v, 11v, 15v, E190/1128/13 fol.13r, 20v, E190/1129/1 fol.4v, 6v, 7r, 12v, 14r, 17r, 17v, 18r, E190/1129/18 fol.8v, 10v, 19r, E190/1129/22 fol.9v.

[77] The most commonly used were the 7-ton *Grace of God*, the 11-ton *Katherine*, the 4-ton *Peter*, and the 12-ton *Elizabeth*, all of Tenby. TNA E190/1128/12 fol.6v, 8r, 10v, 11v, 15r, E190/1128/13 fol.7r, 13r, 20v, 21r, E190/1128/14 fol.4v, 10v, 14r, 16r, E190/1129/1 fol.4v, 6v–7r, 12v, 14r, 16v, 17r–19r, E190/1129/18 fol.4r, 8v–9r, 10v, 12v, 15v, 17v, 19r, E190/1129/22 fol.3v–4r, 9v, 12v, 14r, E190/1130/2 fol.19v.

limited to only Devon traders and were not involved in trade on the Severn, instead travelling between Bristol and Ilfracombe, with occasional detours to Welsh ports. As the Richard Swanley that appeared in these networks was listed as residing in Devon, rather than Gloucester, it is possible that this was not Thomas, George and William's father. However, this Richard was also an occupational mariner and was likely part of the same family as the Gloucester Swanleys, given that they too had a stake in maritime commerce in Devon and that Richard favoured the Swanley sons as shipmasters during periods in which he traded on the Severn.[78] Like many of the traders we have seen to this point, Richard Swanley was flexible in his business approach and would alter his network ties to take advantage of shipmasters who specialised in the trade he was interested in pursuing. However, in this case, we also see a clear preference for family members, suggesting that he took advantage of personal social connections to facilitate trade into regions beyond his typical activity.

As noted above, particularly poor grain harvests in 1575 and 1576 resulted in a general reduction of trade between Bristol and the Severn ports over the latter half of the 1570s, and this particularly impacted the Bristol brewing networks. By 1576, the Swanley family had all but disappeared from the Bristol/Gloucestershire trade routes, and the Bristol brewers with whom they typically engaged largely withdrew from coastal commerce with them. While members of the Swanley family did appear in the customs records in 1576, a large proportion of their voyages bypassed Bristol entirely in order to travel between Gloucestershire, Welsh, and Cornish ports.[79] This is indicative of broader trends in the region whereby a general reduction in trade between Bristol and the Severn ports resulted in various networks of Severn traders taking their leave of Bristol and instead trading coastwise elsewhere.[80]

This had a significant impact on the networks that were formed and while a number of Bristol brewers did appear in the networks of 1576, they were entirely separate from the brewers that previously interacted with the Swanleys. In particular, unlike the Swanleys, none of the shipmasters commissioned by those brewers to command their journeys had a general preference for working with Bristol brewers or bakers. For example, shipmasters John Chator, Robert Smith and John Lewis only appeared on the coastal routes between Bristol and Gloucestershire in 1576 and Richard James was a prolific shipmaster who would command voyages for a diverse range of merchants, travelling on various trade routes and carrying assorted goods. Likewise,

[78] TNA E190/1128/12 fol.9r, 10v, 11r, E190/1128/13 fol.3r, 7r, 12r, 13r, 14v, 17v, E190/1128/14 fol.4 r, 5r, 9r, E190/1129/1 fol.6v, 10r, 17r, E190/1129/18 fol.16v, E190/1129/20 fol.3r, 4r; Lambert, 'Tudor Shipmasters and Maritime Communities, 1550–1600'.

[79] TNA E190/1129/18 fol.7r, 8v, 16v; Lambert and Baker, www.medievalandtudorships.org.

[80] Hoskins, pp. 45–46.

although shipmaster Thomas Dower appeared in the customs records in 1576 and 1577, his preference for brewers only lasted through 1576, and thereafter he engaged with individuals from various occupational groups and residential affiliations.[81]

This suggests that, in the absence of the Swanleys, there was particular opportunity for shipmasters with diverse interests to interact with craftspeople seeking grains from regions north of Bristol and, as always, local shipmasters took advantage of that increased activity. Furthermore, the fact that brewers and bakers clustered around the same shipmasters suggests that those individuals were able to penetrate a specific occupational group through a single tie and form further connections through that initial contact, much as we saw in the case of the Swanley networks above. However, given that these were entirely separate brewers from those for whom the Swanleys commanded, it seems that the absence of the Swanleys prevented those specific brewers from participating in coastal commercial activity, and highlights that this form of network formation was consistent across different individuals from the same occupational group.

Other craftsmen and small-scale traders

In addition to those three well-defined groups, a number of traders from other occupational groups also operated in the port of Bristol. For example, Lewis Philips was a Bristol baker who hired shipmasters and vessels on an *ad hoc* basis for individual voyages, resulting in the formation of mixed-residency, merchant-centric networks. All of Philips' voyages were one-way, freighting grains into Bristol, presumably to stock his business as a baker. Philips mostly transported goods from Tewkesbury, but also occasionally from locations in Worcestershire or Somerset, hiring shipmasters and ships associated with the port from which he was travelling.[82] Likewise, Richard Lewis Hopkins typically traded from Bristol into Wales and thus favoured particular Welsh shipmasters. However, he too expanded his network when necessary and, in doing so, formed ties with individual shipmasters that more typically traded *ad hoc*.

In the same way, Richard Johnson primarily undertook voyages on which he acted in capacity of both shipmaster and merchant, but during 1570 he extended his activities to form network ties with a grocer and a trowman, forming opportunistic ties with others who operated regularly in the region.[83] Similarly,

---

[81] TNA E190/1128/12 fol.6v, 7v, E190/1128/13 fol.13v, E190/1128/14 fol.6r, 10r, E190/1129/1 fol.6r, 8r, 9r, 15r, E190/1129/18 fol.2r, 3v, 4v, 5v, 10r-v, 11r, E190/1129/20 fol.3r, 7v, E190/1129/22 fol.1r-v, 4r, 9v, 10v, E190/1130/2 fol.14v, 16r.

[82] TNA E190/1128/12 fol.2v–8v, E190/1128/14 fol.6r, E190/1128/18 fol.2r–4v.

[83] TNA E190/1128/13 fol.1r, 5v, E190/1128/14 fol.4r, 8v, 11v, 12r.

pewterer John Burrow and grocer Nicholas Hobbs traded out of Bristol to diverse locations, hiring shipmasters per voyage, usually favouring vessels and shipmasters from the destination port.[84] The fact that these craftsmen were able to opportunistically form ties with a range of individuals from the ports with which they intended to trade speaks to the opportunities available in Bristol as a major commercial centre, and, as we shall see below, increased volumes of trade through the port created greater opportunity for collaboration.

This is also evident in the cases of various shipmasters who elected to dedicate their careers to particular trade routes. For example, John Simons of Instow only travelled on the route between Bristol and Barnstaple, Philip Strange only travelled between Bristol and Chepstow, and John Philips only travelled between Bristol and Welsh ports. All three shipmasters would command voyages for a broad range of merchants from any town, carrying any cargo, but only ever travelled on their established routes.[85] While we do not have residency data for Strange or Philips, Simons hailed from Instow, Strange commanded only ships from Chepstow, and Philips commanded ships from Carmarthen, Milford Haven, Newport and St Davids, suggesting that these men ran regular routes from their home towns to Bristol, on which there would have been much demand for shipping. This suggests that the nature of commercial enterprise in Bristol allowed shipmasters to specialise in particularly busy shipping routes between major commercial centres. In turn, this gave merchants who engaged in coastal commerce only *ad hoc* the ability to seek out shipmasters with relevant knowledge, expertise, and local contacts, creating an environment in which short-term network formation was common.

Finally, the opportunities presented by Bristol as a major provincial port in some cases also offered a form of respite from commercial hardship for craftspeople. For example, John Bones (otherwise known as John Bonnar) was also a sporadic coaster, however, his trade is of particular note since he did not engage in coasting as a part of his primary occupation but instead opted to participate only during periods in which there was a lull in his craft. Bones was a cardmaker, and he even took on an apprentice cardmaker in 1559, suggesting that he ran a reasonably successful business.[86] However, his coastwise voyages

[84] TNA E190/1128/12 fol.2r, 3v–6v, 16r, E190/1128/13 fol.3v, 11r, E190/1128/14 fol.4v–6v, E190/1129/1 fol.13v, E190/1129/18 fol.10v, 11r, 15v, 19v, E190/1129/22 fol.14v.
[85] TNA E190/1128/12 fol.8r, 10r, 12r, 13v, 15r-v, E190/1128/13 fol.5r, 16r, 19r, 21r, E190/1128/14 fol.4r, E190/1129/1 fol.11v, 13v, 14v, 15v, 16v, 17v, E190/1129/18 fol.15v, E190/1129/20 fol.1r, E190/1129/22 fol.3r, 5v, 9v, 11r, 14r.
[86] TNA E190/1128/12 fol.15v, E190/1128/13 fol.13r, 20r, 21r, E190/1128/14 fol.14v, 15v, 16r, E190/1129/1 fol.1v, 14v, 16r, 17r, 17v, E190/1129/18 fol.15r, 19r; Sheila Lang and Margaret McGregor, 'Tudor Wills Proved in Bristol, 1546–1603' (Bristol: Bristol Record Society, 1993), pp. 4, 83, 115.

did not involve the transportation of goods associated with cardmaking, but instead the provision of mixed high-value cargoes from Devon.

Bones specialised in the route between Bristol and Barnstaple and was easily able to form ties with numerous separate Devon shipmasters. He was a desirable merchant and he may well have had particular ties to the Devon area. Bones' wife died a widow in 1602 so it is likely that he either died or began winding down his operations towards the end of the period under investigation, hence his sudden departure from the customs records after 1572.[87] Nonetheless, as a craftsman, rather than an occupational merchant, his networking power is notable, and the network graphs generated as part of this project suggest that he had both the financial stability to run high-value voyages and the social stature to integrate effectively into a maritime community outside of his home town.

Bristol's merchant elite

The final occupational group of interest in this section is Bristol's mercantile elite. The role that elite merchants played in the formation of regional networks is examined in more detail below in the context of wider trends of cross-county integration. However, it is worth first briefly exploring a number of common trends in the formation of networks among such traders. As we shall see, it was common for members of the mercantile elite to engage in coastal trade opportunistically, with many choosing to engage routinely in overseas trade while just occasionally participating in coasting during periods of particularly high levels of coastal activity through the port. During such times, Bristol's merchant elite sought out the most experienced local shipmasters to command their vessels and, like many of the craftspeople discussed in the sections above, they oftentimes prioritised shipmasters who specialised in the trade routes on which they wished to operate.

As a result, their presence on coastal trade routes often pulled apart networks of individuals from other regions as they sought network ties with the most valuable contacts on those routes. For example, in 1580, a cluster of Bristol traders tied to a cluster of Devon traders via merchant John Bush. Like many Bristol merchants, Bush hired shipmasters *ad hoc* but usually had a preference for individuals associated with the port into which he was trading. As his foremost trading activity was with Devon, and he therefore mostly interacted with Devon shipmasters, he was largely absent from the network graphs generated for the period under investigation. However, in 1580 he undertook a rare voyage to a non-Devon port and thus tied to a Bristol shipmaster, highlighting the targeted nature of his network formation.[88]

---

[87] Lang and McGregor, p. 83.
[88] TNA E190/1128/12 fol.8v, 12v, 13r, E190/1128/14 fol.2r, 15v, E190/1130/2 fol.18r.

Similarly, various Bristol merchants opportunistically engaged in trade with Wales and the same trends were evident in the networks of those men. Indeed, although overall trade through Bristol decreased in 1576, trade with the Welsh ports was particularly high and various Bristol merchants elected to take advantage of that opportunity. Again, they utilised the services of local shipmasters to do so and, more specifically, they hired shipmasters that specialised in the trade routes on which they wished to sail. For example, shipmaster Thomas Lewis almost exclusively travelled on the route between Bristol and Tenby, typically engaging with other Welshmen but catering for occupational merchants from Bristol during periods of increased trade.. Likewise, John William operated almost exclusively on routes between Bristol and Welsh ports and was therefore able to attract a substantial body of merchants seeking to trade into Wales.[89] Nonetheless, in every case, these network ties were short-term, and the networking power of Bristol's mercantile elite is again evident.

Finally, as we saw in Chapter 3, the majority of coastal shipments carried the goods of only a single merchant, owing to the generally low risks involved and the desire to increase profit margins. However, individuals could occasionally be persuaded to share their hulls with other merchants, usually as a result of increased risk. Such multi-merchant voyages become very evident when the port book data is visualised using Social Network Analysis and it is possible to identify those who sought out mercantile collaboration. For example, in 1569, only one multi-merchant voyage appeared in the network graphs generated. In this case, Laurence Holiday and John Moore collaborated in order to transport a cargo of linen, canvas, train oil and soap from Bristol to Gloucester. The cargo was of a similar value to other shipments transported on many single-merchant voyages on the same route and the ship was unremarkable in size, being just 4 tons.[90] However, this voyage involved the only two merchants in the full dataset who were defined by the customs officials as 'mercers'. The specific identification of Holiday and Moore as mercers, as opposed to clothiers or merchants, heavily implies involvement in overseas trade. Mercers were traditionally silk traders, but were more broadly involved in the transportation of luxury cloth and were fundamentally intertwined with overseas import. This title carried a mark of status and this characterisation, combined with the formation of a multi-merchant network and the fact that they carried linen and soap, suggests that this voyage may well have been the coastal leg of an incoming overseas shipment, accounting for the extra risk and therefore providing the impetus for collaboration.[91]

---

[89] TNA E190/1128/12 fol.2r, 5v, 16r, E190/1128/13 fol.11r, E190/1128/14 fol.4v, 14r, E190/1129/1 fol.15v, 17r-v, E190/1129/18 fol.10v, 15v, 19v, E190/1129/22 fol.14v.
[90] TNA E190/1128/12 fol.3v.
[91] Anne F. Sutton, *The Mercery of London: Trade, Goods and People, 1130–1578*

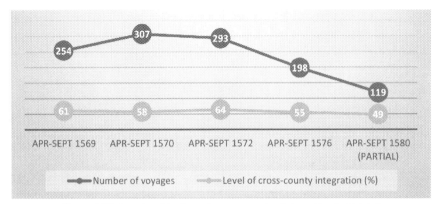

Figure 4.10. Levels of trade and cross-country integration in Bristol.

Changing levels of cross-county integration

As in Southampton, traders from the local region generally dominated coastal commerce in Bristol. However, networks of individuals from elsewhere (primarily Wales, Cornwall and Devon) appeared with more regularity in Bristol than they did in Southampton, owing to the diverse commodities available in the port and the extensive sales market there. As a result, the correlation between levels of trade and levels of cross-county integration in Bristol was less stark than in Southampton, as shown in Figures 4.4 and 4.10. Whereas in Southampton increased cross-county integration resulted from non-local traders travelling to the port *en masse* for short periods in response to specific commercial trends, in Bristol, the presence of external traders was more consistent and did not fluctuate significantly with overarching levels of trade. Instead, levels of integration were most severely impacted by the influx of a number of powerful Bristol merchants, who only substantially engaged in coastal commerce during periods of heightened opportunity and were able to draw Bristol traders into their networks.

More specifically, in April–September 1569 and April–September 1576, when coastwise trade through Bristol was relatively low (at 254 and 198 voyages, respectively), Bristol traders appeared throughout networks of individuals from other regions but rarely engaged with one another and did not form the bulk of the nodes in any given network. However, in April–September 1570 and 1572, when trade through Bristol was greater (at 307 and 293 voyages, respectively), networks involving only Bristol traders were

---

(Oxon: Ashgate, 2005), pp. 1–16.

formed and those that were previously part of more diverse networks were drawn into Bristol-centric groups.

This specific form of interaction resulted from the operational means through which Bristol merchants typically participated in coastal commerce. As noted above, Bristol has a centuries-long history of influential local merchants monopolising its overseas trade. As a result, occupational merchants in the port were usually members of the mercantile elite who were foremost concerned with overseas activity and only occasionally engaged in coastal commerce. However, they occupied a privileged socio-economic position in the port, which allowed them to form business networks very easily when they did elect to participate in coastal commerce, resulting in Bristol's career coastal traders abandoning their regionally diverse networks in order to engage with the mercantile elite during periods of heightened trade.[92]

Coastal networks in Hull

Owing to Hull's commercial characteristics and the nature of its customs records, the analysis in this section is somewhat different from that of Southampton and Bristol. In particular, since 98% of voyages between Newcastle and Hull were undertaken with a single individual acting as both merchant and shipmaster, the methods of Social Network Analysis deployed in this volume are not suitable for examination of Hull's trade with Newcastle.[93] Therefore, this section instead focuses on Hull's other trade routes, most notably trade with London, which was the port's second most abundant coastal connection.

Furthermore, as the Hull port books do not list residences for either shipmasters or merchants, it is difficult to make an informed assumption regarding county affiliations. The only location data available comes from the origin ports of the ships involved and the trade routes on which particular individuals operated. We shall see in Chapter 5 that this information is sufficient to infer residences for a small group of prolific traders, but not for the bulk of the individuals that appear. Likewise, owing to the fact that a large proportion of Hull's trade was with London, fluctuations in levels of commercial activity were minimal and there was limited variation in the number of individuals that engaged in Hull's coastal trade across the five periods. Therefore, this chapter focuses on the structure of the networks that were formed and highlights some particularly important groups for further

---

[92] Carus-Wilson, 'The Merchant Adventurers of Bristol in the Fifteenth Century', pp. 68–82; Flavin and Jones, *Bristol's Trade with Ireland and the Continent 1503–1601: The Evidence of the Exchequer Customs Accounts*, pp. xiii–xiv; Jones, *Inside the Illicit Economy: Reconstructing the Smugglers' Trade of Sixteenth Century*, pp. 138–83.

[93] TNA E190/305/1, E190/305/11, E190/305/12, E190/306/1, E190/306/4, E190/306/16, E190/306/17, E190/307/2, E190/307/3, E190/307/9, E190/307/16.

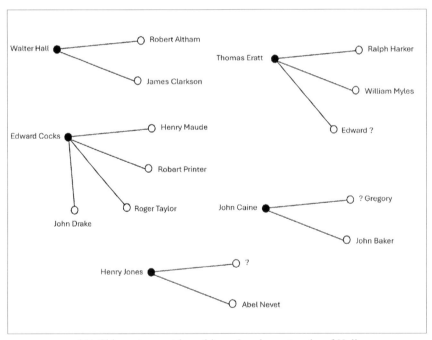

4.11. Shipmaster-centric and large London networks of Hull (shipmasters in black, merchants in white).

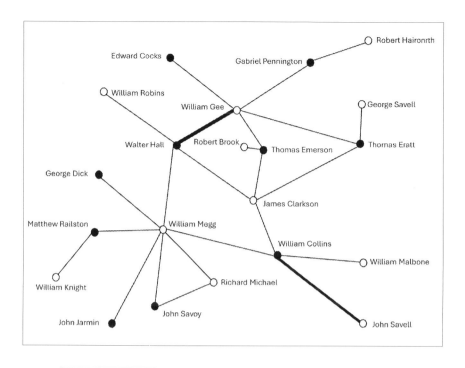
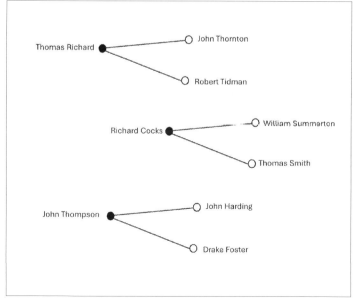

Figure 4.11 (*continued*)

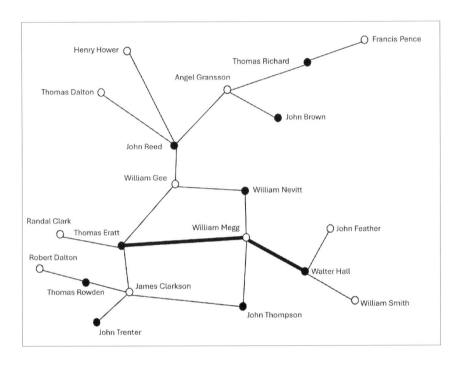

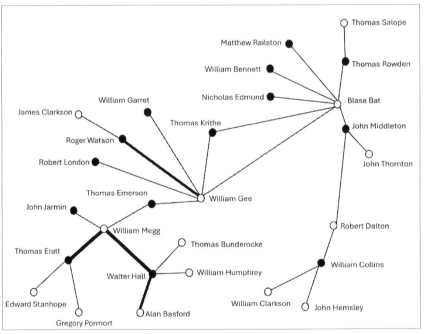

Figure 4.11 (*continued*)

investigation in Chapter 5, rather than exploring the impact of fluctuations in levels of trade or levels of cross-county integration.

Trade with London

Although we are unable to assess the impact of regional affiliation on network formation in Hull, some stark differences between the networks that formed around different types of commercial activity are evident from the network graphs that were generated. Perhaps most startling of these was the clear difference between the networks that formed around trade with London and those that formed around trade with lesser ports. More specifically, in the London trade, a number of particular shipmasters engaged in trade with London regularly and consistently and they commanded voyages for a range of merchants. However, in the case of trade with other provincial ports (such as King's Lynn or Great Yarmouth), which represented more fleeting commercial activity in Hull, merchants more regularly repeated trade and hired shipmasters on a voyage-by-voyage basis, as we shall see below. This difference was the result of the specific nature of the trade undertaken on those routes. London was Hull's second-largest trading partner and, owing to the prevalence of high-value goods such as metals, wine, soap, feathers and butter, could draw particularly high profits for merchants that elected to trade on that route.[94] Therefore, London represented a buoyant and lucrative market for Hull shipmasters that allowed them to interact with local merchants of substantial socio-economic weight, as we shall see in Chapter 5. As a result, there existed a body of occupational mariners that specialised in the route between London and Hull and many of those went on to form the largest and most integrated networks in the region, becoming the core of the local maritime community.

Moreover, as shown in Figure 4.11, shipmasters who engaged in the London trade often began trading within shipmaster-centric networks, with a single shipmaster catering to a range of disconnected merchants, and then leveraged relationships with particularly influential merchants to forge network ties within much more integrated networks of the most prolific merchants and mariners operating with regularity on the Hull–London trade route. Indeed, three of the five shipmasters that appeared in shipmaster-centric networks

---

[94] Directly comparing the value of goods is a challenging endeavour, owing to the varying units utilised for different commodities (or, in many cases, the varying units utilised to measure the same commodities by different customs officials), and the changing Book of Rates over the period. Nonetheless, some goods were clearly of higher value than others, and evaluation of several indicative voyages suggests that London trade was especially lucrative, as shown in Appendix D. See also Flavin and Jones, 'A Glossary of Commodities, Weights and Measures Found in the Sixteenth-Century Bristol Customs Account'.

in September–April 1568/9 had, by 1570/1, transitioned into a much larger, more integrated and well-established network of merchants and mariners who regularly traded into London. Likewise, between 1570/1 and 1571/2, two shipmasters that previously appeared in shipmaster-centric networks shifted into the same large and integrated London network. This trend is evident throughout the period under investigation and there appears to have been a standardised means through which local shipmasters forged network ties with the most important and prolific merchants on the Hull–London trade route.

Indeed, even during periods when the larger and well-established London networks were highly active, smaller shipmaster-centric networks still formed around the London trade route, made up of shipmasters who were new to the route and replacing those who had transitioned into the larger network. While those shipmaster-centric networks involved different individuals, their structure was much the same and many of the shipmasters in those shipmaster-centric networks would go on to transition themselves into the larger London networks in subsequent periods. This suggests that shipmasters seeking to engage in the lucrative and abundant trade between London and Hull typically undertook a number of *ad hoc* voyages for less prolific and lower-status merchants, before shifting to interact directly with the mercantile elite that dominated that route.

However, it is worth noting that economic and commercial factors sometimes impacted the nature of this transition. For example, trade with London accounted for a particularly large proportion of Hull's overall coastal activity in September–April 1573/4 (37% of voyages, compared to 21% in 1571/2, 26% in 1570/1, and 20% in 1568/9). This increase in trade created a particular demand for shipmasters, and therefore new individuals trading on the London–Hull route bypassed the shipmaster-centric phase and engaged directly with core members of Hull's merchant elite, creating a particularly dense and shipmaster-heavy London trade network during this period.

Notably, those shipmasters who had direct access to particular vessels appear to have more easily transitioned from low-level disconnected networks into the core London trade network. For example, all three of the shipmasters that transitioned into the large network between 1568/9 and 1570/1, and the two who transitioned between 1570/1 and 1571/2, appear to have owned or part-owned their own vessels, very likely increasing their desirability as mariners.[95] Likewise, in the earlier periods, there was little consistency in

---

[95] For example, Thomas Eratt was affiliated with (and possibly owned or part-owned) three Hull vessels, the 60-ton *Jesus*, the 50-ton *Daisy* and the 50-ton *Green Dragon*, and Walter Hall was tied to the 40-ton *Jonas* of Hull. Thomas Richard was clearly tied to the 24-ton *Magdalene* of Hull, and John Thompson the 40-ton *Christopher* of Hull; they may have owned or part-owned these vessels or had some form of long-term arrangement for their use. See TNA E190/305/1 fol.1v, 10r, 16v,

the vessels shipmaster Thomas Emerson commanded, and it was only after the first voyage he commanded for elite merchant William Gee on 5 August 1570 that he began using the same ship consistently, commanding the 40-ton *Christopher* of Hull throughout 1570/1 and the 50-ton *Elizabeth* of Hull throughout 1574. This same trend is evident in the case of Roger Watson who likewise commanded a variety of different vessels until his first interaction with William Gee in the 1570s, at which point he began consistently commanding the same *Elizabeth* of Hull. Over that time, both men frequently catered for different merchants but never changed ships. This suggests that these shipmasters had a particular interest in those vessels, and it seems that made them attractive to Gee, enabling them to penetrate the elite London networks. It is difficult to determine whether these shipmasters actually had a share in those vessels, whether they hired them on some kind of long-term lease, or if they were directly employed by the shipowner as shipmasters. However, in all of these cases, they would have had both direct access to and a greater degree of legal or perceived responsibility for the vessel, making them desirable to hire.[96]

In addition to these overarching trends that appear to have been indicative of the general nature of Hull's coastal trade with London, it is also important to highlight the impact that specific individuals had on those same networks. As we saw in Southampton and Bristol, individuals that routinely engaged in the town's largest and most expansive networks were often core members of the local maritime and mercantile communities. In Hull, networks of that sort centred on the trade with London, which was especially lucrative and therefore attracted local traders of substantial wealth and social standing, many of whom appear in the same civic documents, tied together through their engagement in local politics.[97] Of those individuals, William Gee was by far the most influential and the role that Gee had in the formation and maintenance of the large London trade networks is important to highlight.

E190/305/11 fol.1v, 4r-v, 13r, 16r-v, 17r, E190/305/12 fol.1r, 2v, 10v, 13v, E190/306/1 fol.11r, 14r–15r, 20r–21r, E190/306/4 fol.1r-v, 3r, 6r, 8r, 9r-v, E190/306/16 fol.1v, 12r-v, 13v, 17r, E190/306/17 fol.12r–13v, 14v, 15v, 17r, E190/307/2 fol.11r, E190/307/3 fol.8v, E190/307/9 fol.7v.

[96] It should be noted that it is also possible that Gee owned these vessels and hired them to the shipmasters directly, but there is no evidence that Gee was a shipowner in his will or in any civic sources, suggesting that this was not the case. TNA E190/305/1 fol.3r, 11r, 16r, E190/305/11 fol.4r, 16r, E190/305/12 fol.9r, 10r, 12v, 13r, E190/306/4 fol.5r-v, 6r, 8v–9r, E190/306/16 fol.12v, 17r-v, 18r, E190/306/17 fol.12r, 13v, 14r, 16r-v, E190/307/2 fol.7r, 8r, E190/307/9 fol.7r; TNA PROB 11/101/342. See also, Ward, pp. 48–68.

[97] HHC C/DMT/10/1, U/DDFA/6/1, U/DDCB/12/1, U/DDHA/2/18, C/WG/5, C/WG/6, U/DDSY/52/12, U/DDSY/52/19.

Gee entered into the trade between London and Hull in 1570 and journeyed on that route regularly until 1576, primarily trading in lead (usually as part of a larger mixed cargo, often containing butter, pewter, salt, steel and grains).[98] He was often at the centre of the large London trade networks and appears to have been the catalyst for various shipmaster-merchant collaborations, many of which broke apart when Gee departed from coastal commerce in around 1576. William Gee is unusual in that the customs records specifically identify him as a Hull man and he was, in fact, an important member of the wider community. He was a powerful local merchant who served as alderman and mayor, and his son would go on to be an MP. Moreover, he appears in the 1559 and 1590 lay subsidy returns, valued at £30 and £50, respectively, and he controlled various properties in the area, some of which he leased to other traders.[99] Gee's status as an established and wealthy merchant allowed him to form broad networks and trade extensively.[100] However, shipmasters like those mentioned above usually began their involvement in coastal commerce by engaging with merchants of lesser status, becoming more integrated into the local maritime community over time and only then trading with merchants of Gee's social stature.

Nonetheless, once a shipmaster had made the transition to collaborating with Gee directly, this was often a gateway into more extensive network connections. Indeed, it was common for shipmasters to tie to Gee in one period before forming stronger bonds with other members of the merchant elite (such as William Megg, Robert and Thomas Dalton, James Clarkson, Blaise Bat, Thomas Rowden, Alan Basford and Matthew Railson) in a later period. Although sources relating to William Megg are sparse, other merchants in this network are referenced throughout Hull's civic records. For example, Robert Dalton served as mayor in Hull, and various local civic sources show Thomas Dalton and James Clarkson actively engaging in the local community, gathering reasonably large levels of wealth and investing in property in the town. Likewise, several of the merchants that appear in these networks are listed in a number of petitions in which they appealed for restrictions on Londoners trading lead into Hull, pointing to a desire among locals to maintain

---

[98] TNA E190/305/11 fol.16r-v, 17r, E190/305/12 fol.13r-v, E190/306/1 fol.14r-v, E190/306/4 fol.5v–6r, 9r, E190/306/16 fol.17r–18r, E190/306/17 fol.13v–14r, 16r–17v, E190/307/2 fol.8r, 11r, E190/307/3 fol.16r, 17r.

[99] HHC C/DSN/1, U/DDCB/12/1, C/WG/6, C/WG/21, C/WG/38, U/DDWB/11/1, C/BRI/20, C/WW/296, U/DX28/7; TNA E179/203/265 mem.2; John William Clay, 'Dugdale's Visitation of Yorkshire, with Additions' (Exeter: W. Pollard & Co., 1917), p. 21; Andrew Thrush and John P. Ferris, 'Gee, William (?1565–1611), of York Minster Yard and Bishop Burton, Yorks.', www.historyofparliamentonline.org/volume/1604-1629/member/gee-william-1565-1611 (accessed 27 August 2019).

[100] Gee is discussed in more detail below, see pp. 127–29 and 168–70.

control of this important branch of coastal commerce.[101] We can trace the progression of particular shipmasters through this network over time and identify the key nodes that allowed them more extensive access to the core of the mercantile elite.

For example, shipmaster Walter Hall began in 1568/9 in a shipmaster-centric network catering to a range of disconnected low-level merchants, but gradually became more integrated into the core network over time. He slowly transitioned from that initial insignificant network, to engaging directly with Gee, to interacting more broadly with members of the mercantile elite. This trend continued throughout 1573/4, during which time Hall undertook three voyages for William Megg and two for Alan Basford, a level of repeat interaction that was unusual among coastal traders in Hull and is indicative of his increased integration.[102] This was also true of shipmaster Thomas Eratt, who likewise transitioned to commanding voyages for William Megg via William Gee and who, in 1573/4, further strengthened his bond with Megg, commanding multiple voyages for Megg over a six-month period. Likewise, Thomas Emerson first tied to Gee in 1570 and he continued to command voyages for Gee regularly between April 1570 and September 1573, first working with William Megg in 1571.[103] It was through Gee that these shipmasters became acquainted with the larger network and, once they had established themselves as members of the community, they were able to form stronger ties with other local merchants. The case of William Megg is particularly stark, but this trend also applied to the other elite Hull merchants mentioned above and it continued throughout the period under investigation.

Aside from the shipmasters with whom he engaged, William Gee also appears to have had an impact on the network formation of merchants involved in the London trade, and this is particularly evident in the case of merchant Blaise Bat (or Bates). Bat traded in lead and grains and only appeared in the coastal customs records in September–April 1573/4, taking advantage of a particular demand for those products at that time. During 1574, Bat shared a voyage with William Gee, for which they utilised shipmaster Thomas Krithe.[104] This shared voyage was only Bat's second in Hull and the first on which he used a Hull vessel. While he only overlapped with Gee for that one journey, he subsequently tied to other shipmasters that were well established within the large London network (most notably Thomas Rowden and Matthew Railson). We cannot say for certain that Gee was responsible

---

[101] HHC C/BRS/2/1.

[102] TNA E190/306/16 fol. 12r-v, 14r, 17r.

[103] TNA E190/305/1 fol.1v, 10r, 16v, E190/305/11 fol.13r, 17v, E190/305/12 fol.10v, E190/306/1 fol.11r, 14v, 15r, 20r–21r, E190/306/4 fol.1v, 6r, 8r, 9r, E190/306/16 fol.12r-v, 17r, E190/306/17 fol.12r, 13v, 14v, 15v, 17r, E190/307/9 fol.7v.

[104] TNA E190/306/16 fol.17v.

for Bat's ability to forge connections with those key shipmasters, but when we consider Gee's wider significance in network formation, and particularly his role in generating network ties between William Megg and various shipmasters, it seems highly probable.

Such was Gee's influence in Hull that when he withdrew from coastal commerce in 1576, the London trade network broke down completely and the absence of such a network in the graphs generated from the 1577/8 data is startling. In Southampton and Bristol, network changes of this kind usually resulted from fluctuations in levels of trade and in the number of nodes participating at a given time. However, in this case, the network graphs contained approximately the same number of nodes as in earlier periods and there were no significant fluctuations in trade levels. Instead, the key difference was the absence of Gee who, by this time, was winding down his coastal activity to take up a new career as a banker for local merchants, and whose absence had a dramatic impact on the structure of the networks that remained.[105]

Other traders that were central in the large London networks of earlier periods did still engage in coastal commerce in 1577/8, but those individuals clearly played a lesser role in the formation and maintenance of network ties. For example, William Collins, Robert Dalton and Thomas Eratt had appeared in the same network throughout the 1570s, tied together via William Gee, but they split apart due to Gee's absence. Likewise, William Megg still had a strong presence in the port, but his participation was clearly insufficient to keep the network together. In particular, we saw that Thomas Eratt transitioned to commanding voyages on a recurring basis for William Megg via William Gee, but by 1577/8 that relationship had fallen apart, in spite of the fact that Eratt was still active as a shipmaster on the route between Hull and London. In almost every case, the absence of William Gee had a profound impact on the networks of individuals that engaged in trade between London and Hull, and Chapter 5 will bring more depth to our understanding of Gee's pivotal role in Hull's coastal commercial activity.

Finally, to offer some context as to the significance of Gee's influence, it is useful to highlight a case that sits in stark contrast. We saw above that James Clarkson was central among the individuals that traded through London between 1568/9 and 1571/2; however, by 1573/4, he had begun winding down his coastal activity and, as a result, he appeared only on the periphery of the network during that period.[106] Yet in spite of Clarkson's central position

---

[105] Thrush and Ferris, www.historyofparliamentonline.org/volume/1604-1629/member/gee-william-1565-1611.

[106] Between 1568 and 1572, Clarkson typically engaged in at least three coastal voyages per year and sometimes as many as ten or eleven. However, in 1573 this dropped to just one voyage and after 1576 he did not appear in the Hull coastal port books at all. TNA E190/305/1 fol.16v, E190/305/11 fol.13r, E190/305/12 fol.10r-v,

in earlier periods, the network remained intact without his substantial involvement. While the elimination of William Gee had a severe impact on the structure of the network, Clarkson disappeared from the network without affecting the network ties of the other merchants and mariners with whom he engaged. This offers an important juxtaposition against William Gee, and although local records attest to Clarkson being a wealthy and well-established merchant, who was certainly engaged in local community matters, he was less politically inclined than Gee, and the evidence presented here suggests that his overall impact within the community was much less marked.[107]

Trade with East Anglia

As we saw in Chapter 2, Hull's coastal trade was largely dominated by the markets of London and Newcastle. However, some trade was also undertaken with ports in East Anglia, and the commercial nature of that activity had a distinct impact on the networks that formed around it. Most significantly, there was a clear divide between individuals that formed shipmaster-centric networks (who were mostly involved in trade between Hull and London) and individuals that formed merchant-centric networks (who largely traded between Hull and the ports of East Anglia). Thus, in the London trade, a number of shipmasters commanded voyages for a range of merchants, whereas in the trade with East Anglia, merchants more regularly repeated trade and hired shipmasters on a voyage-by-voyage basis.

This applied both to the trade route between Hull and King's Lynn, which we saw in Chapter 2 was highly active during the late 1560s but was near-negligible thereafter, as well as to the trade with Great Yarmouth, which was minimal in the earlier period but much more active during the mid-1570s. Since the trade around which these networks formed did not represent a permanent presence in Hull and these shipments were merely an opportunistic response to demand for foodstuffs, there was little scope for shipmasters or merchants to specialise in these trade routes and most voyages were taken opportunistically by members of the civic elite in East Anglia and Yorkshire. As such, merchants hired shipmasters *ad hoc*, rather than drawing from a pool of mariners that specialised on those routes, and did not therefore form large or integrated networks.

Interestingly, this also applied to the only voyage in the dataset that was undertaken between Hull and Cornwall, when merchant Nicholas Calman journeyed from Looe to Hull in the 20-ton *Martin* of York, commanded by shipmaster Ralph Rackes, and then from Hull to Newcastle in the 22-ton

---

E190/306/1 fol.14r-v, 15r, 20v, E190/306/4 fol.5v–6r, 8r, 9r, E190/306/16 fol.12v, E190/306/17 fol.13r, E190/307/2 fol.6r, 8r, 9v.
[107] HHC C/DSN/1, C/WG/5, C/WG/6.

Francis of Newcastle, commanded by John Waymer, carrying a cargo of barley.[108] Grain-carrying voyages from Cornwall to Newcastle were exceedingly rare and, like the trade with East Anglia, were largely undertaken in response to a particular demand for foodstuffs. As a result, few or no mariners specialised in that route and network ties were thus formed *ad hoc* per voyage, with merchants taking advantage of any shipmaster that could accommodate the journey. This is consistent with themes we saw in Bristol and in Southampton, and suggests that trends in network formation were sometimes consistent across wholly disconnected ports on the basis of the form of commercial activity being undertaken.

Other trade

Aside from the principal trade networks already discussed, a number of outlier networks also operated in the port of Hull, the most notable of which revolved around shipmaster Robert Duffield. Robert Duffield was a prolific mariner, he was principally a coastal trader who occasionally engaged in overseas voyages to France and the Low Countries, and he may well have had a share in the 30-ton *Greyhound* of Keadby (sometimes listed as the *Greyhound* of Hull).[109] The coastal voyages Duffield commanded were extremely varied; he transported feathers to London as part of a large mixed cargo, malt to Berwick-upon-Tweed, and iron and hops into Hull from Lincoln.[110] Duffield catered to a broad range of merchants on an array of trade routes and, unlike the individuals discussed above, appears to have had little preference for the trade in which he engaged.

As a result, Duffield formed trade networks that were more complex than many other Hull networks, reflective of the broad trade interests of the individuals involved. Interestingly, however, a large number of the other shipmasters that appeared in his networks operated in much the same way as Duffield, being hired largely *ad hoc* to command vessels on a range of voyages.[111] This suggests that these individuals were part of a pool of shipmasters that were available for hire in the region, who were willing to cater for any trader on any route without the promise of a longer-term business partnership. As a result, they formed broad networks and incidentally tied to some of the same

---

[108] TNA E190/305/11 fol.3v.

[109] TNA E190/305/1 fol.11r, 16v–17r, E190/305/11 fol.4r, E190/305/12 fol.2r, 4r, E190/306/1 fol.10r, E190/307/2 fol.2r, E190/307/9 fol.1v, 6r, E190/306/17 fol.1r; Lambert and Baker, www.medievalandtudorships.org.

[110] TNA E190/305/12 fol.2r, 4r, E190/306/1 fol.10r, E190/306/17 fol.1r, E190/307/2 fol.2r, E190/307/9 fol.1v.

[111] For example, E190/305/1 fol.11v, 16v, 17r.

merchants who operated in much the same way (hiring *ad hoc* per voyage without forming stronger relationships with particular mariners).

It should also be noted that a number of these shipmasters, including Robert Duffield, also undertook numerous voyages carrying Newcastle coal. However, in those cases, they adjusted their operations and elected to act in the capacity of both shipmaster and merchant.[112] Shipmasters like Duffield were probably career mariners and often owned or part-owned vessels. They mostly commanded their own ships, carrying cargo belonging to a single merchant, but would occasionally invest in the coal trade as an aside. Similarly, merchants operating in the port of Hull would, for the most part, transport only their own goods on individual voyages. However, as in Southampton and Bristol, some would occasionally shift their operational approach and share hull space with other merchants. Those voyages spanned a range of trade routes, were unrelated to each other, and the impetus to share hull space was specific to the characteristics of each shipment.

For example, high-value shipments, such as that carried on a February 1578 voyage commanded by Richard Ward, which contained products such as olive oil, soap, tin, wine, whale fins, and miscellaneous haberdasher and grocery wares, or that carried on an October 1577 voyage commanded by John Clark, which included raisins, salt, wine and grocery wares, often provided the motivation to collaborate with other merchants in order to reduce risk.[113] Similarly, the cargo carried on a shared voyage between William Megg, Ralph Blake and [first name unknown] Rawson was also fairly valuable, including pitch and tar, oil, ropes, soap, metals, grains and fish. However, these commodities were normal for Megg to carry and he typically undertook voyages of a similar value as a single merchant. As such, it seems that the impetus in that case was the extended length of the voyage.[114] Indeed, unlike his other voyages, this shipment only briefly docked in Hull after embarking from London and the final destination was Newcastle. It is therefore probable that the longer distance travelled created a higher level of risk and motivated these merchants to share hull space.

Likewise, the cargo carried by Laurence Hassowle and William Harrison on a journey between King's Lynn and Hull in 1578 was unremarkable in value,

---

[112] TNA E190/305/12 fol.2r, 4r, E190/306/1 fol.10r, E190/306/17 fol.1r, E190/307/2 fol.2r, E190/307/9 fol.1v–2r, 3v.

[113] On the voyage commanded by Richard Ward, the 3 tons of olive oil alone were likely worth around £24, making this a particularly high-value shipment, without even considering the value of the other commodities. Likewise, on the John Clark voyage, just the salt and raisins would likely have been valued at around £17. TNA E190/307/9 fol.5r-v; see Flavin and Jones, 'A Glossary of Commodities, Weights and Measures Found in the Sixteenth-Century Bristol Customs Account', pp. 64, 76, 80.

[114] TNA E190/307/9 fol.4v.

consisting primarily of fish. However, that voyage was undertaken during a period in which trade between Hull and King's Lynn was almost negligible, and thus the risk may have come from the lack of regular trade between the two towns.[115] As we have seen throughout this chapter, the desire to adapt modes of transportation heavily depended on the commodities transported, but could also be a response to other external factors. We see here prolific merchants adapting their practical methods to account for a certain level of risk, and we shall see in Chapter 5 that the same can be said of the Newcastle coal traders.

Conclusions and common threads

A number of notable trends have become apparent throughout this chapter, some of which were common across all three ports, and some of which were regionally varied. For example, we have seen across all three ports that the vast majority of trade was undertaken with just the cargo of a single merchant on board. However, in many cases, individuals were willing to alter their operational approach and expand their networks in order to reduce risk for particularly high-value or high-risk journeys. For each multi-merchant voyage, we can identify particular factors that caused increased risk, such as the inclusion of high-value commodities or the nature of the trade route plied. In such cases, individuals that would typically fill a vessel with only their own goods instead collaborated with other merchants to split that investment between multiple traders. In Southampton, this was especially common in the transportation of Cornish tin, in Hull it was the high-value London trade that prompted the shift, and in Bristol shared voyages were most common in the trade with Cornwall and Devon.

Such adjustments also applied to other elements of network formation, and it was common for individuals to adjust their approach to adapt to particular trade routes. In Hull, for example, a willingness to shift operational approaches in response to specific commercial activity was particularly common among those who both traded into London or East Anglian ports (where they forged networks with other traders) and engaged in the transportation of coal between Newcastle and Hull (where they acted as both shipmaster and merchant). As coal was particularly low-value, individuals who would otherwise act as either shipmaster or merchant shifted to undertake voyages on which they acted in both capacities, and in doing so limited their network ties for those voyages. Likewise, in Southampton, members of the mercantile elite typically hired shipmasters *ad hoc* per voyage and those mariners were usually sourced from the surrounding area. However, on occasions when merchants sought access to trade with a particular region outside of their

---

[115] TNA E190/307/9 fol.5v.

typical commercial activity, they would then shift their network ties to accommodate, such as in the case of trade with Sussex.

This was also true of Bristol traders, who also typically formed ties *ad hoc* and who often favoured shipmasters with links to the port with which they wished to trade. In particular, during periods of increased trade between Bristol and Wales, Bristol merchants utilised shipmasters that regularly traded between Bristol and Welsh ports, but that typically engaged within networks of Welsh traders. As in Southampton, physical proximity within a large commercial centre undoubtedly played a role in the ability of traders to form diverse network ties, as was the case for the various craftspeople that engaged widely with individuals from broad locations. However, the fact that occupational merchants (both from the port of Bristol itself and from other commercial centres, such as Bridgwater merchant Robert Blake) attracted shipmasters from other established networks suggests that they were desirable trading partners.

Nonetheless, personal attributes and economic status could also have the opposite effect, and the impact of individual difference should not be overlooked. For example, merchant John Crook occupied a privileged position within Southampton, being a prolific overseas merchant and being landlord of a prestigious Southampton inn. In theory, he should have been at the heart of maritime commerce in the port. However, his catalogue of personal disputes and failed overseas voyages made him an undesirable trading partner and throughout the dataset we see him gradually separate from the central community. That being said, although the influence of his network ties were limited by his personal business approaches, his socio-economic status appears to have put him in good stead to branch out and form ties with traders from outside of the town's maritime elite, allowing him to continue a steady stream of coastal voyages.

Crook's strained relationships with individuals from the core maritime community in Southampton sat in stark contrast to the activities of individuals such as Sussex merchant John Harman, or shipmasters John Cotton and John Holford, all of whom engaged consistently on the same routes and forged successful businesses based on regular, if perhaps slightly unambitious, trade routes. These traders often sat at the centre of their maritime communities and made themselves reliable and trustworthy business associates, forming tight and consistent networks. Moreover, it appears that ownership of a vessel had a direct impact on the hireability of Cotton and Holford as shipmasters, and while those two men had very different coastal operations, the fact that they both owned vessels had a clear bearing on their ability to form network ties with a range of merchants. In particular, John Cotton was able to dramatically increase his network connections after he purchased a share in a reasonably large Southampton vessel, shifting from sporadic to highly consistent engagement in coastal commerce and becoming substantially involved in the lucrative London trade.

This was also true of individuals operating in Bristol and the occupation data provided by the Bristol customs officials adds another layer of detail regarding the formation of networks around specific trades. For Southampton and Hull, it was possible only to establish that the commodities transported, or the trade routes plied, shaped the formation of networks. However, while this was also true in Bristol, networks were also clearly divided by occupational group. This was most evident within the networks of traders that operated on the River Severn, namely trowmen, maltmakers, and those that catered to Bristol brewers. While the majority of the individuals that fit into these categories altered their approaches and expanded their networks during periods of heightened activity, most usually retained a core of stronger ties to individuals from within their own occupational group. These well-defined networks formed around tight-knit communities of mariners and merchants that frequently incorporated family units, usually revolved around the same small port towns, and often involved repeated use of the same selection of local vessels.

Similarly, trade between London and Hull represented a stable and lucrative part of the commercial landscape in the region and, therefore, a body of dedicated shipmasters and merchants formed long-term businesses on that route. As a result, many of those individuals formed the largest and most complex networks in the port, which were made up of core members of the mercantile elite who dominated Hull's trade with the capital. Those networks often centred on one man, William Gee, who played such a pivotal role in their formation that when he took his leave of the coastal trade sometime between 1574 and 1577, the network collapsed. This example makes clear that the way in which networks were formed hinged not only on the commercial activity around which they were based but also on the specific character of the traders that participated. Conversely, in the case of Hull's trade with King's Lynn and Great Yarmouth, we mostly saw the formation of merchant-centric networks, with few shipmasters repeating engagement. Since these trades were a reaction to specific regional demands, merchants dipped into those routes intermittently and were almost certainly involved more regularly in other commercial activity in their own regions. As a result, they hired shipmasters and vessels *ad hoc*, and the graphs generated from the data were dominated by small networks that did not represent a permanent presence in the port.

Clearly, then, in spite of a number of underlying trends that were common across all three ports, there were also significant regional differences, and this was perhaps most obvious in the differences in fluctuations of cross-county integration in Southampton and in Bristol. In Southampton, there was a clear and measurable correlation between levels of trade and levels of cross-county integration. During periods of increased trade, individuals from a broad region (including numerous London merchants) were drawn into Southampton, and their presence allowed for the formation of business networks. Moreover, the more extensive networks that were formed during periods of increased opportunity could sometimes endure through periods of reduced trade. This resulted in levels of trade decreasing to a greater extent than levels of integration during the latter years and was particularly evident in the case of the networks involving London merchant John White. Stephen Gadd has suggested that the farming of Southampton's custom to Thomas Smyth in 1576, and the subsequent reduction in local customs, drew more outside merchants into Southampton, particularly from London. While this may account for some degree of the increased engagement in 1576, the higher numbers of external traders primarily came in 1575, before Thomas Smyth took over, as a reaction to the increased levels of trade in Cornish tin and Sussex iron. It was during such periods that individuals like White were able to integrate well into the local maritime community and those ties sometimes persisted for extended periods.[116]

However, in Bristol, the correlation between levels of trade and levels of cross-county integration was far less stark. While levels of integration in Southampton were shaped by the degree to which individuals from other towns engaged in commercial activity through the port, external traders operated within Bristol regularly and the number of traders from other domestic ports that were present in Bristol did not fluctuate substantially between periods. As a result, apart from times when heightened trade encouraged Bristol merchants who normally focused on overseas trade to become involved in coasting, levels of cross-county integration in Bristol were fairly stable across the dataset. Nonetheless, the socio-economic/socio-political position of Bristol's mercantile elite allowed them to easily form network ties when they chose to engage in coastal commerce, which drew local traders out from regionally diverse networks into networks that were more Bristol-centric.

In general, these trends suggest that coastal trading could be a highly flexible and adaptive endeavour. Individuals could engage in coasting in such a way that suited their personal preferences and business ambitions. Some merchants and shipmasters established long-term trade on set routes that involved specific occupational networks, whereas others participated as a response to particular commercial trends or during periods of reduced activity in their primary craft. Nonetheless, most individuals shifted their operational approach in order to facilitate particular types of commercial activity, opportunistically forming network ties that suited the route on which they wished to trade, and occasionally engaging in multi-merchant voyages when levels of risk were especially high.

[116] Stephen Gadd, 'Illegal Quays: Elizabethan Customs Reforms and Suppression of the Coastal Trade of Christchurch, Hampshire', *The Economic History Review*, 71 (2018), 737–38.

5

The socio-economic position of coastal traders

So far this book has examined coastal commerce in broad terms, only occasionally focusing on the socio-economic position of coastal traders and rarely examining the lives and careers of those individuals in detail. In particular, Chapters 2 and 3 aimed to solidify our understanding of the commercial nature of coasting in Bristol, Southampton and Hull, and Chapter 4 focused on the business networks that formed around that trade. However, in order to develop a rounded image of coastal commercial activity, we must look in more detail at the socio-economic and socio-political role coastal traders played within their towns, assessing how their engagement in the activity described above impacted their ability to accumulate wealth and garner political and social influence.

In order to assess these factors, customs records have been cross-referenced with lay subsidy returns and local civic records. However, since the customs accounts do not generally list the residences of shipmasters, analysis in this chapter is more focused on merchants (as defined by their role in the port books) than shipmasters. While it was possible in Chapter 4 to discuss the regional affiliations of shipmasters in broad terms, this is a problematic approach when supplementing the evidence in the customs accounts with other sources. As mentioned above, commercial affiliation with a particular county did not necessarily equate to residency in that area, therefore reliance on estimates of regional affiliation would be problematic in terms of nominal linkage and would almost certainly result in incorrect identification of individuals in different sources. Nonetheless, a reasonable cross-section of traders has been identified, and the case studies below allow us to explore the lives and careers of those individuals in some detail.

Occupations

As discussed in the Introduction, it is important to note that a distinction must be made between the titles of shipmaster and merchant as defined by the roles individuals played on specific voyages and the occupations they were assigned in civic records. For the most part, references in this volume to merchants and shipmasters indicate their positions within the port books, and where reference is instead made to their civic titles the terms 'occupational mariner' or 'occupational merchant' are used. Throughout this chapter, we will explore the occupational groups that participated in coastal commercial activity through English and Welsh ports, and we shall see that their levels of wealth, the nature of their career progression, and their physical locations within the town were often tied to their occupational titles, although there was a significant overlap between groups.

It is important to note that the degree to which we are able to analyse the occupational titles of seafarers varies between ports owing to differences in the customs records kept by the customs officials in the port. For example, in Bristol, the customs officials provided an occupational title for each merchant that passed through the town and thus it is possible to identify occupations for a particularly large sample, including all individuals that traded through Bristol, rather than just those that resided in the port itself. Indeed, it has been possible to identify an occupational title for some 700 merchants and shipmasters that traded through Bristol over this period. Conversely, in Southampton, the customs officials did not routinely record the occupational titles of merchants or shipmasters, but they did offer residential information for merchants, making nominal linkage with other sources relatively straightforward. Thus, in Southampton, it has been possible to ascertain the occupational titles of around fifty merchants and shipmasters living in the port.

Unfortunately, the customs officials in Hull only very rarely recorded occupational titles or residences for merchants or shipmasters that traded through the port, making determination of occupational titles somewhat difficult. Nonetheless, it has been possible to identify a number of specific merchants and shipmasters in lay subsidy returns and local civic records, especially in the case of individuals that were particularly prolific in Hull's coastal trade. However, while these examples are telling of the commercial environment in Hull, they are clearly less representative than the numerous examples for Bristol and Southampton. In total, fifteen individuals listed in the port books have been identified in the lay subsidy returns (including five merchants, six shipmasters, and four individuals that routinely acted in both capacities). Therefore, for Hull, the focus will be on the characteristics of the Newcastle coal trade, allowing us to explore the nature of a specific element of north-eastern commerce in a slightly different, albeit equally useful, manner. Examination of Hull traders that engaged in other activity through the port (most notably those who travelled between Hull and London) will take place primarily in the context of wealth and social standing, later in the chapter.

In the section that follows, various occupational groups or trades will be examined in turn, allowing us to compare the practical trading activities of individual seafarers with the occupational titles they were allocated by civic authorities. In this way, we will challenge preconceived notions regarding the meaning of particular occupational titles and explore the reliability of the occupations allocated to individuals in contemporary civic records. We will also explore the overlap between seemingly disparate occupational groups and tie back to the Social Network Analysis undertaken above to examine the importance of occupational groupings to the practical character of early modern maritime trading.

Occupational mariners and Gloucester trowmen

We turn first to those individuals who forged careers as shipmasters and mariners. As noted above, the names of shipmasters were often listed in the port books without any other identifying information (occupation, residency) and therefore the identification of occupational mariners is somewhat difficult. As such, there almost certainly existed a body of occupational mariners that engaged in coastal commerce who have not been identified here. However, we must limit our investigations to the individuals for whom we have reliable data and, even with this limitation, a large sample of occupational mariners have been identified in all three ports and a number of notable characteristics come to light from that sample that differ between regions.

For example, in Bristol, eighty separate individuals were allocated the title of 'mariner' by the customs officials and the majority of those engaged in coastal commerce in the same way: acting in dual capacity as shipmaster/merchant, with very few routinely commanding voyages for separate merchants. These individuals seem to have had little or no interest in overseas trade, yet they traded coastwise with much frequency, usually carrying large mixed cargoes including wine and cloth.[1] This was somewhat different from the typical operations of occupational mariners for whom overseas trade was their primary business interest, who more often commanded vessels for a separate merchant (or merchants), perhaps taking some share of the hull space as partial payment, but rarely carrying only their own goods.[2] It may have been that this classification was applied in the coastal records to those that had been apprenticed, but this is unlikely to have been the case for all or even the majority of the individuals listed.[3] Therefore, the allocation of this occupational title to these traders is somewhat surprising and is complicated further by the fact that a number of 'mariners' undertook coastal activity through Bristol that was

---

[1] TNA E190/1128/12 fol.3r–6v, 7v, 9v, 10r, 11r-v, 12r, 13r, E190/1128/13 fol.1r, 3r-v, 5r, 6v, 11r, 12r, 13v–14v, 15v, 16r, 19v, 20r-v, E190/1128/14 fol.4r, 5v–6v, 7v, 8v, 9v, 11v–13r, 15r, 16r, E190/1129/1 fol.3v, 4v, 5v, 9v, 10r, 11r–12r, 13r, 15r, 16v, 18v, 19r, E190/1129/18 fol.3r, 4r–6r, 7r, 8v–9v, 10v, 12r, 15v, 16r–17r, E190/1129/20 fol.1r-v, 3r–4r, 7v, E190/1129/22 fol.5v, 9v, 11r, 12r, 14r, E190/1130/2 fol.6v, 15r; Lambert and Baker, www.medievalandtudorships.org.

[2] Fury, 'The Elizabethan Maritime Community', pp. 117–20.

[3] Fury, 'Training and Education in the Elizabethan Maritime Community, 1585–1603', pp. 117–20.

near-identical to that undertaken by trowmen, and that they operated markedly differently from mariners in Southampton and Hull.

Indeed, as we saw in Chapter 4, the only notable difference between those two groups appears to have been their preference to look inwards to their own communities, such that they rarely overlapped in their trading networks. Interestingly, this shows trowmen in a substantially different light from their portrayal in the traditional historiography and, in fact, from their portrayal by Bristol merchants who sought to downplay the professional nature of Gloucester's wider mariner community.[4] The commercial importance and social standing of trowmen has traditionally been minimised and early scholars did not consider it plausible, for example, that trowmen could also be trow owners, due to the low calibre of their social-economic positions.[5] However, the sources analysed here show that individuals defined as trowmen operated in a broad variety of forms, with some reaching much higher levels of commercial stature than acknowledged by scholars like Grahame Farr.

Indeed, some trowmen appear to have neither commanded nor owned the vessels on which they transported goods, acting instead in the capacity of merchant and appearing to have been established traders more akin to occupational merchants.[6] Conversely, some trowmen more routinely acted in the capacity of shipmaster, usually commanding voyages for other trowmen and only occasionally carrying their own goods.[7] Likewise, others again routinely acted as both shipmaster and merchant, only occasionally interacting with other individuals.[8] Furthermore, there is evidence to suggest that individuals that operated in all three ways may have owned or part-owned the vessels on which they traded, challenging the assessment of trowmen put forward by Farr.[9] In addition, it may be suggested that the allocation of this title

[4] Alexander Higgins, 'The Establishment of the Head Port of Gloucester, 1565–1584' (MPhil thesis, University of Bristol, 2012), pp. 40–42.

[5] Farr, pp. 93–94.

[6] For example, Thomas Brown, Richard Caper, Hugh Evans: see TNA E190/1128/12 fol.2v, 4r, 7r, 8r, 9r, E190/1128/13 fol.3v, 13v–14r, 15r-v, E190/1128/14 fol.1v, 2v, 8r, 10r, E190/1129/18 fol.5r, E190/1129/20 fol.6v, 8r, E190/1129/22 fol.1v, 5r, 6r–7r, 8r-v, 10r, E190/1130/2 fol.15v, 16v, 17v.

[7] For example, John Aware, Thomas Beal, Hugh Sallarwaye: see TNA E190/1128/12 fol.2v, 4r, 5r, 7r, 11r, 13r, E190/1128/13 fol.3v, 6r, 12v, 14r, 15r, E190/1128/14 fol.2v, 5v, 7r, 9r, E190/1129/18 fol.2v, 4r–6v, 8r, 10v, 12r, E190/1129/1 fol.10r, E190/1129/20 fol.5r–6v, 7v, 10r–11r, E190/1129/22 fol.4r–6r, 7r, 9r, 14r.

[8] For example, Humphrey Barnsley, John and Roger Brook, James Chamberlain, Samuel Hooper: see TNA E190/1128/12 fol.11v, 13v, 14v, E190/1128/13 fol.3r, 12v, 13v, 14v, 15v, 16v–17v, E190/1128/14 fol.2v, 7v, 8v, 11r, E190/1129/1 fol.4r, 5r, 6r, 7r, 11r, E190/1129/18 fol.4r, 5r, 7r, 8r, E190/1129/20 fol.5r, 6v, 7v, E190/1129/22 fol.1v, 4v, 5v–7r, 9r, 11v, E190/1130/2 fol.14r, 15r-v, 16v, 17r–18r, 19r, 20r.

[9] For example, the port book data suggests that shipmaster Hugh Sallarwaye may

was merely a reference to the vessels on which they traded (i.e. the trow barge), but the sources assessed here do not support that assertion. In fact, a substantial number of the vessels commanded by those listed as trowmen were also routinely utilised by individuals listed as mariners.[10] Thus, there is very little support here for the idea that trowmen were principally sailors who worked for trow owners. Instead, we see a range of individuals running their businesses in quite different ways: acting in various capacities on board, at least sometimes owning the vessels on which they traded, and being almost indistinguishable from individuals listed as mariners.

Conversely, in Southampton, far from the home of the Gloucester trow, only some of the individuals identified as mariners carried only their own goods and a larger proportion catered to the needs of other coastal traders, including craftsmen and occupational mariners. As we shall see below, a number of occupational mariners forged lucrative careers in Southampton and many also engaged in overseas trade. Perhaps because of this overlap, the distinguishing line between mariners and merchants was sometimes difficult to determine. Indeed, the practical activities of some of Southampton's mariners appear to

---

have had a share in the 16-ton *Matthew* of Bewdley, and that merchant Thomas Brown may have had a share in the 15-ton *Leonard* of Bewdley. Of the twenty-nine voyages commanded by Sallarwaye over the full twelve-year span, only four were undertaken on a ship other than the *Matthew*, and Sallarwaye continued to utilise the *Matthew* even when commanding voyages for a broad array of other merchants. Likewise, Brown appeared on fifteen voyages over an eight-year span and in that time he only appeared on a ship other than the *Leonard* on one occasion, even though he employed the services of an array of different shipmasters. Moreover, that one occasion was the only time that he traded outside the Bristol/Worcester route, trading instead into Wales and utilising a Welsh vessel. As noted throughout this volume, this repeated use of the same ships may have resulted from another form of legal arrangement, such as long-term waged employment, but given the small size of the ships, their confinement to the Severn river system and their fundamentally local character, it seems likely that they were either owners or part-owners. TNA E190/1128/12 fol.2v–3r, 4r, 5r, 7r, 8r, 9r, 11r, 13r, E190/1128/13 fol.3v, 5r–6r, 7r, 11v, 12v, 13v, 14r–15v, E190/1128/14 fol.1v, 2v, 5v, 7r, 8r, 9r–10v, E190/1129/1 fol.1r, 3v, 10v, 15v, E190/1129/18 fol.6v, E190/1129/22 fol.14v, E190/1130/2 fol.15r, 18v; see also Andrews, 'The Elizabethan Seaman', p. 257; Childs, pp. 25–26; Farr, pp. 66–95; Kowaleski, 'The Shipmaster as Entrepreneur in Medieval England', pp. 165–72; Donald Woodward, 'Ships, Masters and Shipowners of the Wirral 1550–1650', *The Mariner's Mirror*, 63 (1977), 240–42.

[10] For example, the 8-ton *Margaret* of Carmarthen, the 12-ton *Margaret* of Tewkesbury, the 15-ton *Trinity* of Gloucester, the 10-ton *Peter* of Bewdley and the 14-ton *Arnold* of Worcester: see TNA E190/1128/12 fol.2r, 3r, 4r, 6r–7v, 8v, 9r-v, 10r, 11r-v, 12r-v, 13r-v, 11v, E190/1128/13 fol.1r-v, 3r, 4r, 5r, 6v, 11r, 12v, 13v, 14v, 15v, 16v, 17v, E190/1128/14 fol.2r-v, 7v, 11r, E190/1129/1 fol.4r-v, 7r, 10v, 11v, E190/1129/18 fol.6v, E190/1129/20 fol.1v, 7v, E190/1129/22 fol.1r, 3r-v, 5v–7r, 9r, 10r, E190/1130/2 fol.14r, 15v.

have somewhat puzzled the civic authorities. For example, Francis Hobbs was identified by the Admiralty Court as a mariner, but Southampton's 'Stall and Art' records list him as a merchant. Various civic records suggest that Hobbs was, in fact, a prolific salesman who ran a market stall in the wealthy ward of Holy Rood from at least 1565 to 1589, and the customs records see him commanding various coastal voyages for established local merchants.[11] However, his trading activities do not reflect the typical pursuits of individuals commonly recognised as merchants, suggesting that the identification of an individual as a merchant was not necessarily the mark of status that might be expected.

In fact, Hobbs' classification as a merchant seems to have been made solely on the basis that he sold goods on the market and sailed ships. He did not even transport his own goods by water and, in the context of his coastal activity, only ever worked as a hired shipmaster for other merchants.[12] Moreover, in spite of Hobbs having a dual identity as a mariner and a merchant, he was not particularly wealthy and he had not achieved burgess status. Although, as we shall see below, being a non-burgess was common among mariners engaged in coastal trading, it was not common among their mercantile counterparts.[13] Thus, this example demonstrates that we cannot assume that a civic record of an individual listed as a merchant correlates to a particular level of wealth or status, or even an anticipated commercial activity.

Moreover, Hobbs' maritime activities aligned more closely to those identified as mariners in the traditional historiography (in that he commanded various voyages for a range of occupational merchants) than individuals who were listed as mariners in the Bristol port books (whose practical activities would suggest they were merchant/mariners, rather than purely occupational mariners). This suggests that the classification of individuals within particular occupational categories varied substantially between ports, as well as between specific civic authorities operating within the same port. As we shall see throughout this chapter, the practical trading activities of those operating within English ports were substantially varied, making the

---

[11] The 'Stall and Art' rolls were kept as part of Southampton's 'Court Leet', and contained lists of non-burgesses who were licensed to run a market stall that year, detailing the licence fee and the parish in which they were entitled to operate. In most years, the rolls simply recorded a list of names and the licensing fee, but in 1551, 1552 and 1566 the clerk recorded more detail, including occupations of the individuals listed and the grounds of their assessment. See Fossey Hearnshaw, 'Southampton Court Leet Records, A.D. 1550–1577' (Southampton: Southampton Record Series, 1905), p. xv.

[12] TNA E190/815/1 fol.1r, 3r.

[13] Of the 14 shipmasters and 39 merchants for whom a burgess status can be determined, 4 shipmasters (29%) and 27 merchant (69%) were burgesses: see Butler, http://www.tudorrevels.co.uk/records.php.

distinguishing of individuals from different occupational groups somewhat challenging, and the perceptions of civic authorities were as complex as the occupations themselves.

Owing to source limitations within the Hull customs records, it is even more difficult to identify occupational mariners who operated in the North East. However, some specific trends are apparent from the records that survive and there was undoubtedly a body of individuals operating in the port of Hull who forged careers as occupational mariners. Moreover, as we shall see below, a number of mariners of this kind, who dedicated their careers to commanding coastal vessels for members of the mercantile elite engaging in the high-value London-Hull trade, managed to accumulate respectable levels of wealth as career mariners. Nonetheless, generally speaking, the operational approaches of Hull's shipmasters varied substantially depending on their chosen trade and, in the case of the Newcastle coal trade, many of those individuals blurred the line of what it meant to be a mariner, much like Francis Hobbs or the mariner/trowmen of Bristol. While it is difficult to determine the specific character of Hull's mariner community, examination of the Newcastle coal trade undertaken separately below shines much light on the specific approaches of Hull's seafarers and, in many ways, this solidifies the argument that mariners often toed the line between mariner, merchant, and craftsperson.

Occupational merchants

Much like in the case of occupational mariners, the degree to which the practical trading activities of those identified as occupational merchants aligned with their titles varied substantially between individuals and between ports. However, the impetus for civic authorities to consider an individual a 'merchant' is a particularly important line of enquiry owing to the commercial and social significance typically attributed to the 'mercantile class'. Indeed, the term 'merchant' is used widely and carelessly within the field of maritime history, and indeed in wider social and political histories. Historians use the term to refer to an individual of a specific and well-defined occupation, but also use it in a broad sense to refer to anyone participating in the exchange of goods, regardless of the form that trade took. Equally, the term is often used to refer to a specific socio-economic group (characterised in this volume as the 'mercantile elite'), but historians frequently fail to define the boundaries of that community.[14]

---

[14] Dana Durkee has offered an excellent explanation of this problem, and has noted that there has been a tendency for historians of all kinds to divide the early modern world into two tiers, with merchants a level above individuals engaged in all other forms of commercial activity, to 'pit a well-defined mercantile oligarchy against everyone else': Durkee, pp. 150–55.

Likewise, within contemporary society, the term merchant was sometimes considered a mark of status but was at other times allocated to individuals with limited commercial significance, as we saw in the case of Francis Hobbs above.[15] For the purposes of this volume, merchants are defined by their position within the customs records, including anyone freighting goods on a ship. However, when we turn to civic sources, the preconceptions of the compiler of the record, or of the individual being identified, had an impact on the title that was allocated. As a result, use of the term merchant is highly problematic and, in reality, as noted by Robin Ward, 'there was no impermeable barrier between the categories of those engaged in sea ventures, and a trader could, if he wanted, act in several capacities at the same or at other times'. This could include acting as a shipmaster, a member of the ship's lesser crew, or as a trader transporting goods by water.[16]

Ward's assertion is supported by the data analysed here. Indeed, of the 947 voyages through Southampton that appear in the full dataset, 181 (19%) were commanded by a merchant carrying goods on the ship.[17] In approximately 80% of those cases, the shipmaster/merchant was the only individual carrying goods on board and those traders often plied the same trade routes repeatedly. There were approximately 100 individuals covering 165 voyages through Southampton that fitted into that category and they mostly traded in low-value commodities, such as firewood, coal, or beer, suggesting that they utilised this operational approach as a means to reduce costs and maximise returns on voyages with limited potential for profit. Similarly, a number of individuals that routinely acted as either shipmaster or merchant in Southampton would change their approach to act in both capacities on specific voyages in order to undertake exceptional shipments of coal, which we shall see was also a common means through which individuals traded between Newcastle and Hull.[18]

Conversely, in the remaining 20% of cases, the shipments contained the goods of multiple merchants in addition to those of the shipmaster, suggesting that their cargo was either a partial payment for their services as a hired shipmaster or was part of their investment in the voyage as a partner.[19] For

---

[15] For discussion regarding the use of the term merchant to indicate social/commercial stature, see Derek Keene, 'Changes in London's Economic Hinterland as Indicated by Debt Cases in the Court of the Common Pleas', in *Trade, Urban Hinterlands and Market Integration c. 1300–1600*, ed. by James A. Galloway (London: Centre for Metropolitan History, Insitute of Historical Research, 2000), pp. 59–81.

[16] Ward, p. 105.

[17] TNA E190/814/5, E190/814/6, E190/814/7, E190/814/11, E190/814/12, E190/815/1, E190/815/2, E190/815/8.

[18] For example, TNA E190/814/7 fol.4v, E190/814/11 fol.2r, 5r, 7r, E190/815/1 fol.8v, E190/815/2 fol.1v–2r, E190/815/8 fol.1v–2r.

[19] For a detailed explanation regarding the various mechanisms through which

example, on 14 August 1577, the 100-ton *Primrose* of Poole embarked from Southampton for Poole carrying the Spanish salt and wine of various merchants, including the shipmaster John Christian, who transported 2 tons of sack wine, very likely offered as partial payment for his services as shipmaster.[20] This was also true in Bristol, where 364 (23%) of the 1,549 voyages undertaken through the port were commanded by a shipmaster who was also a merchant carrying goods on board.[21] As in Southampton, a very small proportion of those were multi-merchant voyages on which the shipmaster was allocated space in the hull among other merchants, each of which was probably the coastal leg of an overseas voyage.[22] This suggests that, in the majority of cases, rather than occupational mariners commanding voyages for parties of merchants, these traders were either mariners dabbling in mercantile activity, merchants taking the decision to avoid hiring a shipmaster and commanding themselves, or individuals from another occupational group commanding and filling a vessel for their own business needs, adjusting their operational approach to suit the commodities traded. In all cases, this figure represents a large body of individuals that had the necessary skill, desire, and financial means to take command of a vessel and to invest in their own commodities as 'merchants'. Many coastal traders sat in the grey area between merchant, seafarer and craftsperson, taking on a broad range of roles and complicating notions that these were entirely separate communities.

Interestingly, unlike in Southampton and Hull, where individuals from the ports themselves frequently occupied the dual position of merchant and shipmaster, those trading in such a way through Bristol were usually from other domestic ports in the local region. More specifically, traders that resided in the ports of the River Severn accounted for 75% of the voyages on which the shipmaster was also the merchant, and Welshmen for a further 14%. As discussed in Chapter 4, Bristol traders tended to fit into the category of 'mercantile elite' and more routinely engaged in overseas commerce, only

---

shipmasters were paid for their services, see Fury, 'The Elizabethan Maritime Community', pp. 118–20; Scammell, 'Manning the English Merchant Service in the Sixteenth Century', pp. 10–11; Ward, pp. 48–68.

[20] TNA E190/815/2 fol.7v.

[21] TNA E190/1128/12, E190/1128/13, E190/1128/14, E190/1129/1, E190/1129/18, E190/1129/20, E190/1129/22, E190/1130/2.

[22] In one case, the 4-ton *Julian* of Workington travelled from Workington to Bristol, and we can see from the data contained within the Medieval and Tudor Ships Project that this voyage went onwards from Bristol to Ireland. Similar evidence is not available for the second voyage, but it was commanded by one of only six traders in the full dataset identified as 'alien', suggesting that this was also likely part of an overseas operation. TNA E190/1129/18 fol.19r, E190/1130/2 fol.6v; Lambert and Baker, www.medievalandtudorships.org.

occasionally participating in coastal trade during periods of increased activity. Individuals from that group tended to hire shipmasters *ad hoc*, often formed charter parties with other merchants, and rarely commanded their own vessels. However, individuals from the broader region that routinely acted in both capacities typically had a larger stake in coastal commerce and engaged in the maritime industry rather differently. In particular, in the case of traders from Gloucestershire, Worcestershire and the West Midlands, partial confinement to an inland river system influenced the nature of their engagement in coastal commerce and created much scope for dual roles, as we saw in the case of the Gloucester trowmen above.

The large number of individuals that were able to act in the capacity of both merchant and shipmaster shows that there was clearly overlap in the skills present within the coastal trading community, which gave individuals the means to switch between maritime and mercantile activities. However, civic authorities had their own understanding of the occupational categories into which specific individuals fitted and it is often difficult to determine how these classifications were made. In particular, the term 'merchant' was used by customs officials loosely, and many individuals were listed variously with mercantile and non-mercantile occupations. In the case of Francis Hobbs in Southampton, we saw that the threshold to be considered a merchant by the civic authorities could be very low, and the same appears to have been true in Bristol. Indeed, although some 400 individuals were listed in the Bristol port books with the title of 'merchant', their practical trading activities varied greatly, from highly prized shipments of luxury goods on several-hundred-ton vessels, to shipments of low-value goods carried on vessels of under 10 tons.[23] Moreover, various individuals were listed with specific mercantile occupations, such as clothiers, drapers, grocers and vintners, but the degree to which the trading activities of such individuals aligned with their occupational titles varied substantially between traders.[24]

In some cases, the practical activities in which such traders engaged aligned clearly with their occupational title. For example, clothiers typically shipped cloth or wool into Bristol from Wales or Gloucestershire and returned carrying mixed cargoes including wine, iron, dry wares or cheese.[25] Likewise, vintners

---

[23] For examples of low-value shipments on small ships, see TNA E190/1128/12 fol.13v, 16r, E190/1129/1 fol.13r, 17r, E190/1130/2 fol.8v, 10r. For examples of high-value shipments on voyages above 100 tons, see TNA E190/1130/2 fol.1r, 4v, 5v, 6v.

[24] For broader discussion regarding the various forms of mercantile occupation, see John Oldland, 'The Allocation of Merchant Capital in Early Tudor London', *The Economic History Review*, 63 (2010), 1073–75.

[25] TNA E190/1128/12 fol.12v, E190/1128/13 fol.3v, 5r–7r, 12r, 13r, 15v, 19r, E190/1128/14 fol.8v, 9v, 15r, E190/1129/1 fol.1r, 7r, 9r, 11r, 13v, 15v, 17r–18v, E190/1129/18 fol.9v, 10r, 12r, 15r–17r, 19r, E190/1129/20 fol.1r–3r, 10r–13v, E190/1130/2 fol.19r.

almost exclusively transported wine, only occasionally carrying other commodities, and grocers routinely transported mixed cargoes, usually including a high proportion of foodstuffs and beer.[26] However, some mercantile occupations seemingly had little or no connection to the coastal trade undertaken. In particular, of the thirty-nine voyages on which the merchant was a draper, only ten included a cloth product in their inventory, and Bristol's customs officials had a particular tendency to switch between the titles of draper and merchant.[27] The routes plied by grocers, merchants and drapers were as diverse as the cargoes they carried, and the vessels they utilised originated from a broad range of locations and ranged from 4 to 200 tons. This suggests that many individuals identified as having mercantile occupations partook in a broad range of commercial activity, and the allocation of titles by the customs officials was not necessarily reflective of a particular set of criteria, but rather a vague indication of their primary trade interests. This again supports the assertion that we cannot necessarily take the title of merchant as a mark of status, and the sources examined here suggest that many other occupational titles allocated to mariners and merchants were only vaguely defined.

From the various examples explored through this section, it may be possible, to a limited extent, to apply to the merchant group a similar classification to that Cheryl Fury has applied to the seafaring community. In her investigations into the role of apprenticeships in the maritime community, she divided mariners into the 'elite' classes and 'ordinary seamen'. Fury noted that in order to be part of the maritime elite, an individual needed to have completed an apprenticeship under an experienced seafarer and, therefore, the status of 'elite' was primarily reserved for the wealthy, whose parents could afford the indenture.[28] The situation for merchants was a little more complex since the ability to transport goods on a ship did not rely so heavily on practical skills, but was more dependent on financial resources, especially given that engagement in coastal commerce did not depend on membership of a merchant

---

[26] TNA E190/1128/12 fol.13v, 16r, E190/1128/13 fol.20v, E190/1129/1 fol.1v, 16r, 17v, E190/1129/18 fol.3v, E190/1129/20 fol.7v, E190/1129/22 fol.5v, 10v, 11r, 12r, E190/1130/2 fol.14v, 15v, 18v, 19r.

[27] For example, both Luke Garnons and Thomas Sarle were recorded variously as draper and merchant, but neither routinely transported cloth. Luke Garnons only ever appeared in the coastal port books transporting grains into Bristol from Gloucestershire, and Thomas Sarle tended to transport mixed cargoes of largely overseas commodities, only occasionally including small quantities of cloth among other goods. See TNA E190/1128/12 fol.3r-v, 6r, 8r, 13v, 14r, 16r, 20v, 21r, E190/1128/14 fol.1v, 4r, 6v, 10r, 11r, 12v, 13r, E190/1129/1 fol.1v, 3r-v, 4v, 10r, 13v, 16r, E190/1129/18 fol.3v, 6r-v, 7r, 10r, 12r, E190/1129/20 fol.3v, E190/1129/22 fol.7v, 11r, E190/1130/2 fol.3r-v, 8v.

[28] Fury, 'Training and Education in the Elizabethan Maritime Community, 1585–1603', pp. 149–51.

company or society, unlike much overseas trade. In the case of coastal trading, the financial collateral required could be very low and thus even those with limited socio-economic weight could participate, and those lesser merchants fitted into a markedly different socio-economic and socio-political group than very wealthy and politically-inclined members of the mercantile elite. A similar categorisation can therefore be applied to merchants that engaged in coastal commerce, with individuals of substantial wealth and influence at one end, and those with limited wealth and local importance at the other, albeit with a substantial 'grey area' in the middle. In other words, the allocation of the title of 'merchant' did not necessarily equate to a ranking among the 'mercantile elite', although individuals that were of significant wealth and social influence were an important element of that community.

Furthermore, the line between merchant and mariner was inherently blurred at both ends of the hierarchy, both for merchants and seafarers. Many established mariners appear in the customs accounts as merchants, operating as both elite seafarers and small-scale traders. Likewise, established members of the merchant elite would occasionally command their own vessels, demonstrating that they had the necessary skills and knowledge to command ships travelling on routes of a range of distances and complexities. However, many historians do not consider merchants to be true members of the maritime community. David Loades noted that:

> Established merchants did not normally command or sail in their own ships, and although their role in the maritime community was very important, they were not its core members. At the heart of that community lay those who actually built and sailed the vessels that carried the cargo.[29]

Nonetheless, a number of more recent regional studies have shown that many merchants were also shipowners. And, while many large-scale overseas merchants likely engaged in ship ownership without ever sailing vessels themselves, evidence from the coastal port books paints a picture of significant occupational overlap, with many merchants able and willing to command, and many shipmasters acting in the capacity of merchant, with both groups occupying primarily maritime wards, as we shall see below.[30] It is questionable both to place merchants in a single distinctive category and to consider them a

---

[29] David Loades, 'The English Maritime Community, 1500–1650', in *The Social History of English Seamen, 1485–1649*, ed. by Cheryl A. Fury (Woodbridge: Boydell Press, 2012), pp. 5–26 (p. 6).

[30] Among others, see Andrews, 'The Elizabethan Seaman', p. 257; Jones, 'The Bristol Shipping Industry in the Sixteenth Century', pp. 27–29; Kermode, 'The Merchants of York, Beverley and Hull in the Fourteenth and Fifteenth Centuries', pp. 180–82; Craig Lambert, *Shipping the Medieval Military: English Maritime*

separate entity from the wider maritime community. After all, their businesses depended on the maritime community, and, as we shall see below, they lived and worked in the same places, often interacting on a daily basis. Vincent Patarino has argued that seafarers took aspects of landborne culture and aspects of seaborne culture and formulated a distinctive cultural paradigm that was unique to those who earned their living from seaborne trade.[31] If we cultivate a much broader definition of the term 'merchant' than Loades, it becomes evident that merchants operated within the same cultural space as mariners, and their communities were often one and the same. To separate merchants entirely from the seafaring community is to misunderstand the socio-political spectrum into which sea traders fitted.

Craftspeople

Aside from those identified as merchants and mariners, members of various other occupational groups also participated in coastal commerce. Those included occupations associated with the production of textiles (including tanners, shoemakers, upholsterers, fletchers, glovers, saddlers, tailors), those involved in the supply of foodstuffs (fishmongers, halliers, brewers, maltmakers, publicans, bakers), and producers of supplies and industrial wares (pewterers, hoopers, soapmakers, cardmakers, braziers).

In Bristol, some such traders, particularly fishmongers, hoopers and halliers, participated in coastal commerce entirely separately from their primary crafts, carrying mixed cargoes on diverse trade routes. However, individuals of this sort appeared only sporadically and seem to have opportunistically dabbled in maritime commerce, rather than utilising it as a central part of their business model.[32] More commonly, craftspeople participated in coastal commerce as a means to accommodate their primary careers. For example, tanners almost exclusively transported salted hides or calfskins into Bristol and finished leather products to regions across the South West. Likewise, most shoemakers who traded through Bristol were Welsh and primarily transported finished leather out of Bristol into the Welsh ports on one-way voyages.[33] Similarly, brewers resided in either Bristol or Cardiff and all transported grains from Gloucestershire into Bristol or the Welsh ports for use in beer brewing.

Logistics in the Fourteenth Century (Woodbridge: Boydell Press, 2011), pp. 193–96; Mate, pp. 96–99; Ward, pp. 48–68.

[31] Patarino, p. 192.

[32] TNA E190/1128/13 fol.11v, E190/1129/1 fol.11r, E190/1129/18 fol.4r, 12v, E190/1129/22 fol.3v.

[33] TNA E190/1128/12 fol.8v, 10r-v, 11v, 12r–13r, 15r-v, E190/1128/13 fol.5v, 11r, 13v, 14r, E190/1128/14 fol.2r, 9r, 11v, 12r, 13r, 14r, 15v, E190/1129/1 fol.10v, 13r, E190/1129/18 fol.2v, 6v–7v, 9r, 11v, 12r, 13v, 14r, 15r, 19r-v, E190/1129/22 fol.6v–7v, 13v–14v, 16r, E190/1130/2 fol.14v, 15r, 16r–17v, 18r–20r.

Brewers would occasionally carry mixed cargoes on the outward journey to Gloucestershire, but this was clearly an exercise in maximising profits on voyages where the primary concern was the collection of grain.[34] The same trend is evident in the case of Gloucestershire's maltmakers who tended to supply malted barley and wheat to Bristol and occasionally onwards to the Welsh ports.[35]

In each of these cases, there is little question that the occupations provided by the customs officials corresponded to the activity undertaken, and this perhaps suggests that the exercise of categorising craftspeople was less challenging than categorising mariners or merchants. Nonetheless, there was still clearly overlap with the mercantile and maritime communities, especially in the case of maltmakers, who plied the same routes and occupied the same physical spaces as mariners and trowmen, as we saw in Chapter 4. This is consistent with the findings of Alexander Higgins, who found that a number of Gloucester men that occupied non-maritime occupations owned small boats and plied trade on the Severn.[36] Thus, these occupational titles cannot be taken to encompass all possible forms of engagement in specific crafts, and many individuals in these groups straddled the line between crafter and merchant.

Such trends are of course much more difficult to observe in Southampton owing to the source deficiencies discussed above, but some similar themes emerge from the sources that do survive. For example, bakers John Sowter and Thomas Courtney both transported wheat into Southampton, presumably as a supply for their bakeries.[37] Likewise, brewers Bernard and William Courtney transported beer and malt from Southampton out to the Channel Islands and Devon.[38] Interestingly, the networks of Thomas, William and Bernard Courtney were discussed in Chapter 4, and it was shown that these men were part of the same family, operating within Southampton and becoming well-integrated members of the mercantile community. Each member of the Courtney family acted variously as mariner, merchant and craftsperson, which allowed them to form a multifaceted business that benefited from numerous revenue streams.

---

[34] TNA E190/1128/12 fol.2v, 4r–5v, 6v–9r, 12v–13v, E190/1128/13 fol.1v, 5r–6v, 12r–13v, 15r, 16r, 18r, E190/1128/14 fol.4r–5r, 7r, 8r, 9v, 12v, E190/1129/1 fol.1r, 3r–4v, 6v–8r, 9r, 14r–v, E190/1129/18 fol.2r–4r, 5r–v, 10r, 11r, E190/1129/20 fol.1r, 3v, 4r, E190/1129/22 fol.1r–v, 3r–4r, 5v, 9v–11r.

[35] TNA E190/1128/12 fol.2r–9r, 12v, 13v, E190/1128/13 fol.3r–v, 5r–7v, 10r–11v, 12r, 13r–18r, E190/1128/14 fol.2r, 4r–5v, 7r–10r, 13r–14v, E190/1129/1 fol.1r–10v, 13r, 14r–15v, E190/1129/18 fol.2r–5v, 10r–11r, E190/1129/20 fol.1r–3v–4r, E190/1129/22 fol.1r, 3v–5v, 9v–11r, E190/1130/2 fol.14v, 16v–17v, 18r.

[36] Higgins, p. 27.

[37] TNA E190/814/11 fol.4r, 7r–v.

[38] TNA E190/814/7 fol.1v, E190/814/11 fol.5r, E190/814/12 fol.9v, E190/815/1 fol.2r, 3v, E190/815/8 fol.5r.

It is perhaps unsurprising that bakers and brewers operating on river systems would take advantage of coastal trading to sell their products and supply their businesses, buying goods wholesale and avoiding costly local markets, but this again supports the assessment that the low financial threshold and limited need for extensive sailing experience meant that individuals from across the socio-economic and occupational spectrum could take advantage of coastal trade routes.

This was also true in the case of those who were responsible for the running of drinking establishments, many of whom were, first and foremost, coastal traders. In fact, of the twelve Southampton shipmasters identified in local civic sources as mariners, five were also 'publicans'. Four of those fell into the category of 'tippler' or 'alehouse-keeper', who typically sold beer from domestic dwellings, and have been described as being 'by the poor, for the poor', and one was the keeper of a high-status Holy Rood inn.[39] However, unlike the bakers and brewers discussed above, whose engagement in coastal commerce only extended as far as to assist their primary craft, these men appear to have subsidised their maritime careers with the sale of alcohol. For example, we saw in Chapter 4 that John Crook was a prolific merchant, but he was also a publican, and he occasionally appears in the customs accounts domestically importing hops and wheat into Southampton, and exporting beer to London.[40] Likewise, Nicholas Roche was listed in civic sources as being a mariner, lighterman, shipmaster, and alehouse keeper, and he routinely commanded around ten to thirteen voyages per year through Southampton, carrying high-value goods for elite merchants to London and Cornwall.[41] Similarly, Reginald Barber, who we saw above was a key link in the commercial ties between Southampton and Sussex, was listed in civic records as a mariner and as a tippler, and he too commanded numerous voyages per year for high-status local merchants.[42] This suggests that these men were firstly mariners, and secondly publicans, and we shall see below that participation in the running of drinking establishments, be they small-scale breweries within private dwellings or prestige public houses, fitted well alongside engagement in maritime trade. Both commercial ventures encouraged engagement with

---

[39] Peter Clark, 'The Alehouse and the Alternative Society', in *Puritans and Revolutionaries: Essays in Seventeenth Century History*, ed. by Donald Pennington and Keith Thomas (Oxford: Clarendon Press, 1978), pp. 47–72 (p. 48).

[40] TNA E190/814/11 fol.1r, 2v, E190/814/12 fol.10r, E190/815/1 fol.8v, E190/815/8 fol.2r; Butler, 'John Crooke (1563–1600)', http://www.tudorrevels.co.uk/records.php.

[41] For example, TNA E190/814/5 fol.14r, E190/814/6 fol.2v, E190/814/7 fol.2v, 4r-v, 8r; Butler, 'Nicholas Roche (1540–1594)', http://www.tudorrevels.co.uk/records.php.

[42] For example, TNA E190/814/5 fol.2r, 4v, 6v, 9v, E190/814/6 fol.1v–2r, E190/814/7 fol.3v; Butler, 'Raynold Barber (1570–1577)', http://www.tudorrevels.co.uk/records.php.

the local community and coasting allowed for the supply of raw materials, as well as providing broader markets for the sale of finished goods.

The Hull–Newcastle coal trade

As mentioned above, source deficiencies for Hull have meant that analysis of the occupations of Hull merchants and mariners has had to take a slightly different form from that of Southampton and Bristol. Rather than looking in turn at particular occupational groups, it has been necessary to focus on the trade in Newcastle coal. We will look first at the general operational character of the Newcastle coal trade, before examining in turn those who specialised in that industry and those who dabbled in the trade only occasionally. It is important to note that the organisation of the Newcastle coal trade has been extensively studied and many have attempted to lay out the privileges of the Newcastle burgesses and of the Company of Hostmen in detail.[43] While it was not until 1600 that the Company of Hostmen was incorporated by charter, Newcastle merchants had sought monopolisation of the Newcastle coal trade for the preceding three centuries, and the sixteenth century saw control over the coal trade increasingly dominated by the Hostmen. As a result, and as laid out in some detail by John Hatcher, the east coast coal trade into London operated within a complex organisational structure, consisting of colliery owners, hostmen, shipmasters, brokers, woodmongers, lightermen, crimps, factors, wholesalers, and retailers.[44]

However, to date, the historiography has almost exclusively focused on London, and Newcastle's coal trade with other domestic ports is largely ignored. As a result, the literature on this topic does not satisfactorily cover the transportation of coal between Newcastle and Hull, and the evidence evaluated here suggests that Newcastle traders did not dominate that route, and that the mechanics of the coal trade in Hull were markedly different from those of the coal trade in London. In particular, Nef noted that shipmasters transporting coal into London were often employed directly by colliery owners, for whom they acted in multiple capacities.[45] However, there is little evidence in the civic sources that individuals from Hull worked in that way, and there is no indication in the customs records that they acted as agents. Instead, Hull traders that transported coal into Hull from Newcastle appear to have primarily carried their own product and they developed a specific operational approach that suited their chosen commodity, as discussed briefly in the section that follows.

---

[43] Blake, pp. 11–26; Hatcher, pp. 508–46; Willan, *The English Coasting Trade: 1600–1750*, pp. 34–37.

[44] Hatcher, pp. 508–46.

[45] Nef, p. 35.

The operational nature of Hull's coal trade

In a survey of the port of Hull undertaken in 1565, the commissioners emphasised the dangers of trading on England's north-eastern coast. They noted that the area was prone to bad 'stormes' and 'wyndes' and highlighted that ships passing through the stretch between the mouth of the River Humber and Holy Island (off the coast of Berwick-upon-Tweed) were often forced into Scarborough by bad weather.[46] As we saw in Chapter 3, heightened risk typically resulted in traders implementing methods to protect their investment and reduce risk (such as hiring a separate shipmaster or sharing hull space with other merchants). However, even though the route between Hull and Newcastle involved passing through a particularly dangerous stretch of water (at least by coastal standards), efforts to reduce risk were minimal. On none of the 734 voyages between Hull and Newcastle did more than one merchant carry cargo, and 98% of those trips were undertaken with a single individual acting in the capacity of both shipmaster and merchant. This apparent discrepancy resulted from the exceptionally low value of Newcastle coal. Not only was coal a more financially viable cargo when volumes were maximised, but the transportation of a large quantity by a single merchant meant that the full consignment could be placed directly into the hold without the cost of labour and materials needed for packaging the load into smaller batches.

While scholars exploring the seventeenth and eighteenth centuries have shown that much wealth could be accumulated from the sale of coal in London, even those later traders engaged in questionable tactics to increase the value of their shipments, and coal could fetch a much higher price in London than it could in Hull.[47] As shown in Appendix D, and discussed in more detail below, the transportation of coal into Hull during this period was a particularly low-value venture. Therefore, traders engaged in the coal trade would reduce expenditure by sacrificing a separate shipmaster and would maximise profits by carrying as much product as possible in a single shipment, without the need to separate it into individually packaged batches. Indeed, the very few voyages between Hull and Newcastle on which the merchant did not also command the vessel, involved the transportation of goods other than coal.[48] As a result, coastal commercial activity between Hull and Newcastle took on a unique character and was undertaken by individuals from a specific socio-economic group that was quite different from those explored in Southampton or Bristol, or from those Hull traders that instead engaged in commerce with London.

---

[46] TNA E159/350 fol.151d–152d.

[47] Hatcher, pp. 508–46, 77–78, 88–89.

[48] TNA E190/305/11 fol.3r-v, 10v, E190/305/12 fol.1v, 12r–13r, E190/306/1 fol.13r, E190/306/4 fol.2v, E190/306/16 fol.1v, E190/306/17 fol.1v, 13r, 17v, 18r, E190/307/2 fol.10r-v, E190/307/3 fol.1v, 16r, 17r, E190/307/9 fol.7v, 8r, E190/307/16 fol.2v.

Thus, in spite of the significant shortfalls in the sources available, Hull makes an important case study for an examination of English coastal commerce.

Across the full dataset, nineteen individuals specialised in the transportation of coal, and a further twelve appear to have had a particular interest in that trade. While the customs records do not provide residences for any of these individuals, the frequency and consistency with which they occupied specific vessels can give an indication of affiliated town. It is not possible to predict affiliated regions in this way for a large sample, but it is possible to make an informed assumption for a small group on a case-by-case basis, and it is evident that specialist coal traders originated from five main locations, namely Hull, Newcastle, York, Keadby, and Scarborough. That traders from Newcastle, Hull and Scarborough would dominate is unsurprising, given that they were the largest ports on the route between Hull and Newcastle. However, the prevalence of individuals from Keadby and York is notable as it speaks to the role of Hull as a gateway to the Humber river system. While the continuation of coal to York and Keadby cannot be observed in the customs records (as discussed in Chapter 2), much of the coal transported on York and Keadby vessels undoubtedly made its way to those ports after arriving in Hull.

For the most part, these individuals typically acted in the capacity of shipmaster, commanding vessels carrying the goods of merchants travelling on other trade routes, but they would also occasionally command voyages on which they carried only their own quantities of coal. For example, Richard Percy typically commanded ships transporting barley between Norfolk and Hull, and William Collins commanded voyages for a diverse range of merchants on the Hull/London route, but both men would occasionally command their own coal-carrying voyages from Newcastle.[49] Moreover, a number of these individuals regularly commanded vessels on behalf of members of Hull's mercantile elite, suggesting that they may have been occupational mariners, and their ability to invest in their own product implies that they had some degree of personal wealth (or capacity for credit).[50] As already noted, there is a possibility that some of these individuals were hired by colliery owners to transport coal. However, given that this type of opportunistic mercantile activity was very common among members of the seafaring community, and that this trade was sporadic, it seems more likely that these shipments were occasional investments by individuals that had separate primary careers.

In addition, there were also a small number of individuals that more routinely appeared on coastal voyages in the capacity of merchant, but who

---

[49] TNA E190/305/1 fol.2v, 11r, E190/305/11 fol.1r, 3v, 13r, 16r, E190/305/12 fol.1r, 10v, E190/306/1 fol.10v–11r, 13r, E190/306/4 fol.2r, 4v, 8v, E190/306/16 fol.12r, 13r, E190/306/17 fol.3r, 4r, 16v, 17v, E190/307/2 fol.1v, 3r, 6r-v, 7v, 10r-v, E190/307/3 fol.9r, 17r, E190/307/9 fol.1r, 2r, 3v, 7r-v, E190/307/16 fol.2r.

[50] TNA E190/306/4 fol.8v, E190/306/17 fol.12v, 16v.

would occasionally command vessels to transport coal. For example, George Anderson principally undertook voyages between Whitby and Hull carrying grains and herring, for which he hired various separate shipmasters, but he also occasionally invested in coal shipments from Newcastle, on which he acted in the dual capacity of shipmaster/merchant. As we have seen in Southampton and Bristol, this suggests that merchants engaging in coastwise trade often had dual skillsets that allowed them to take charge of vessels on those occasions when it was more cost-effective to do so. Moreover, as noted, these vessels were often of a substantial size, and the journey involved navigation of some difficult coastline, suggesting that these merchants were also skilled shipmasters, again blurring the line between merchant and mariner.

The civic elite

Finally, in both Bristol and Hull there is evidence that members of the civic elite also engaged in coastal commerce. Turning first to Bristol, and a number of individuals were listed in the port books with civic titles, including 'esquire', 'armiger' and 'gentleman', all of whom transported grains. Only a few of these individuals appear in the dataset, but they are of note as their engagement in coastal commerce correlates with trends in the quality of grain harvests. More specifically, the three years in which individuals with civic titles engaged in coastal trading to transport grain (1569, 1571 and 1576) were years in which Hoskins observed a kingdom-wide deficiency in grain or particularly poor harvests in the West Country.[51] However, in the five years for which we have a sufficient body of port book data, but in which no individuals of civic positions appear (1570, 1572, 1577, 1579 and 1580), kingdom-wide harvests were either good or average (not deficient) and the South West was no worse off than other regions.[52] This suggests that those of high social calibre stepped in to participate in the supply of grain during times of exceptional need.

Similar trends are evident in Hull, where individuals who appear to have been members of the civic elite sporadically engaged in the transportation of grain into Hull from Berwick-upon-Tweed and King's Lynn. While the Hull port books did not often list the home towns or occupations of the merchants that traded through the port, there are various factors that suggest that these were individuals of high status. First, individuals involved in the transportation of grain were granted an occupational title by the Hull customs officials with an unusual degree of frequency. Of the 589 separate merchants that appeared in the Hull port books, only forty-three were listed with an

---

[51] TNA E190/1128/12 fol.4v, 6v, 8r-v, 10v, E190/1128/13 fol.14v, 16v, 17r, 19r, E190/1128/14 fol.5r, E190/1129/18 fol.4r, 12r-v, 15r, 17r-v, E190/1129/22 fol.5v, 6r, 12r, 13r, 14r, E190/1130/2 fol.16v, 17v.

[52] Hoskins, pp. 45–46.

occupational title. Of those, forty were given a mercantile occupation, and the remaining three were an armiger, a mariner, and a maltmaker.[53] That these men were allocated an occupational title, while others were not, may imply that they were of particular importance, especially given that elite merchant William Gee was listed with the title of merchant. Furthermore, the majority of grain traders were listed as occupational merchants and one was listed as an armiger. The title of armiger was overtly high-status and, while we saw in Bristol that the title of merchant was more loosely applied, this was open to the interpretation of the customer taking the record, and the fact that individuals from other occupational groups were rarely granted a title implies some degree of affluence.

Secondly, we can substantiate this suggestion with three specific examples. First, armiger Valentia Brown was the only individual in the Hull customs records to be listed with a civic title. Brown only appeared in the port books for three short periods but during those times he undertook numerous voyages on which he supplied grain to Berwick-upon-Tweed from Hull.[54] Secondly, although no other individuals were listed with civic titles of this kind, we saw above that James Clarkson and William Megg were members of the mercantile elite in Hull, and they also partook in the grain trade for short but intensive periods.[55] It would be unrealistic to think that these examples could necessarily be extrapolated to apply to all individuals that traded through Hull carrying grain. However, it is notable that this trend is consistent with themes seen in Bristol and suggests again that individuals of civic positions engaged in the coastal transportation of grain during times of dearth.

Whether these were opportunistic voyages in an effort to make money or a response to social pressure to provide grain and prevent social unrest is not entirely clear. However, various devotions by the town clerk to Bristol merchant Thomas Aldworth for his provision of grains 'to the greate good of the whole comunaltie of the cittie' attest to the fact that there was an expectation on the mercantile elite to ensure that grain supplies were healthy.[56] Nonetheless, given that the merchants involved in the grain trade through

---

[53] TNA E190/305/1 fol.10r, 11r–12r, 16r–17r, E190/305/11 fol.2r, 4r-v, 13r-v, 16r-v, E190/305/12 fol.1r, 2v, 9r–10v, 12r-v, E190/306/1 fol.14r–15r, 20r-v, E190/306/4 fol.5v, 6r, 8r–9v, E190/306/16 fol.12r-v, 17r, 18r, E190/306/17 fol.12r–16r, 17r, E190/307/2 fol.2r, 3r, 6r–7r, 8r, 10r–11r, E190/307/3 fol.1r, 8r, 9r–10v, 16v, 17r, E190/307/9 fol.1v, 2v, 4v, 6r, 7r-v, E190/307/16 fol.2v.

[54] TNA E190/305/11 fol.16r, E190/305/12 fol.12r, E190/306/17 fol.15v, 16r, 17r, E190/307/2 fol.5v, 10r, 11r.

[55] TNA E190/305/1 fol.11v, 16v, E190/305/11 fol.2r, 4v, 13r-v, E190/305/12 fol.9r–10v, E190/306/1 fol.14r–15r, 20r-v, E190/306/4 fol.5v–6r, 8r–9v, E190/306/16 fol.12r-v, 17r, E190/306/17 fol.12r–15r, E190/307/2 fol.6r–7r, 10v, E190/307/9 fol.4v, 6r, 8r, 9v.

[56] TNA E190/1130/2 fol.4r-v, 8v; Lucy T. Smith, *The Maire of Bristowe Is Kalendar*

Bristol were rarely from the port supplying or receiving grain (but rather from a third unconnected location), it seems plausible that this was a matter of opportunistic business engagement. The evidence presented here is not necessarily indicative of a kingdom-wide trend and this matter deserves further attention across a broader range of case study ports. However, while it is beyond the scope of this volume to examine this matter in more detail, the sources investigated here certainly hint at a wider trend relating specifically to the coastwise supply of grain.

Wealth, political engagement and career development

Having now examined the occupational character of those who engaged in coastal commerce and explored the varying ways in which such individuals integrated domestic exchange into their wider careers, it is now necessary to establish their broader socio-economic position. This section will therefore utilise a variety of national and local civic records to determine the wealth, political positions, and occupational elevation that could be obtained by those who engaged in coastal commerce, again looking in turn at a variety of occupational groups.

Merchants and shipmasters

As discussed above, it is important to distinguish between the occupational titles applied to individuals by civic authorities and the role they played on the voyages in which they engaged. As such, this section will first address any wealth discrepancies between those who acted in the capacity of merchant on coastal voyages and those who acted in the capacity of shipmaster, before moving on to look at the wealth and social position of individuals in relation to their allocated occupational titles.

As evident in the figures displayed in Appendix C, broadly speaking, those who acted in the capacity of shipmaster were less wealthy than those who acted in the capacity of merchant. This is particularly obvious in Southampton and Hull, where a large proportion of local shipmasters did not appear in the lay subsidy returns at all, and those that did tended to sit in the lowest wealth tier, generally being less affluent than their mercantile counterparts. Some of those missing individuals may have had more than one residence and were thus taxed in a separate return, but that cannot have been the case for all of the missing masters and at least some of those must have been below the threshold required to pay tax.

Indeed, although their trading patterns suggest that the majority of shipmasters engaged in the lucrative trade between Hull and London were

---

by Robert Ricart, Town Clerk of Bristol 18 Edward IV (Westminster: Camden New Series, 1872), pp. 61–62.

Hull residents, they were notably absent from local civic sources. There is little evidence that they were made freemen or burgesses, there is a telling lack of evidence of them controlling any property or lands, and they clearly had very little involvement in local politics. Moreover, the small number of those shipmasters that *did* appear in the lay subsidy returns were significantly less wealthy than the merchants that traded on the same route. For example, Thomas Emerson was the wealthiest of the coastal shipmasters identified in Hull and was valued higher than all but seven individuals in his ward in 1571, yet he was still among the least affluent within the wider town and was substantially less wealthy than any of the merchants that traded into London from Hull (see Appendix C).[57]

Owing to the difficulties in positively identifying shipmasters in the Bristol lay subsidy returns, it would be misleading to make similar generalisations regarding their socio-economic position, although some assertions can be made. Shipmasters were again valued, on average, lower than merchants. Individuals that only acted as shipmasters averaged £3, whereas those who routinely acted as shipmaster/merchants averaged £6, and those who only appeared as merchants averaged £9. As the rate of return is so low, we cannot say with certainty that this is indicative of the wider community, but the fact that this is consistent with both of the other case study ports adds weight to that assertion.

This is unsurprising given the social and commercial significance of the mercantile community and their traditional place among the elite. However, it is also worth noting that not all individuals who appeared as merchants in the coastal port books fitted within this category. For example, of the seventy-two separate merchants listed in the customs records as residing in Southampton, only thirteen appear in the lay subsidy returns that were consulted.[58] Again, some may have been taxed in separate returns, but many will have been below the taxation threshold. This shows the broad spectrum of individuals that engaged in coastal trading and again challenges the notion that merchants were inherently wealthy.

Moreover, that the shipmasters listed in Appendix C were tax-liable at all suggests that they were of relative affluence, and some were among the richest in their wards. Interestingly, Craig Lambert has undertaken similar work across a much broader geographic and chronological landscape, which has placed mariners at much the same level of wealth. Notably, Lambert's investigations were not confined to the coastal trade and many of the individuals he identified

---

[57] TNA E179/204/292 mem.1.
[58] TNA E179/174/387; Douglas F. Vick, 'Central Hampshire Lay Subsidy Assessments, 1558–1603; Fawley Division, Southampton, Isle of Wight and Winchester' (Farnham: D. F. Vick, 1987).

engaged extensively in overseas commerce.[59] Broader investigation would be required to determine the precise and overarching differences in wealth and societal position of those traders engaged in coastal versus overseas activity, but there are indications that seafarers that engaged foremost in coastal trade could become as affluent as those engaged mainly in overseas voyages.

For example, the goods of Southampton shipmasters John Cotton and Thomas Hill were valued at just £3 in the 1571 lay subsidy return, whereas those of Nicholas Roche and Thomas Griston were valued at £6. Moreover, both Roche and Griston were shipowners, Roche owning the 16-ton *Elizabeth* and Griston the 10-ton *Anne*, both of Southampton.[60] Yet various sources show that Cotton and Hill participated much more extensively in overseas trade than Roche or Griston.[61] In particular, Nicholas Roche was a well-established and pivotal member of Southampton's maritime community and his £6 valuation places him firmly among the wealthiest in the ward of St Michael/St John, yet his wealth was largely accumulated through coastal trading, rather than any kind of significant position among overseas traders.[62]

Similarly, in Bristol, individuals like Henry Nelson only ever appeared as shipmasters and had very little engagement in overseas trade, but were also able to accumulate reasonably high levels of wealth, at least enough to be tax-liable (as shown in Appendix C).[63] Yet, at the other end of the spectrum, a number of particularly wealthy Bristol individuals also occasionally acted in the capacity of shipmaster on coastal voyages. For example, Walter Standfast was valued at £8 in 1568 and was an established overseas trader, as well as an alderman for Bristol. Standfast's reasonably high level of wealth, along with his engagement in overseas trade and local politics, places him among the mercantile elite.[64] Nonetheless, he had the necessary skills to command his own short-distance voyages, suggesting that the overlap between merchant and seafarer did not only apply to low-level coastal traders, but also to individuals

---

[59] Lambert, 'Tudor Shipmasters and Maritime Communities, 1550–1600'.

[60] SP12/38 fol.77.

[61] Butler, 'John Cotton (1570–1617)', 'Nicholas Roche (1540–1594)', 'Thomas Hills (1564–1596)', 'Thomas Gryston (1552–1600)', http://www.tudorrevels.co.uk/records.php.

[62] While Roche did engage in occasional overseas voyages, his focus was undoubtedly on coastal trade and his travel overseas was unusual. It should also be noted that another Nicholas Roche, who resided in Carmarthen, traded extensively through Bristol throughout this period, and that individual is explored in more detail in Chapter 5. Lambert and Baker, www.medievalandtudorships.org; Lambert, 'Tudor Shipmasters and Maritime Communities, 1550–1600'.

[63] Henry Nelson did undertake occasional voyages to Ireland, but his overseas engagement was limited to those few short trips. See Lambert and Baker, www.medievalandtudorships.org.

[64] Vanes, pp. 37, 84.

of substantial commercial and social importance. These examples demonstrate the range of engagement in coastal commerce, the broad skillsets present in the community, and the surprising capacity for wealth among individuals that specialised in coastal voyages.

Merchants and mariners

Having established the socio-economic differences between those who operated as shipmasters and those who operated as merchants on coastal voyages, it is now necessary to compare and contrast those differences to the occupational titles they were allocated by civic authorities. As noted throughout this volume, there is a great deal that can be established from the occupational titles allocated to individuals who traded through Bristol, owing to the exceptionally thorough record keeping of the Bristol customs officials. From this data, it is immediately clear that individuals associated with mercantile occupations (including clothiers, drapers, grocers and vintners) were generally wealthier than mariners or craftspeople. Indeed, the average lay subsidy valuation of all five mercantile groups exceeded £6, and most groups exceeded £8. The fact that individuals of social significance and relative affluence engaged in coastwise voyages is of note, and exploration of the lives and careers of several occupational merchants that engaged in coastal commerce helps to substantiate their roles in domestic exchange. Furthermore, these traders provide an interesting juxtaposition against the Gloucester merchants explored below, who were also members of the mercantile elite, but were generally valued much lower than Bristol merchants, probably resulting from their lesser engagement in foreign trade.

The first Bristol merchant of particular interest is William Popwell, who received by far the highest lay subsidy valuation of any individual that appeared in Bristol's coastal customs records. He was valued at £30 in 1560, £98 in 1564, and £130 in 1571.[65] Like most of the occupational merchants discussed here, Popwell only briefly appears in the coastal port books, carrying oil and wine into Bristol from Chepstow, but he is notable for two reasons.[66] First, the appearance of an individual of such substantial wealth attests to the fact that traders from a broad socio-economic spectrum partook in coastal commerce. Popwell was a trustee of the Society of Merchant Venturers of Bristol, was deeply involved in overseas trade, and racked up a substantial fortune over his career. There is a dearth of data relating to any political ambitions Popwell may have had, but it seems likely that he was related to Michael Popwell, who acted as mayor of Bristol in 1594, placing him among the mercantile elite.[67] Secondly, that Popwell traded between Bristol and Chepstow suggests that his

---

[65] TNA E179/115/355 mem.2, E179/115/368 mem.3, E179/115/386 mem.3.
[66] TNA E190/1128/14 fol.14r.
[67] John Latimer, *The History of the Society of Merchant Venturers of the City of*

voyages were the coastal leg of incoming overseas shipments. As discussed in Chapter 2, Chepstow was primarily a stopping point for wine-carrying voyages as a means to avoid tax. Therefore, this highlights the broad range of motivations that encouraged engagement in coastal commercial activity and that, in turn, created a diverse workforce of coastal traders.

While no other occupational merchant listed in Appendix C was valued as highly as Popwell, others did operate in the same way and also accumulated high levels of wealth. For example, Thomas Aldworth was valued at £10 in the 1563 lay subsidy return and left substantial financial gifts in his will; he also traded extensively into Spain and Portugal and represented Bristol as an MP on two occasions. Like Popwell, Aldworth was foremost concerned with overseas commerce and just occasionally dabbled in coastal trade as an aside, usually utilising one of two 100-ton vessels, the *Dominic* of Bristol and the *Dragon* of Newport.[68] Likewise, grocer Philip Langley was rated at £25 in the 1571 lay subsidy return, was also an established overseas trader, and engaged in local politics, acting in both the capacity of mayor and as an MP for Bristol. However, Langley is of further interest owing to a significant dispute he had with the Society of Merchant Venturers of Bristol in which he attempted to prevent an impending ban against non-members trading overseas out of the town.

As a man involved in a retail trade, Langley would have been ineligible to enter the Society and, therefore, banning non-members from overseas trade would have been detrimental to his business. Indeed, the records of the dispute show Langley fighting hard to prevent the monopolisation of the overseas trade. Nonetheless, despite being derogatorily characterised by the Society as a 'notorious retailer', his socio-political position and his engagement in coastal trade were very similar to that of admitted members.[69] He primarily took part in overseas trade, only occasionally dabbling in coastal commerce in order to distribute mixed overseas commodities, the ships he utilised were of a similar size to those used by Popwell, and he hired shipmasters and vessels *ad hoc* per voyage.[70] Of course, Langley's overseas trade may have been of a different character, and his non-admission to the Society was a symptom

---

Bristol; with Some Account of the Anterior Merchants' Guilds (Bristol: Arrowsmith, 1903), p. 23; Smith, p. 62.

[68] TNA E190/1129/18 fol.12v, 17r, 19r, E190/1130/2 fol.4r-v, 5v–6v, 12r-v, 8v, 20r, E179/115/373 mem.4; P. W. Hasler, 'Aldworth, Thomas II (d.1599), of Bristol, Glos.', www.historyofparliamentonline.org/volume/1558-1603/member/aldworth-thomas-ii-1599 (accessed 27 August 2019).

[69] TNA E179/115/386 mem.2; P. W. Hasler, 'Langley, Philip (c.1525–92), of Bristol', www.historyofparliamentonline.org/volume/1558-1603/member/langley-philip-1525-92 (accessed 27 August 2019).

[70] TNA E190/1128/14 fol.14r, E190/1129/18 fol.10v, E190/1129/22 fol.3r, E190/1130/2 fol.11r, 12r.

of his engagement in retail business, but his impact on coastal commerce appears to have been very similar to that of Society members, his levels of wealth were much the same, and the customs officials often referred to him as a 'merchant'.[71] Thus, we see Langley sitting in a precarious position between retail and wholesale. Diversifying his business to cover both elements of trade made him ineligible to join the Society of Merchant Venturers, which placed him in a vulnerable position despite his socio-political position and methods of commercial engagement seeming to be similar to those of admitted members.

Regardless of the nuances surrounding the socio-political position of these merchants, they were all of substantial local importance and significant affluence but were only sporadically involved in the domestic distribution of goods. However, at the other end of the spectrum, various other Bristol merchants appeared in the coastal records with much more frequency. Such individuals tended to accumulate less overall wealth and were usually valued at under £8. For example, draper Thomas Sarle was valued at £3 in the 1568 lay subsidy return and £8 in 1571, and merchant Thomas Rowland at £5 in 1560 and 1568 and £4 in 1564.[72] While neither of these men can be characterised as career coastal traders, coastal commerce did make up a large proportion of their overall business dealings.[73] The weighting of their commercial activity to include a larger proportion of coastal trade appears to have had a direct impact on their affluence and, although they were tax-liable, they were at the lower end of the wealth spectrum.

This sits in direct contrast to career coastal merchants in Southampton, some of whom reached the highest levels of wealth, despite not engaging in overseas trade. This difference likely resulted from the dominance of overseas merchants in Bristol, which limited the possibility that coasters could compete with the class of established overseas traders. The case of iron merchant John Knight best exemplifies this trend since we have evidence of his continuous engagement in coastal commerce and a telling lack of additional evidence pointing to any involvement in overseas trade.[74] As we saw in Chapter 4, Knight substantially increased his levels of trade through Southampton after 1574, and that increase in activity correlated with expansion and diversification

---

[71] TNA E190/1129/22 fol.3r, 16r, E190/1130/2 fol.10v; Brenner, *Merchants and Revolution: Commercial Change, Political Conflict, and London's Overseas Traders, 1550–1653*, pp. 69–70; Vanes, p. 26.

[72] TNA E179/115/355 mem.2, E179/115/368 mem.2, E179/115/373 mem.4, E179/115/386 mem.3.

[73] TNA E190/1128/12 fol.8r, 21r, E190/1129/1 fol.3v, 10r, 13v, 16v, E190/1129/18 fol.10r, E190/1130/2 fol.4v, 6r, 7r, 8v.

[74] Knight's continuous appearance in the coastal customs accounts can be seen throughout TNA E190/814/5, E190/814/6, E190/814/7, E190/814/11, E190/814/12, E190/815/1, E190/815/2, and his lack of overseas involvement is evident from Butler, 'John Knight (1555–1603)', http://www.tudorrevels.co.uk/records.php.

of his business networks. Furthermore, examination of Knight's biographic information also shows an upward trajectory of political significance in line with his increased coastal trading activities.

Knight was granted his burgess status in 1556/7 and until 1569 was an active member of the community, renting a property in Holy Rood, bearing witness to various wills, paying alms, and acting as water bailiff in 1565/6, but was not involved in the town's politics. Then, in 1569, he was made sheriff and from then on retained a position within the town's governance. He became mayor in 1571, alderman in 1574, and Justice of the Peace in 1576. Knight was also listed as a 'gentleman lieutenant' in a 1589 muster roll, suggesting he had become a man of significant local standing.[75] By the 1590s, he had clearly accumulated some substantial wealth; he loaned the town £5 to accommodate a visit from the queen in 1590 and contributed an exceptionally high payment of £18 for the Cadiz campaign (an initial payment of £13 in 1595 and then an additional £5 in 1596).[76]

Such an elevated position was common among merchants, but examination of such individuals has been largely confined to overseas traders and it has been widely assumed that coastal trading was not an especially lucrative business.[77] Knight's position within the town and his level of wealth directly contradict that established narrative. As a career coastal trader specialising in a much-needed product (and one that was especially necessary in the years building up to the Anglo-Spanish war), he was able to establish a healthy and lucrative maritime career, through which he was granted a privileged position within the town's elite, fulfilling an important role within the Southampton community.

However, that being said, John Knight was unusual and most of the wealthiest Southampton merchants displayed in Appendix C were also substantial overseas traders. In particular, the three wealthiest merchants, John Crook,

---

[75] Butler, 'John Knight (1555–1603)', http://www.tudorrevels.co.uk/records.php.

[76] This figure is substantially higher than the other individuals identified here, including many who engaged in overseas trade. For example, John Caplein and Paul Elliott both contributed just £10 over 1595/6: Butler, 'John Capelyn (1516–1570)', 'Paul Elliott (1550–1613)', ibid.

[77] For examination of the mercantile elite in Bristol, Southampton and the North East, see Brown; Carus-Wilson, 'The Merchant Adventurers of Bristol in the Fifteenth Century'; Childs; East, 'The Port of Kingston-upon-Hull during the Industrial Revolution'; Flavin and Jones, *Bristol's Trade with Ireland and the Continent 1503–1601: The Evidence of the Exchequer Customs Accounts*; Jones, *Inside the Illicit Economy: Reconstructing the Smugglers' Trade of Sixteenth Century*; Kermode, *Medieval Merchants: York, Beverley and Hull in the Later Middle Ages*; Lamb; Merson; Platt; Ruddock, 'Alien Merchants in Southampton in the Later Middle Ages'; Ruddock, 'London Capitalists and the Decline of Southampton in the Early Tudor Period'; Ruddock, *Italian Merchants and Shipping in Southampton, 1270–1600*; Ruddock, 'Merchants and Shipping in Medieval Southampton'; Stone, 'The Overseas Trade of Bristol before the Civil War'; Taylor; Tavener; Welch.

Richard Goddard Senior and Nicholas Caplein, were heavily involved in overseas ventures.[78] Crook traded extensively overseas and became a privateer after 1585, much like Goddard's nephew and apprentice Richard Goddard Junior who has been described by Kenneth Andrews as a 'powerful [man] in [the] Iberian trade, in oceanic projects and in privateering'.[79] Likewise, it is evident from other sources that Nicholas Caplein traded frequently overseas, primarily into La Rochelle and Bordeaux, and often on voyages with Crook and the Goddards.[80] Much like in the case of Bristol, these traders demonstrate that individuals from a broad socio-economic and socio-political spectrum engaged in coastal commercial activity, and yet situational factors could have a marked impact on the form that mercantile success could take, with coastal trade sometimes forming a significant part of the broader business models of Southampton merchants.

Interestingly, equally diverse maritime careers were also evident among some mariners who operated in the port of Southampton, and case studies of two such individuals can help to demonstrate the broad range of careers that could be forged, as well as the socio-economic characteristics of individuals that opted to pursue coastal trade in different ways. First, as mentioned in Chapter 4, John Cotton appears to have made a concerted effort to develop his career and expand his reach as a mariner. Until around 1575, Cotton's appearance in the coastal port books was sporadic and his engagement in overseas trade was minimal (although he did undertake some voyages to La Rochelle in the early 1560s). However, his career trajectory changed dramatically after 1576 when he purchased a share in the 28-ton *Mayflower* of Southampton and he thereafter interacted with many affluent Southampton merchants, establishing a consistent stream of trade between Southampton and London.

Moreover, his engagement with those merchants on the Southampton/London route appears to have enabled him to extend the trajectory of his voyages and he subsequently undertook shipments for various charter parties, one of which was planned to travel to Bayonne (France), Viana (Portugal) and Bruges (Flanders). Although we only have a lay subsidy valuation for Cotton for 1571, in which he was valued at £3, he went on to purchase a larger 50-ton vessel sometime before 1579 and he sold a hulk that he owned for an

---

[78] Andrews, *Elizabethan Privateering: English Privateering during the Spanish War, 1585–1603*, pp. 92, 113, 39, 41–42, 46; Butler, 'John Crooke (1563–1600)', 'Richard Goddard (1555–1573)', 'Nicholas Capelyn (1532–1590)', http://www.tudorrevels.co.uk/records.php.

[79] Andrews, *Elizabethan Privateering: English Privateering during the Spanish War, 1585–1603*, pp. 113, 46.

[80] Butler, 'Nicholas Capelyn (1532–1590)', http://www.tudorrevels.co.uk/records.php.

impressive £100 in 1581/2. Moreover, his will shows over fifteen beneficiaries, although their individual gains appear to have been limited.[81] It is clear that Cotton was a mariner of some stature; he interacted with the mercantile elite, invested in ships, and undertook various voyages overseas. His ownership of a vessel almost certainly enabled him to trade extensively with a range of significant merchants, and the rapid nature of his career development suggests that this was a strategic business decision made in order to expand his career as a dedicated mariner.

Conversely, oyster dragger John Holford used his fishing vessel to opportunistically engage in coastal commerce through Southampton when there was a demand for ships and shipmasters, usually in response to large incoming overseas shipments. Interestingly, Holford did not live within Southampton and instead resided in Dibden (slightly further down the estuary, near Hythe). Yet in spite of his geographic distance from the broader Southampton maritime community, Holford formed and maintained strong business ties with many important Southampton traders, as explained in Chapter 4. Moreover, while the lay subsidy returns explored here do not include Holford, and there is limited evidence relating to his wealth, he was called to present as a juror at the court leet and was paid £3 19s 2d for his engagement with the Lord Admiral in 1587. However, he was also frequently in trouble with the local admiralty, often fishing and selling goods outside the designated areas and, at one point, becoming the victim of an assault that caused bloodshed.[82] Holford was a very different type of trader from Cotton and, in spite of his prolific engagement in coastal trade and his ability to form extensive local ties, his career was turbulent and he does not appear to have ever transitioned from oyster dragging to more substantial maritime activity.

Before moving on to the North East, it is worth briefly examining similar socio-economic differences that existed between Bristol merchants and Gloucester merchants, as mentioned above. As may be anticipated, Gloucester men listed with mercantile occupations (including merchants, drapers and mercers) were the wealthiest of the Gloucester traders to engage in coastal commercial activity through Bristol. However, while the average valuation of Gloucester merchants was approximately the same as Bristol merchants, the upper range of those valuations was much lower, peaking at £16 rather than

---

[81] TNA E190/815/2 fol.1r, 2r-v, 3r, 4v, 6r; Butler, 'John Cotton (1570–1617)', http://www.tudorrevels.co.uk/records.php.

[82] A number of lay subsidy returns for Hampshire do survive but, unfortunately, they do not contain pertinent information relating to the parish of Dibden. In particular, while TNA E179/174/434 contains a section on Dibden, it is substantially damaged and the names are illegible. See Butler, 'John Holford (1566–1588)', http://www.tudorrevels.co.uk/records.php.

£130.[83] This is unsurprising and we would expect merchants from one of the largest port towns in England to occupy a higher socio-economic position than individuals from a much smaller subsidiary port. Nonetheless, within the context of their own region, several Gloucester traders gained substantial socio-economic and socio-political stature.

For example, Thomas Francombe appeared in the coastal port books transporting cloth and wine, but also acted as a sheriff in Gloucester in 1560 and mayor in 1570. Francombe was the highest valued of the Gloucester traders identified, and the fact that he was also substantially involved in local politics places him among the mercantile elite. Similarly, Luke Garnons also acted as both sheriff and mayor in Gloucester and additionally served as MP for Gloucester on four occasions.[84] Garnons was listed as a draper by the customs officials, but Duncan Taylor has defined him as a 'grain merchant', and certainly his practical coastal activities better fit the latter title.[85] However, unlike the Bristol merchants discussed above, there is little evidence that these individuals engaged in overseas trade, instead being foremost concerned with supplying grains into Bristol and returning with mixed overseas commodities to supply the Gloucestershire hinterland.[86] Conversely, the two men listed as mercers very likely did trade overseas (since we saw above that mercers were intrinsically linked to foreign import), and these men were no more wealthy than merchants that engaged in only coastal trade. This speaks to the importance of coastal commerce in the region and suggests that in some ports coastal enterprise could equate to substantial affluence, much as we saw in Southampton. Moreover, the individuals highlighted here demonstrate that coastal merchants were central to civic life in Gloucester, engaging in local politics, influencing maritime policies, and gaining substantial notoriety.

Notably, evidence from the Bristol port books also suggests similar trends among traders from other ports. For example, as mentioned above, 14% of voyages through Bristol on which the merchant and shipmaster were the same person were undertaken by Welshmen. However, this practical approach was not representative of the typical means through which Welshmen participated in coastal commerce, and the high shipmaster/merchant figure in that case was

---

[83] TNA E179/115/353, E179/115/367, E179/115/382, E179/115/385.

[84] P. W. Hasler, 'Garnons, Luke (d.1615), of Southgate Street, Gloucester', www.historyofparliamentonline.org/volume/1558-1603/member/garnons-luke-1615 (accessed 27 August 2019); Samuel Rudder, *The History and Antiquities of Gloucester: Including the Civil and Military Affairs of That Antient City; with a Particular Account ... Of the Cathedral Church; and All Other Public Establishments, from the Earliest Period to the Present Time* (Cirencester: S. Rudder, 1781), pp. 73, 145; Taylor, pp. 6, 155.

[85] Taylor, p. 155.

[86] TNA E190/1128/12 fol.3v, 6r, E190/1128/14 fol.1v, 12v, E190/1129/18 fol.1r, 2r, 3r–5r, E190/1130/2 fol.14r, 16v, 18v.

instead the result of the activities of two particularly prolific traders, Nicholas Roche and Thomas Fisher. As Roche and Fisher were not Bristol residents, they are somewhat beyond the scope of this volume, but are nonetheless worth mentioning briefly in the context of this matter.[87] Both men ran regular voyages between Carmarthen and Bristol, usually commanding the same ships and carrying mixed cargoes. On only one occasion did Roche carry another person's goods, when in July 1576 he transported calfskins, tanned hides, and leather for shoemaker David Peter.[88] Neither Roche nor Fisher deviated from the trade route between Bristol and Carmarthenshire, and there is no evidence in the data made available by the Medieval and Tudor Ships Project that they participated in overseas trade.[89] Thus, these men exemplify that dual mariner/merchant skillsets could enable individuals to build up healthy careers regularly shuttling short distances along the coast.[90]

Importantly, this also applied to many merchants operating in the port of Hull. Although source deficiencies in Hull make it difficult to determine the precise nature of the occupations of those trading coastwise through the port, it is clear that those individuals who routinely engaged in the transportation of goods between Hull and London unequivocally fitted into the category of mercantile elite. They often accumulated substantial wealth, had a strong presence within the town, and actively participated in local (and sometimes regional) politics. In fact, the average valuation for tax-liable merchants who specialised in the Hull/London trade was £31 10s, far outranking both the shipmasters that specialised on that route, who averaged £4 4s, and the Newcastle/Hull specialists, who averaged just £5 6s.

This stark difference can be credited to the nature of the commercial activity in which they engaged. As shown in Chapter 2, shipments of goods traded between London and Hull usually consisted of mixed cargoes, including

---

[87] Note that this is a different Nicholas Roche from the man we saw above that was involved in trade in Southampton. For Nicholas Roche of Southampton, see TNA E190/814/5 fol.2r, 4v, 6v, 9v, E190/814/6 fol.1v, 2r, 3r. For Nicholas Roche of Carmarthen, see E190/1128/12 fol.12r, E190/1128/13 fol.6v, 11r, 12r, 14v, 15v, 19r–20v, E190/1128/14 fol.9v, 15r, 16r, E190/1129/1 fol.13r, 15r, 16v, 18v–19r, E190/1129/18 fol.3r, 4r, 5v–6r, 9r, 10v, 12r, 15v–17r, E190/1129/20 fol.1r-v, 9v, 11r, 12r, 14r.

[88] TNA E190/1129/18 fol.9r.

[89] Lambert and Baker, www.medievalandtudorships.org.

[90] Roche and Fisher typically undertook at least five to six voyages every six months between Bristol and Carmarthenshire, Fisher on the 8-ton *Margaret* of Carmarthen and Roche on the 20-ton *Matthew* of Carmarthen. Their shipments usually contained products of high value such as wine, lead, iron, salt and soap, thus they demonstrate not only regularity in trade but also profitability. TNA E190/1128/12 fol.12r, 13r, E190/1128/13 fol.3r, 5r, 6v, 11r, 12r, 14v, 15v, 19r–20v, E190/1128/14 fol.9v, 15r, 16r, E190/1129/1 fol.4v, 11v, 13r, 15r, 16v, 18v, 19r, E190/1129/18 fol.3r, 4r, 5v–6r, 9r–10v, 12r, 15v–17r, E190/1129/20 fol.1r-v, E190/1129/22 fol.9v, 11r, 12r, 14r.

industrial goods, wine, oil, haberdasher wares, and foodstuffs. Not all of these shipments would have necessarily garnered huge profits, but a review of several indicative shipments suggests that they were often substantially more valuable than voyages that involved the transportation of coal. As shown in Appendix D, a 30-ton vessel travelling into Hull from London could typically accumulate a value of at least £100, whereas a 30-ton shipment of Newcastle coal tended to hold a maximum value of £20–30.[91]

There are, of course, various issues with assessing the value of commodities, especially across different ports. However, even taking into account the possible discrepancies, the difference in value was so great that it is reasonable to assert that London voyages were generally more profitable than Newcastle voyages. The result of this commercial difference was that London trade tended to attract merchants with substantial initial wealth and allowed those individuals to continue to grow their fortunes, whereas traders working the coal routes could do so with minimal expenditure, but the returns were less great. Likewise, although shipmasters that engaged in the trade with London failed to reach the same exceptionally high levels of wealth as their mercantile counterparts, they were still able to forge respectable careers as coastal mariners on that route.

Indeed, that they appear in the lay subsidy returns at all demonstrates that there was some scope for the accumulation of wealth among shipmasters that facilitated trade between Hull and London and, importantly, there is also much evidence to suggest that many shipmasters that traded between Hull and London owned a share in the vessels they utilised.[92] Furthermore, the tax-liable shipmasters from this group were the same individuals that formed central nodes in the London networks explored in Chapter 4, namely Thomas Emerson, Thomas Eratt, Roger Watson and Walter Hall.[93] While these men

---

[91] TNA E190/305/11 fol.1r, 4v, E190/306/1 fol.11v, 20r, E190/307/3 fol.10r, E190/307/9 fol.1r.

[92] For example, Thomas Emerson commanded the 40-ton *Christopher* of Hull for nine of the eleven coastal voyages he undertook throughout 1570 and 1571, and then throughout 1574 he commanded the 50-ton *Elizabeth* of Hull for all six of his coastal journeys. Likewise, Thomas Eratt always commanded either the 60-ton *Jesus*, 50-ton *Daisy* or 50-ton *Green Dragon*, all of Hull. However, conversely, William Gee was a prolific merchant and a very wealthy man but the ships he utilised almost always shifted with the shipmaster commanding the voyage, many of whom repeatedly used the same ships regardless of the trade route, cargo, or merchant involved, and there is no mention of any vessel in his will. TNA E190/305/1 fol.1v, 10r, 11r, 16v, E190/305/11 fol.4r, 13r, 16r, 17r, E190/305/12 fol.10r-v, 12v, 13r, E190/306/1 fol.11r, 14v, 15r, 20r-v, 21r, E190/306/4 fol.1v, 5r–6r, 8r–9r, E190/306/16 fol.1r, 12r-v, 17r, 18r, E190/306/17 fol.12r, 13v, 14v, 15v, 16r, 17r, E190/307/9 fol.7v, PROB 11/101/342.

[93] TNA E190/305/1 fol.1v, 3r, 10r, 11v, 16r-v, 21r, E190/305/11 fol.3v–4v, 10r, 13r-v, 16r–17r, E190/305/12 fol.9r–10v, 12r, 13v, E190/306/1 fol.11r, 14r–15r, 20r-v, E190/306/4

were clearly less wealthy than their mercantile counterparts, they were among the wealthiest coastal mariners in the port, and this appears to reflect their privileged position as preferred shipmasters for members of the mercantile elite. This data aligns Hull with the trends established in Southampton and Bristol, whereby occupational merchants who clearly fitted into the category of mercantile elite dominated the most profitable trades, and while the shipmasters engaged in those trades could accumulate some wealth, they were typically of lower status.

Of the merchants that routinely participated in trade between Hull and London, four individuals deserve particular attention, namely, William Gee, James Clarkson, Robert Dalton and Thomas Dalton. Gee was by far the most notable of these men and we saw in Chapter 4 that he was at the very centre of the networks of London/Hull traders, tying together otherwise disparate groups. Deeper investigation into local civic records suggests that Gee was not only at the centre of the trade with London but was at the very heart of the maritime community in Hull. In a letter to Lord Burghley in June 1595, Gee was commended for his contribution to the town. He was said to have 'benefitted the town more than any in the memory of this age', always giving 'charitably and liberally for the good of the town' and never being 'sued nor called into question for usury or hard dealing'. It was noted that he had been 'mayor three times with great credit' and had contributed more than £1,800 to the establishment of a school and a poor hospital, and to general upkeep in the town, including repairs to the 'great church', the marketplace, the highways and the water supply. He had 'spent his life and substance most Christianly both to the public and private good'.[94]

Aside from being three-time mayor, Gee also served as alderman, acted as a banker for the merchants of the town, and owned numerous properties, various of which were rented out to merchants and other craftspeople, and for use as Gee's hospital.[95] His personal engagement in the social fabric of the region is evidenced further in his will, in which he left cash sums to over twenty-five separate beneficiaries. Aside from his family, this included sums for the poor of Hull and the surrounding region, various sums to ensure the upkeep of the highways, and a sum to his 'neighbours in the street where [he lived]'.[96] Clearly, Gee was extremely wealthy; the cash sums left in his will

---

fol.1v, 4v–6r, 8r–9v, 11r, E190/306/16 fol.12r–14v, 17r–18r, E190/306/17 fol.12r–16v, 17v, E190/307/2 fol.6r-v, 7v–8r, 10r–11r, E190/307/3 fol.2r, 8v, 9r, 10r, 16r, 17r, E190/307/9 fol.2v, 7r-v.

[94] Green, pp. 49–50.

[95] HHC U/DDCB/12/1, C/WG/6, C/WG/21, C/WG/38, U/DDWB/11/1, C/BRI/20, U/DX28/7; Thrush and Ferris, www.historyofparliamentonline.org/volume/1604-1629/member/gee-william-1565-1611.

[96] TNA PROB 11/101/342.

equated to more than £3,000 (not including various gold and silver items he left to his children), and in the 1594 lay subsidy return he was valued at £50, far outranking any other individual in the town at that time.[97]

Furthermore, Gee's philanthropic activity in the Hull region ensured that he was a well-liked and well-respected member of the mercantile elite, and he was considered a reliable and trustworthy businessman. He is very likely to have traded overseas, especially given that his will references 'a dozen silver spoons bought in Flanders', but he had allegedly retired from maritime trade in the early years of the reign of Elizabeth I.[98] That he is visible in the coastal customs accounts as late as the 1570s suggests that he was able to continue to trade coastwise even when his overseas trade was winding down to make space for his role as town banker. Gee's wealth and social privilege, combined with his apparently fair and honest approach to trade, goes a long way in explaining his pivotal role in the networks of merchants explored above. Gee's significance in the region did not stop at the city walls and his dedication to the upkeep of towns outside Hull demonstrates his remarkably broad socio-political influence. However, Gee did not engage with the coal traders discussed above, highlighting the extent of this maritime divide.

The other three merchants noted above were of less regional significance than Gee but still fitted within the category of mercantile elite. The first of these was James Clarkson, who also appeared in the London network graphs of Chapter 4 but, unlike Gee, had minimal impact on the overall structure of those networks. Nonetheless, Clarkson was a wealthy and regionally important merchant. In both the 1559 and 1571 lay subsidy returns, he was valued at £20, outranking all but four individuals in his ward in 1559 and all but five in 1571.[99] In addition, Clarkson was made freeman in 1577 and purchased four tenements and an orchard from William Gee in 1578, demonstrating not only his wealth and social status but also his close ties to the broader mercantile community.[100] Further information on Clarkson is scarce, but the few sources that do survive place him within a similar socio-economic bracket to the other traders that engaged in commercial activity into London and suggest that he was markedly more affluent than Hull's typical coal traders.

The same is true of Robert and Thomas Dalton, who were also actively engaged in the networks of London traders that were identified in Chapter 4. Both men traded extensively between London and Hull over the 1570s, utilising various shipmasters and vessels, and carrying mixed cargoes. Like

---

[97] TNA PROB 11/101/342, E179/204/328 fol.1v; Thrush and Ferris, www.historyofparliamentonline.org/volume/1604-1629/member/gee-william-1565-1611.

[98] TNA PROB 11/101/342; Thrush and Ferris, www.historyofparliamentonline.org/volume/1604-1629/member/gee-william-1565-1611.

[99] TNA E179/203/265 mem.3, E179/204/292 mem.1.

[100] HHC C/DSN/1, C/WG/5, C/WG/6.

Clarkson, Thomas and Robert were made freemen in 1577 (the year in which the Hull Merchant's Society was incorporated by charter), and appear in various property documents, both purchasing and selling land, and acting in the capacities of witnesses and administrators.[101] Moreover, both men served as mayor and as aldermen and Thomas even served two terms as MP for Hull, in 1555 and 1572.[102]

Much like in the case of William Gee, the documents of the Hull corporation leave a plethora of clues that the Daltons were at the centre of the mercantile elite in the port. In a property deed relating to lands owned by Gee's hospital, Thomas Dalton is referred to as 'our truly and well beloved', hinting at his esteemed position within the town.[103] Likewise, in a petition of 1588, Robert Dalton collected signatures of nine high-ranking local merchants (including William Gee) in an attempt to block crown requisitioning of Hull vessels that he claimed was putting great strain on local commerce.[104] Both men also appear in the 1559 and 1571 lay subsidy returns, in which they were listed as the wealthiest in their respective wards, with Robert valued at £20 and Thomas at £66 13s 4d.[105]

Like Gee and Clarkson, these individuals were at the centre of trade and commerce in Hull and were the core of the mercantile elite. They engaged in local politics, invested in property and land, and accumulated substantial wealth. That these men were engaged in Hull's trade with London is

---

[101] HHC C/DSN/1, C/BRD/1/107, U/DDFA/6/1, U/DDHA/2/18, U/DDSY/52/12, U/DDSY/52/19, C/WG/21, U/DDWB/11/1.

[102] HHC C/BRD/1/34, U/DX28/7, C/BRI/20; Stanley T. Bindoff, 'Dalton, Thomas (1516/17–91), of Kingston-upon-Hull, Yorks.', www.historyofparliamentonline.org/volume/1509-1558/member/dalton-thomas-151617-91 (accessed 27 August 2019); P. W. Hasler, 'Dalton, Thomas (1517–91), of Kingston-upon-Hull, Yorks.', www.historyofparliamentonline.org/volume/1558-1603/member/dalton-thomas-1517-91 (accessed 27 August 2019).

[103] HHC C/WG/21.

[104] HHC C/DMT/10/1.

[105] It should be noted that another Robert Dalton appeared in the 1594 return valued at £6. However, given that the original Robert Dalton would have been at least 76 (and probably older) by 1594, that his younger brother Thomas had already died in 1591, and that the valuation was unusually low, it seems likely that this was another Robert Dalton, possibly a son of one of the brothers Thomas, Robert or John. Likewise, another Thomas Dalton appeared in the lay subsidy return of 1563 valued at £6. However, given that in 1559 and 1571 he was listed as residing in Trinity ward, and the Thomas Dalton of 1563 resided in South ward, and that the valuation was unusually low, this was likely a different Thomas Dalton, again potentially a son of one of the brothers. TNA E179/203/265 mem.3, E179/204/274 mem.5, E179/204/292 mem.1, E179/204/328 mem.1; Bindoff, www.historyofparliamentonline.org/volume/1509-1558/member/dalton-thomas-151617-91.

symptomatic of their privileged positions within the community. As in Bristol and Southampton, the commodities transported and the trade routes plied had a direct impact on the socio-economic and socio-political position of the individuals involved, and these four examples highlight the wealth and political influence that could be obtained through engagement in the trade between Hull and the capital.

Conversely, while individuals from various ports specialised in Hull's trade in Newcastle coal, Hull traders were by far the most dominant group on this route. Yet details relating to their lives and careers are difficult to ascertain from the sources that survive owing to their limited social and political influence in the port and region. Nonetheless, several key points are evident and deserve particular examination. First, across all residential groups, there are many indications that these shipmaster/merchants either owned or had a particular interest in specific vessels, with most coal specialists utilising the same ships for every voyage, often over many months or years. For example, Francis Hedley appears in the port books repeatedly over a six-year span, during which time he commanded the 24-ton *Francis* of Newcastle for every voyage and, likewise, Ralph Rackes commanded the 34-ton *Trinity* of York for fourteen of the fifteen voyages he undertook over a seven-year period. Similarly, although Peter Corbet utilised two vessels, he never deviated from commanding either the 30-ton *Andrew* or the 30-ton *Lion* (both of Newcastle) over a four-year span.[106]

As we have seen throughout this volume, this is not a completely reliable means of determining ownership. Nonetheless, frequency of ship usage is indicative of individuals that had at least some share in the vessels they utilised, especially considering that they transported only their own goods. Notably, these ships averaged 30 tons and some were as large as 60 tons, making them much larger than most coastal vessels utilised in Southampton or Bristol. The size of these colliers was shaped by the fact that they transported a bulky and low-value product, meaning that large vessels were required to maximise profits. Nonetheless, this is noteworthy as larger vessels were more costly to build and more challenging to command, suggesting some degree of wealth and skill among the individuals who specialised in the coastwise transportation of coal.

However, while these traders appear to have had some form of interest in the vessels they utilised, and they clearly had either the wealth to invest in shipments of coal or the means to obtain credit, they tended to be of limited socio-economic and socio-political stature. Of the Hull traders that specialised in the transportation of coal from Newcastle, only four appear in the lay

---

[106] TNA E190/305/1 fol.2v, 3r, 15r, E190/305/11 fol.1r, 3r, E190/305/12 fol.2v–5v, E190/306/1 fol.11r, E190/306/4 fol.1r, 3r, 4v, E190/306/17 fol.1r–4v, 4v, 5r, E190/307/2 fol.1r–2r, 8r, 10r, E190/307/3 fol.1v–3v, 7v, E190/307/16 fol.1r–2r.

subsidy returns that have been assessed, and none appear in the surviving lists of freemen and aldermen.[107] Furthermore, as shown in Appendix C, those that did appear in the lay subsidy returns received low valuations, primarily being valued at under £5. John Thompson bucked this trend, being valued at £12, and Robert Wardall was valued at £8 in 1559, but coal specialists were rarely the wealthiest in their wards and were certainly not among the most affluent in the town.

For example, although Wardall was wealthy among coal traders, he was one of the poorest tax-liable individuals in his ward, outranking only two of the nineteen persons listed as residing in St Mary's in 1559, and only fifteen of the thirty-two that were tax-liable in that ward in 1571.[108] Moreover, the valuations for specialist coal traders averaged around £5 6s, a measly sum compared to the £31 10s average for merchants that engaged in London trade. In addition, there is little reference to these individuals in local civic records, suggesting that they were neither engaged in local politics nor owned property in the town. Thus, while these traders were clearly skilled (being able to command ships of over 20 tons in difficult waters), evidently had the means to invest in cargo, probably owned or part-owned the vessels they utilised, and were central to coastal commercial activity in the region, they were of limited socio-political influence.

Unlike their counterparts on the London route, this group built up a steady stream of commercial activity and forged long-term careers based on the transportation of a specific commodity. However, the low value of their chosen product limited their opportunity to obtain wealth and social influence. Engagement in an abundant and reliable trade that involved relatively low levels of investment was one of several options for maritime traders in Hull and was markedly separate from trade between Hull and London. The approach individual traders took to their businesses was a personal decision and hinged on a number of factors related to their socio-economic background and their general outlook, as discussed by Robert Brenner.[109]

As in Southampton and Bristol, some traders found the risks associated with transporting high-value goods unappealing and, for them, the benefits of a steady career in a reliable and secure industry outweighed the drive for personal economic expansion. There was undoubtedly a degree to which members of the mercantile elite monopolised trade in higher-value goods, but there is no evidence in the civic records of these lesser traders attempting to penetrate that industry. Yet while traders that specialised in the transportation

---

[107] TNA E179/203/265, E179/204/274, E179/204/292, E179/204/328; HHC C/BRI/20, C/DSN/1, U/DX28/7.

[108] TNA E179/203/265 mem.2, E179/204/274 mem.2, E179/204/292 mem.2.

[109] Brenner, 'The Social Basis of English Commercial Expansion, 1550–1650', pp. 361–62.

of Newcastle coal occupied a low socio-economic position, their role in the region was very important. They not only contributed to the upkeep of the town and to the port's ship fleet, but they were pivotal in the supply of a much-needed product to the region's vast hinterland, in this case revealing a clear distinction between socio-political dominance and commercial significance.

Finally, aside from those who specialised in the transportation of Newcastle coal, various shipmaster/merchants also occasionally dabbled in that trade as an aside to their typical maritime activities, and those individuals tended to occupy the same socio-economic position as coal specialists. Much like the specialist coal traders discussed above, these individuals were affiliated with ports in the local region, namely Hull, Newcastle, York and Keadby. Likewise, in the case of the shipmasters, there are many indications that these traders had an interest in the vessels they utilised. Not only did they use the same ships over sustained periods, but they commanded the same vessels even when the merchant carrying cargo on board shifted. For example, John Norris commanded the 30-ton *Elizabeth* of Hull for every voyage in which he participated during 1573 and 1574, even though he commanded for a range of separate merchants. The same can also be said of William Parrett in the case of the 50-ton *Daisy* of Hull, and Robert Duffield in the case of the 34-ton *Greyhound* of Keadby.[110]

This does not appear to have been the case for those individuals who more typically acted as merchants, and those traders usually hired the ship and shipmaster together during their routine trade. Nonetheless, individuals from both categories very rarely appeared in Hull's civic records and only three appear in the lay subsidy returns, two of whom typically acted in the capacity of shipmaster on London voyages, probably accounting for their higher valuations. Yet, even those traders that did appear in the lay subsidy returns were valued at £5 or under, placing them among the middling ranks of individuals in their wards, and again aligning these men with those that specialised in the coal trade.[111]

Like the specialist coal traders discussed above, those who only sporadically transported coal had sufficient wealth to invest in their own product and benefited from substantial maritime skill and knowledge, but rarely achieved a high level of wealth or social stature. Again, these individuals occupied a

---

[110] TNA E190/305/1 fol.2v–3r, 16r, E190/305/12 fol.5r, 9r, E190/306/1 fol.14v, E190/306/16 fol.12r, 13r, 17r-v, E190/306/17 fol.2v, 3v, 12r, 14r, 16r, 17r, 18r, E190/307/2 fol.6r, 7r, 8r, 10r, E190/307/9 fol.5v–6r, 7r.

[111] In 1563, Walter Hall appeared in a ward with twenty-five other individuals, only thirteen of whom were valued at £5 or under. Likewise, in 1571, Hall appeared in the same ward as Robert London and of the twenty-six individuals that appeared in that ward, only seventeen were valued at £5 or under. TNA E179/204/274 mem.2, E179/204/292 mem.1.

very different socio-economic and socio-political position in the town from the merchants that engaged in trade with London. The Hull/London trade was dominated by Hull's mercantile elite, and neither the shipmasters that engaged on that route nor the shipmaster/merchants that instead transported coal were able to reach the same level of affluence as those traders. Moreover, the divide between these groups was stark, and merchants that specialised in the trade with London do not appear to have engaged in the transportation of coal to any extent, in spite of the important role the coal trade played in the town's commercial landscape. This suggests that the coal trade was the preserve of lesser shipmaster/merchants, who rarely expanded their commercial reach to participate in higher-value trade, and this is reflected in their socio-economic position within the town.

Publicans and brewers

As we saw above, aside from occupational merchants and mariners, various individuals of other crafts also engaged in coastal exchange. This was especially true of those involved in the production and sale of beer, many of whom utilised the complementary characteristics of alcohol distribution and coastal commerce to establish highly successful careers. Nonetheless, the success such individuals found in their merging of those two trades was not necessarily reflected in their socio-economic positions. For example, in Bristol, although some brewers were able to accumulate substantial wealth, in some cases being valued at upwards of £10 and finding a place among the civic elite, they were generally less wealthy than occupational merchants. Moreover, some brewers that were exceedingly prevalent in Bristol's coastal trade never appeared in the lay subsidy returns. There are clearly flaws in assuming that absence from the subsidy returns necessarily confirms a lower level of wealth, since those individuals arguably could have resided elsewhere or had multiple residences. However, there were a number of brewers who resided in Bristol at the time of the assessments and who do not appear in the tax returns, probably because they were not wealthy enough to reach the tax threshold.[112]

Moreover, while we saw in Chapter 4 that brewers who employed the Swanleys as shipmasters engaged in coastal trading most frequently through Bristol and formed the tightest occupational networks, they were not the wealthiest brewers to engage in coastal activity through the town. Instead, that accolade goes to Robert Smith and John Stone who appeared in the

---

[112] For example, John Kedward appears in the port books listed as a Bristol resident consistently throughout 1570, 1571, 1576 and 1577 but did not appear in the 1572 return. See TNA E179/115/386, E190/1128/12 fol.5v, E190/1128/13 fol.13r, 16r-v, E190/1129/18 fol.2r–3v, 5r-v, 11r, E190/1129/22 fol.1v, 4r, 10v.

coastal customs records only a few times and who engaged with other Gloucestershire shipmasters. This is notable as it suggests that participation in coastal commercial activity in order to support a primary craft was not always the most effective means to acquire wealth. Nonetheless, while brewers from the Swanley networks were less wealthy than Smith and Stone, they were often still tax-liable and some were particularly affluent.

For example, William Blast was valued at £8 in 1568 and £5 in 1571, between which he invested in property, perhaps accounting for his reduction in goods valuation.[113] This puts Blast among the wealthiest of all coastal traders examined here, and especially among other brewers. Moreover, Blast was occasionally assigned the title of 'merchant' by the customs officials, reflecting his prolific engagement in maritime trade.[114] Likewise, Anthony Hodge also ran regular grain voyages between Gloucestershire and Bristol and formed strong ties to the Swanley networks.[115] Hodge was valued lower than Blast at just £3 in 1568 and 1571 but was still tax-liable and again exemplifies that establishment of a steady and reliable trade could enable individuals to gain some socio-economic stature. Furthermore, William Watford's valuation increased between 1568 and 1571 from £5 to £10, and that increase correlated with increased engagement in coastal commerce.[116] This suggests that Watford began engaging in coastal trade once he had established a sufficient level of wealth and that, in some cases, engagement in coastal commercial activity did correlate with socio-economic position.

It is impossible to determine using this data whether engagement in coastal commerce allowed individuals from these occupations to accumulate greater wealth than comparable individuals that did not partake in maritime trade. Indeed, Richard Hoyle has shown that craftspeople of all kinds could gain substantial wealth in non-port towns.[117] However, this data does suggest that some individuals incorporated engagement in coastwise trade into their businesses as a means to cut out costly third parties from supply and distribution. The accessible nature of coastal commerce allowed individuals from a broad spectrum of backgrounds to take advantage of their geographic position on the coast and, in some cases, this created an environment in which strong business models could be established and substantial wealth accumulated.

---

[113] TNA E179/115/373 mem.3, E179/115/386 mem.3; BRO P.AS/D/LM/A/15.

[114] Blast usually undertook around four to six voyages through Bristol every six months, almost all of which involved a member of the Swanley family as shipmaster. See TNA E190/1128/12 fol.2v, 4v, 6v, 8r, E190/1128/13 fol.1v, 5r, 8r, 12r, 13r, 18r, E190/1128/14 fol.4r, 5v, 7r, E190/1129/1 fol.3r, 6v, 8r, 14r.

[115] TNA E190/1128/13 fol.13v, 15r, 16r, E190/1129/1 fol.7v, 9r, 14v.

[116] TNA E190/1129/1 fol.3r, 6v–7r, 14r.

[117] Richard Hoyle, 'Taxation and the Mid-Tudor Crisis', *The Economic History Review*, 51 (1998), 662–69.

This was also evident in Southampton, where various publicans engaged in coastal commerce, such as tipplers Nicholas Roche, Reginald Barber, Thomas Griston and John Cavil, and innkeeper Peter Janverin, who occupied *The Star*.[118] Notably, unlike the mariners described above, all except John Cavil appear in a lay subsidy return and two of those were valued at £6, putting them among the wealthiest in their wards.[119] The fact that these men were victuallers goes some way in explaining these valuations since they probably had inventories of stock that were counted towards their wealth assessments. In addition, Nicholas Roche owned a storehouse on the West Quay and therefore most likely had a substantial quantity of rateable goods at the time of valuation.[120]

Nonetheless, it is clear that shipmasters could forge lucrative careers through the dual occupation of mariner/publican, and seemingly to a greater extent than mariner/brewers. Aside from the obvious financial benefits that came from having two revenue streams, it seems that these individuals were particularly well integrated members of the Southampton community and their close social ties very likely afforded them greater business opportunities as victuallers and as mariners. Indeed, there is much suggestion that the wives and widows of publicans were engaged in the running of public houses, meaning that, even when seafarers were at sea, their alehouses continued to run and their wives remained in community-facing roles on land. This is evident in the case of both Thomas Griston, whose widow Alice was listed as 'tippler' and continued to pay the 'scavage rate' after his death, and Peter Janverin, whose wife Mary inherited *The Star* from her father and played a pivotal role in the running of the establishment throughout her life.[121]

Nicholas Roche, whose goods were valued at a higher rate of £6, was particularly well known in the town and was affectionately referred to as 'French Nick'. While he often found himself at the centre of disputes, this appears to have been a result of his constant interaction with a broad social circle rather than a result of an antagonistic temperament, as we saw in the case of John Crook.[122] Likewise, there is some evidence that Thomas Griston, whose goods were also valued at £6, was similarly integrated into the broader town; he interacted extensively with other mariners, drew up probate

---

[118] James Brown has provided a thorough analysis of the different tiers of public houses in Brown, pp. 23–29.

[119] Thomas Griston and Nicholas Roche were valued at £6 in 1571, making them wealthier than ten of the sixteen tax-liable individuals that resided in their ward in that year: TNA E179/174/387 mem.1.

[120] Butler, 'Nicholas Roche (1540–1594)', http://www.tudorrevels.co.uk/records.php.

[121] Butler, 'Alice Griston (1570–1613)', 'Mary Janverin (1539–1608)', ibid.

[122] Brown, pp. 84, 131; Butler, 'Nicholas Roche (1540–1594)', http://www.tudorrevels.co.uk/records.php.

inventories for various townspeople, assisted with repairs to the town's walls and quays, and contributed alms.[123] Barber and Cavil are less well represented in the sources that survive, but they too had a broad range of local contacts, suggesting that they were also well connected within the port.[124] Apart from in the case of Peter Janverin, these traders all demonstrate the potential benefits of multiple occupations, especially when both careers were beneficial to and benefited from having close-knit ties within the local community.

However, as discussed in Chapter 4, Peter Janverin was a slightly different case, being a member of a large and important maritime family that operated out of the Channel Island of Jersey.[125] In spite of his establishment as keeper of a pivotal Southampton inn, he continued to engage almost exclusively with Islanders in his position as shipmaster. Moreover, unlike the majority of the individuals discussed here, Janverin lived in St Lawrence, although this resulted from his marriage to the widow owner of *The Star*, rather than any conscious decision to live away from the wider maritime community. There are some parallels here between John Crook (discussed in more detail in Chapter 4) and Peter Janverin.

They were both outsiders, Crook from Poole and Janverin from Jersey, and both entered Southampton to marry widow innkeepers, taking control of important Southampton public houses.[126] Moreover, after moving into Southampton, both men forged mercantile careers but remained distant from the core of the Hampshire maritime and mercantile communities. Crook did have close societal connections to many important Southampton merchants, and he dwelled within Holy Rood and St Michael/St John but, as we saw in Chapter 4, this did not help him to forge strong business networks and he remained detached from the core community in the context of his coastal activities. Similarly, Janverin's record is one of continual dispute within the town. He earned his burgess status in 1564 but was later stripped of that privilege, and he frequently appeared in court to settle disputes with neighbours.

While Janverin appears to have engaged heavily with the townspeople, lending and borrowing extensively and appearing in court as a pledge, this seems to have centred on his status as a publican rather than his maritime activities.[127] No doubt, Janverin earned an important place within the community by claiming ownership of *The Star*, but his focus after taking on the inn shifted and his career as a mariner remained tied to the Channel Islands for the short

---

[123] Butler, 'Thomas Gryston (1552–1600)', http://www.tudorrevels.co.uk/records.php.

[124] Butler, 'Raynold Barber (1570–1577)', 'John Cavell (1551–1584)', ibid.

[125] Jamieson, p. 79; Syvret and Stevens, pp. 90–91.

[126] Brown, pp. 81–82; Butler, 'John Crooke (1563–1600)', 'Peter Janverin (1559–1596)', http://www.tudorrevels.co.uk/records.php.

[127] Butler, 'Peter Janverin (1559–1596)', http://www.tudorrevels.co.uk/records.php.

time it continued, again demonstrating the impact that personality traits and individual decision making could have on the position occupied by specific merchants and mariners.

Gloucester mariners, trowmen and maltmakers

Finally, as discussed above, it has been very difficult to determine exactly how customs officials distinguished between mariners, trowmen and maltmakers; they plied the same routes, carried the same cargoes, and utilised the same vessels. Unfortunately, the data analysed in this chapter does little to answer this question as these individuals also occupied broadly the same socio-economic position. All of those identified in the lay subsidy returns were valued at under £10 (as shown in Appendix C), and there is a notable lack of evidence that they engaged in local politics, although some leased properties in the town.[128] This was even true of members of the Swanley family, who we have established were central to maritime activity in Gloucestershire. Although Craig Lambert points out that Richard Swanley was among the wealthiest in Gloucester's West ward, various merchants located in other wards who also engaged in coastal commerce outranked him in terms of wealth and were markedly more influential in the town.[129] Thus, while Gloucester mariners, trowmen and maltmakers were the most prolifically engaged in coastal maritime commerce in the region, they did not rank among the local elite.

As we saw above, these individuals established regular and low-risk trading activities, sticking to their local region, rarely deviating from their established routes, and remaining within stable networks, forming strong business ties with reliable individuals and creating a steady stream of income. This way of operating was safe, but it did create a political and financial ceiling for the individuals involved. Each merchant and mariner faced a choice of whether to remain engaged in low-risk ventures that often had limited returns, or to extend their reach, increasing their investments and seeking out ventures of a grander scale with potentially higher rewards. The traditional historiography, focusing as it does on overseas commercial trade, has overlooked individuals that opted to remain engrossed in coastal commerce, who we have shown were crucial to the maritime successes of the kingdom and were often able to maintain a decent standard of living. As shown in Appendix C, even trowmen, who have typically been considered of the lowest social calibre, could obtain reasonable wealth and benefit from the less sensationalised side of the maritime industry.

---

[128] Barbara Drake, 'The Development of an Urban Site 1455–1750, the Island and Lower Part of Westgate Street', *Gloucestershire History*, Special Extra Edition (1990), 7, 12.

[129] Lambert, 'Tudor Shipmasters and Maritime Communities, 1550–1600'.

Inner-town residence

Aside from their allocated occupations, forms of career development, and levels of wealth, the physical spaces shipmasters and merchants occupied within their ports are also of interest. However, as source deficiencies in the Hull port books have made it very difficult to ascertain ward residences for any notable number of seafarers, this section will focus on Southampton and Bristol.

Turning first to Southampton and, as indicated in Map 5.1a below, two residences have been identified for nine of the thirty-nine Southampton merchants under examination. This was usually the result of a subsidy being taken before and after a change of location and, for those individuals, a node has been placed in all wards in which a residency has been identified. Of those nine, one was recorded as residing in both St Lawrence and Holy Rood, two in All Saints and St Lawrence, two in All Saints and Holy Rood, and four in St Michael/St John and Holy Rood. Of the remaining thirty merchants, one resided in All Saints, three in St Lawrence, twelve in St Michael/St John, and fourteen in Holy Rood. Finally, ten of the twelve listed shipmasters resided in St Michael/St John, with just one residing in Holy Rood, and one in St Lawrence.

Maps 5.1a and 5.1b indicate that both shipmasters and merchants living in Southampton had a preference to reside in the wards of Holy Rood and St Michael/St John, although shipmasters were more confined to those wards than merchants.[130] This tendency is unsurprising since those were the largest wards in the town and were in close proximity to the customs house, the two docks (West Quay and the Watergate), the local market, and two important public houses (*The Dolphin* and *The Crown*).[131] Moreover, while it is difficult to definitively determine which of those two wards was the more affluent during this period, the historiography suggests that Holy Rood may have been slightly wealthier than St Michael/St John.[132] Thus, it is reflective of the high concentration of wealth among occupational merchants that they tended to congregate in Holy Rood, whereas occupational mariners were more likely to reside in St Michael/St John.

Furthermore, individuals who resided outside of Holy Rood or St Michael/St John were principally those that were allocated an occupational title other

---

[130] This map has been reconstructed using the findings of James Brown and Colin Platt. The positioning of the public houses varies slightly from record to record, but their approximate location has been provided. Brown, pp. 1–76; Platt, pp. 215–24.

[131] The Maritime Museum of Southampton, *Southampton in 1620 and the "Mayflower": An Exhibition of Documents by the Southampton City Record Office to Celebrate the 350th Anniversary of the Sailing of the "Mayflower" from Southampton in 1620* (Southampton: Southampton City Record Office, 1970), p. 14.

[132] Ibid., pp. 14, 28, 35, 43, 61, 78; Brown, pp. 34–35; Platt, p. 218.

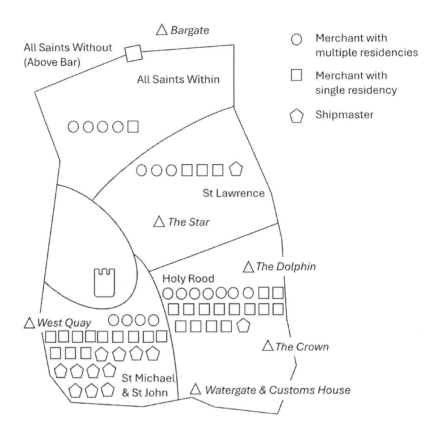

Map 5.1a. Ward residences of merchants and shipmasters living in Southampton.

than mariner or merchant. For example, fisherman John Holford was the only shipmaster identified to reside outside of the city walls, being instead based in Dibden, and tallow chandler Paul Elliott resided in St Lawrence.[133] These trends generally support the assertions of historians such as Cheryl Fury and Craig Lambert, who have argued that seafarers tended to form distinctive communities on land within which they established strong maritime subcultures. Lambert has termed these 'proto-sailor towns' as a nod to the clearly defined sailor towns of later centuries, and this suggestion certainly appears

[133] Butler, 'John Holford (1566–1588)', 'Paul Elliott (1550–1613)', http://www.tudorrevels.co.uk/records.php.

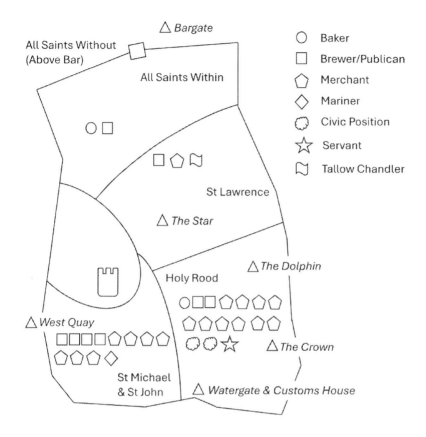

Map 5.1b. Ward residences of merchants and shipmasters living in Southampton.

to hold some weight for Southampton during the period under examination.[134] However, it is also evident from this data that merchants too occupied those spaces, suggesting that the communities of mariners and merchants that engaged in coastal commerce were closely tied.

The lives and careers of some of these individuals were explored in more detail above, but it is worth also paying particular attention to the career paths of the individuals for whom two residences are listed, as their detailed biographies allow for a more comprehensive overview of the impact of commercial

---

[134] Fury, 'The Elizabethan Maritime Community'; Lambert, 'Tudor Shipmasters and Maritime Communities, 1550–1600'.

activity on personal circumstances. Since Holy Rood was a traditionally wealthy ward and St Michael/St John was the centre of maritime activity in Southampton, it is fair to assume that a move into Holy Rood or St Michael/St John represented an improvement in personal circumstances or, at the least, a closer tie to the maritime community. Of the nine merchants for whom two residences are listed, five moved from one location to another, one owned multiple properties, and the remaining three are unclear. Of the five that moved, two left All Saints to live in Holy Rood, and the timing of their move coincided with a clear career progression.

More specifically, in 1575 (the same year he first appears in the coastal port books) Richard Willmott moved from his family home in All Saints to Holy Rood in order to become a servant to established merchant John Crook, suggesting that his employment as Crook's servant enabled him to participate in coastal commerce.[135] Similarly, Richard Biston had a bumper year of coastal trading in 1575, running thirteen voyages, mostly to London, during which time he lived in All Saints. However, in the latter part of the 1570s, he moved to Holy Rood and this change coincided with a shift towards greater involvement in more lucrative overseas voyages.[136]

In other cases, the correlation between career and residence was less clear. For example, as Holy Rood and St Michael/St John were of similar socio-economic character, moves between those two areas were less telling of changes in personal circumstances, but the fact that wealthy and high-status merchants Emery Lake and John Crook moved between the two wards suggests that both areas could attract an affluent crowd.[137] Likewise, Reginald House, David Morell and Alexander Payton all appear to have owned homes in both Holy Rood and St Michael/St John, some of which they rented out for a subsidiary income.[138] Again, this suggests that these were wealthy individuals with some degree of financial stability, and their affluence was reflected in their tax valuations. Ward residence was certainly determined to some degree by wealth, and Holy Rood and St Michael/St John were desirable areas of the town in which to reside. However, the degree to which the wards were divided by mercantile and maritime affiliation suggests that the decision to reside in a particular part of the town also depended on practical

[135] Importantly, the voyages undertaken by Willmott contained only his own goods, rather than goods that he was transporting on Crook's behalf. See TNA E190/814/11 fol.1v; Butler, 'Richard Willmott (1557–1579)', http://www.tudorrevels.co.uk/records.php; TNA E190/814/11 fol.1v.

[136] TNA E190/814/11 fol.1r, 7v–8r, E190/814/12 fol.1r, 3r, 5r, E190/815/1 fol.8r.

[137] Butler, 'Emery Lake (1539–1594)', 'John Crooke (1563–1600)', http://www.tudorrevels.co.uk/records.php.

[138] Butler, 'Alexander Payneton (1566–1616)', 'David Morell (1550–1616)', 'Reginald House (1542–1573)', ibid.

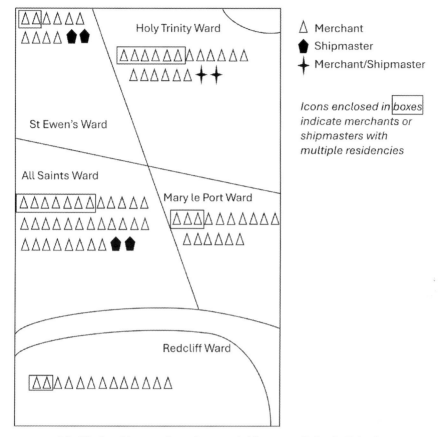

5.2. Ward residences of merchants and shipmasters living in Bristol.

elements, such as proximity to the quayside and integration with members of the same occupational group.

Similar trends are also evident in Bristol, where ward locations have been identified for around eighty shipmasters and merchants, as shown in Map 5.2 below. Of those individuals for whom only a single location has been identified, twenty-four merchants resided in All Saints, thirteen in Mary le Port, ten in Redcliff, nine in St Ewen's, and nine in Holy Trinity. The two shipmasters resided in St Ewen's, and the three individuals listed as both shipmaster and merchant were split between Holy Trinity and All Saints.

Just as in Southampton, and as shown in Map 5.2, while coastal traders appeared in all areas of the town, they had a preference for certain wards, in this case All Saints and, to a lesser extent, Mary le Port.[139] The four wards north of the River Avon (St Ewen's, Holy Trinity, All Saints and Mary le Port) were the original constituent parts of the walled town, and Redcliff (or Mary Redcliff) was formed as Bristol's fifth ward after the twelfth century when the city walls were expanded to include the wealthy parts of the suburb. However, while Redcliff was Bristol's newest ward, Christian Liddy has highlighted its long history as one of the wealthiest areas of the town, contributing a higher proportion of the 1373 tenth and fifteenth than any other ward, and being home to the bulk of Bristol's cloth industry.[140] Nonetheless, Redcliff was markedly separate from the original four wards, which were tightly-knit, had easy access to the waterfront, and were well established as the centre of the old town.

All Saints was perhaps better placed to accommodate those engaged in maritime commerce since it was particularly close to the customs house, and Fleming has identified All Saints and St Ewen's as the wealthiest of the central quadrant.[141] Holy Trinity was the poorest of the central wards but was still wealthy in the context of the broader region beyond the walls, and Mary le Port sat somewhere in the middle.[142] Unfortunately, aside from one return from 1564, the tax returns for Bristol do not generally include the external wards. Nonetheless, no coastal traders appeared outside of the walls during 1564 and, while we cannot say for certain that coastal traders did not reside outside of the five core wards, this omission is telling and supports Sacks' research that places traders and marketeers in the central parishes.[143]

Taking the socio-economic geography of the port into account, it is again possible to assess the correlation between levels of wealth, nature of commercial activity, and physical location within the town. As in Southampton, we can assume that a move from a poorer area into a wealthier area represented an

---

[139] Unlike Southampton, each Bristol ward spanned a number of the small parishes into which the town was divided. Moreover, the Bristol parish boundaries changed fairly significantly over the course of the sixteenth, seventeenth and eighteenth centuries, were far more complex than the parishes of Southampton, and no single study has conclusively determined where the boundaries lay during the Tudor period. Nonetheless, it has been possible to reconstruct the approximate positions of the wards using records from the Bristol Record Office. The four northern wards were divided by four streets, namely, Corn Street, Wine Street, High Street, and Broad Street. BRO BristolPlans/Arranged/193, BristolPlans/Arranged/234, BristolPlans/Arranged/237; Christian D. Liddy, *War, Politics and Finance in Late Medieval English Towns: Bristol, York and the Crown, 1350–1400* (Woodbridge: Boydell Press, 2005), pp. 82–83.

[140] Liddy.

[141] Peter Fleming, 'Time, Space and Power in Later Medieval Bristol', *Working Paper*, University of the West of England (2013), www.eprints.uwe.ac.uk/22171/2/TimeSpacePowerFinalVersion%20%283%29.pdf (accessed 2 April 2019), pp. 160–82.

[142] Ibid., p. 180.

[143] Sacks, pp. 147–53.

improvement in personal circumstances. Therefore, we would expect that a move from Holy Trinity or Mary le Port into any of the other three wards would coincide with increased wealth, and a move in the reverse direction would coincide with lower levels of affluence. This applied to a number of coastal traders that lived within the town, and their lay subsidy valuations allow us to determine their levels of wealth and ward residences. For example, merchant Dominic Chester resided in Holy Trinity in 1560 and 1568, during which time his lay subsidy valuation increased from £5 to £15, enabling him to make the move to the wealthier ward of All Saints, where he was again valued at £15 in 1571. However, John Webb moved from All Saints to Mary le Port and, between those returns, his valuation dropped from £5 to £4. Likewise, Robert Smith and John White both moved from the wealthy ward of All Saints to the poorer ward of Holy Trinity and, over that period, their valuations decreased (from £10 to £6 for Smith, and from £6 to £3 for White).[144]

However, wealth was not the only factor that influenced the residences of individuals within the town, and three examples demonstrate that occupations and commercial activity also had a bearing on residency. First, Thomas Pitt moved between the wealthy wards of Mary Redcliff and All Saints, and his valuation remained steady at £10. Pitt was a wealthy Bristol draper, shipowner, and chamberlain to the town, and so his tendency to reside within wealthy wards is unsurprising.[145] Yet, while Pitt's valuation remained constant, his occupation as defined by the customs officials changed over time and he was more frequently referred to as a draper during the period in which he was listed as residing in Redcliff, and more frequently referred to as a merchant when he lived in All Saints.[146]

Given that Pitt's will shows that he leased at least two properties in Redcliff (including *The Saracen's Head* pub), he probably had property in both wards, but Hoyle has shown that the residence listed in the lay subsidy return tended to be the principal home of the individual at the time of the assessment.[147] Therefore, his move from the ward most associated with the cloth industry to the ward most associated with maritime trade coincided with a perceived

---

[144] TNA E179/115/355 mem.2, E179/115/368 mem.2, E179/115/373 mem.2, 4, E179/115/386 mem.2.

[145] Edythe J. R. Whitley, *Red River Settlers: Records of the Settlers of Northern Montgomery, Robertson, and Sumner Counties, Tennessee* (Baltimore: Genealogical Publishing Company, 1980), p. 61.

[146] TNA E190/1128/14 fol.10r, 11r, E190/1130/2 fol.5r, 8v.

[147] John Bennett Boddie, *Seventeenth Century Isle of Wight County, Virginia: A History of the County of Isle of Wight, Virginia, during the Seventeenth Century, Including Abstracts of the County Records* (Chicago: Genealogical Publishing Company, 1973), pp. 505–10; Hoyle, *Tudor Taxation Records: A Guide for Users*, p. 33.

change of occupation in the eyes of the customs officials, suggesting that he may have adjusted his personal circumstances to accommodate a shift away from cloth production and towards broader mercantile activity. That Pitt's valuation remained at the high rate of £10 is reflective of the fact that he was part of an established mercantile family and, in this case, it seems that his move was a practical response to the type of activity he was undertaking, rather than a reflection of his level of affluence.

Similarly, Anthony Hodge and William Watford both moved into Holy Trinity from traditionally more wealthy wards during the early 1570s (Watford from All Saints and Hodge from St Ewen's), although their lay subsidy valuations remained steady.[148] Both men were brewers and engaged in coastal commerce to support their principal careers by shipping barley and hops from Gloucestershire into Bristol. Furthermore, both individuals frequently utilised the services of Thomas Swanley as shipmaster, who we saw in Chapter 4 forged a career through catering to Bristol brewers.[149] We shall see below that brewers tended to congregate in Holy Trinity and that the individuals with whom the Swanleys interacted were particularly likely to reside in that ward. Neither Watford nor Hodge appeared in the coastal port books before 1570, and then traded extensively over 1571, 1572 and 1576.[150] The reasons for this sudden increase are not clear, but those dates correlate with their moves between wards and with a sudden increase in interaction with the Swanley family. Such residence patterns suggest that individuals gravitated towards those parts of the town that were most closely associated with the industry to which they were connected, and support suggestions made in Chapter 4 that geographic proximity between individuals had a bearing on the formation of network ties.

Finally, Dominic Chester was from a wealthy Bristol mercantile family. He was bequeathed a Dominican friary by his father and held some significant social stature but was less prominent than his brother Thomas, and did not begin trading until the late 1540s, by which time he was probably in his forties or fifties. Chester resided in the poorer ward of Holy Trinity in 1560 but moved to the wealthier ward of All Saints in 1568 and still resided in All Saints in 1571. Over this time, his valuation increased from £5 to £15, and this correlated with a significant increase in his maritime activity that saw him trade to Spain, France and the Iberian Peninsula, although he died in 1575.[151] While it was not a single notable event that saw Chester rise to prominence, his

---

[148] TNA E179/115/373 mem.2, 4, E179/115/386 mem. 2.
[149] TNA E190/1128/13 fol.13v, 15r, 16r, E190/1129/1 fol.3r, 6v–7v, 9r, 14r-v.
[150] TNA E190/1128/13 fol.13v, 15r, 16r, E190/1129/1 fol.3r, 6v–7v, 9r, 14r-v.
[151] TNA E179/115/355 mem.2, E179/115/373 mem.4, E179/115/386 mem.3; Joe Inwood, 'The Chesters of Bristol: A Tudor Merchant Dynasty' (BA thesis, University of Bristol, 2006), pp. 45–51.

THE SOCIO-ECONOMIC POSITION OF COASTAL TRADERS 187

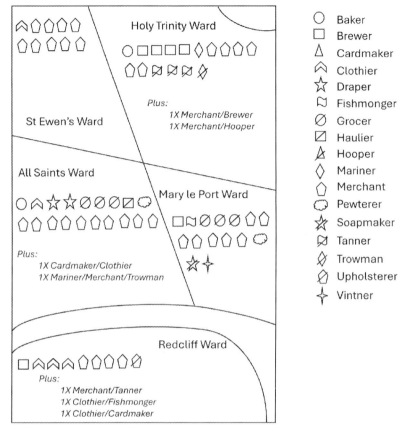

Map 5.3. Ward residences of coastal traders living in Bristol, organised by occupation.

movement in the town is reflective of his broad career development, although this was largely in overseas, rather than coastal, commerce.

These specific case studies suggest that individuals from different occupations may have, in some cases, been drawn to particular parts of the town for practical reasons related to their occupation, and this idea is supported further by broader evidence from the Bristol port books, as shown in Map 5.3.[152]

---

[152] There are two methodological factors of Map 5.3 that should be noted. First, for those individuals for whom two residences are recorded, the most pertinent location at the time in which the individual was trading in Bristol has been noted. For example, John Rowland appeared in the lay subsidy return of 1568 in Mary le Port and the return of 1572 in All Saints. As Rowland was most active in Bristol's coastal trade between 1570 and 1572, his residency from the 1572 return has been noted. Secondly,

Four groups are of particular interest here and are explored separately below: merchants, brewers, mariners, and individuals involved in the cloth industry.

First, individuals from mercantile occupations (including clothiers, drapers, grocers and vintners) were clearly attracted to the wealthiest wards. In the most affluent wards of St Ewen's, All Saints and Redcliff, more than 83% of the traders identified were allocated mercantile occupations. In the middling-wealth ward of Mary le Port, that figure dropped to 81%, and in the poorer ward of Holy Trinity, it reduced to 44%. This meshes with the social geography established in Southampton, whereby the mercantile community dominated the wealthier parts of the town and individuals from lesser occupations occupied poorer regions. This not only supports assumptions regarding the wealth and social status of different occupational groups but also feeds back to the networking chapter above and highlights that coastal traders tended to operate within communities somewhat defined by their occupations.

For example, occupational merchants John Bodell and Nicholas Blake both resided in Mary le Port, and we saw in Chapter 4 that they appeared on a multi-merchant voyage together, indicating some form of business partnership.[153] Likewise, merchants Luke Cocks and Edward Roberts also shared a voyage and both resided in Redcliff ward.[154] This was not the case for all Bristol traders and indeed many individuals identified as occupational merchants interacted with other traders without any discernible pattern of interaction, but these two examples suggest that propinquity played some role in the formation of business ties.

Secondly, although All Saints mostly contained individuals of mercantile occupations, it was also home to a number of coastal traders who were engaged in non-mercantile crafts, including a brewer, a pewterer and a haulier. However, these were unusual and most craftspeople gathered in the less affluent wards, with most brewers residing in Holy Trinity. Moreover, three of the brewers that lived in that ward (William Blast, Anthony Hodge and William Watford) were those that most consistently engaged in coastal commerce and they also appeared in the Swanley networks discussed in Chapter 4.[155] The other two

---

several individuals appear listed in the port books with more than one occupation. In these cases, the nodes have been split to indicate the various occupational titles that were allocated. See E190/1128/13 fol.17v, E190/1128/14 fol.11v, E190/1129/1 fol.7v.

[153] TNA E190/1128/12 fol.16r, E190/1128/13 fol.20v–21r, E190/1128/14 fol.14r–16r, E190/1129/1 fol.13v, 17r–18r, E190/1129/18 fol.16r–17v, 19v, E190/1129/20 fol.5r, E190/1129/22 fol.5v–6v, 12r–13v, E190/1130/2 fol.7v, 9v 10v, E179/115/373 mem. 2, 3.

[154] TNA E190/1128/14 fol.15r, E179/115/386 mem.6.

[155] William Blast was by far the most prolific, undertaking sixteen voyages between Bristol and Gloucestershire across the dataset, followed by Anthony Hodge at six voyages, and William Watford at five. For completeness, Thomas Balding appears three times, Simon Habert and Robert Smith twice, and John Stone just once. TNA

Holy Trinity brewers (Robert Smith and Simon Habert) did not engage with the Swanleys, but their engagement in coastal commerce was minimal, and they appeared in the dataset for just two voyages each.[156] This suggests that the brewers engaged in the Swanley networks mostly centred on the ward of Holy Trinity, and it may have been that their close physical proximity enabled the Swanleys to so successfully penetrate the Bristol brewing market. Thomas Balding is the clear exception to this rule as he was both very prolific in coastal trading and was tied to the Swanleys, but he resided in Mary le Port. However, Thomas Balding first traded coastwise in August 1569 and immediately employed the services of Thomas Swanley, suggesting that he may have been part of the same community, even if he resided apart from the other brewers investigated here.

As has already been noted, difficulties in ensuring reliable nominal linkage mean that very few occupational mariners have been identified. However, we can add to the mariner nodes visible in Map 5.3 the two shipmasters displayed in Map 5.2 who resided in St Ewen's. Although the port books lack occupational titles for shipmasters, evaluation of data provided by the Medieval and Tudor Ships Project suggests that these two men were probably career mariners (at least insofar as their practical engagement in maritime trade was concerned).[157] Therefore, although the data for mariners is limited, there is some suggestion of maritime clustering in the northern wards, and especially in St Ewen's. Since St Ewen's was close to the waterfront, it makes sense that mariners would be keen to reside there, but the fact that they too appeared in the wealthiest wards in the town suggests that those who engaged in coastal commercial activity as shipmasters could occupy a privileged social position. This data again supports assertions made above that occupational mariners clustered in specific parts of the town, forming 'proto-sailor towns', and that merchants were very often attracted to those same areas, occupying the same social space and adding weight to the suggestion that they were part of the same community.[158]

Finally, owing to the specific socio-geographic character of Bristol, individuals engaged in the cloth industry also require brief mention. As discussed above, Liddy and others have highlighted that Redcliff ward was dominated by the cloth industry from as early as the thirteenth century, and the coastal data assessed here supports that assertion for the later period.[159] Of

---

E190/1128/12 fol.2v, 4v, 6v–7v, 8r, 13r, E190/1128/13 fol.1v, 5r, 12r, 13r–13v, 15r, 16r, 18r, 20v, E190/1128/14 fol.4r, 5v, 7r, 9v, E190/1129/1 fol.3r, 6v–9r, 14r–4v, E190/1129/18 fol.2r, 4r.

[156] TNA E190/1128/12 fol.7r, 8r, E190/1129/18 fol.2r, 4r.
[157] Lambert and Baker, www.medievalandtudorships.org.
[158] Lambert, 'Tudor Shipmasters and Maritime Communities, 1550–1600'.
[159] Liddy, pp. 82–83.

the twelve men identified as living in Redcliff, six were listed with occupations linked to the cloth industry (three clothiers, one upholsterer, one clothier/fishmonger, and one clothier/cardmaker). Individuals listed as clothiers and drapers did reside in other wards, but Redcliff was dominated by traders that worked within that sphere, again supporting the assessment that the town was somewhat divided by occupational group.

Conclusion

This chapter has tied together the previous strands of analysis concerning the nature of English coastal commerce and of the individuals that allowed that trade to function. More specifically, it has examined the socio-economic and socio-political positions of coastal traders that resided within the case study ports, including their occupations, levels of wealth, and residences. Owing to the limitations present in the sources relating to Hull, analysis of occupations and residential data has focused on Southampton and Bristol, with analysis of Hull coastal traders taking a slightly different form, focusing largely on case study groups and individuals within the port, rather than analysing overarching figures relating to the socio-economic position of coastal traders. Nonetheless, utilising the data that can be obtained from the port books, the lay subsidy returns, and a body of local civic sources, it has been possible to observe significant trends and themes present across all three regions.

First, we have seen that occupational titles that were applied to merchants and shipmasters by civic authorities were somewhat varied, suggesting that coastal traders were drawn from a number of separate occupational communities and formed a complex social group. In particular, the vigilant record keeping of the Bristol customs officials allowed us to evaluate in more detail the specific nature of the occupational titles that were allocated to coastal traders, and the ways in which those titles related to their practical trading activities within the port. We saw that a number of the distinctive occupations assigned to coastal traders in the Bristol port books were linked to their maritime activities. For example, clothiers principally traded in textile products, vintners in wine, grocers in foodstuffs, tanners and shoemakers in leather, and brewers and maltmakers in grain.

However, the categorisation of individuals into certain groups did not always reflect the practical coastal activities of the individuals involved. For example, drapers transported large mixed cargoes that rarely contained textile products, and those listed as mariner, trowmen or maltmaker were indistinguishable from one another, trading on the same routes, carrying the same goods, utilising the same ships, and running their businesses in the same ways. This was also true in Southampton, where a number of the traders that appeared in the coastal port books as merchants were principally engaged in other occupations, and some were listed in various civic sources as being both merchants and members of other occupational groups. Those individuals engaged in coastal commercial activity to varying extents, with some becoming career coastal traders, some being more primarily focused on overseas trade, and some being foremost concerned with another craft.

Likewise, this also applied to Southampton shipmasters, many of whom engaged in work that directly benefited from or was beneficial to a maritime career, such as a secondary occupation as a publican, or a primary career as a fisherman.[160] This suggests that individuals partaking in coastal commerce, including occupational mariners, could be enterprising and entrepreneurial, often seeking multiple revenue streams and adjusting their operational approaches in order to engage in different forms of trade. These are characteristics that have generally been reserved for the mercantile elite and, while various recent scholars have acknowledged that maritime and mercantile occupations could overlap, few have appreciated the occupational breadth of the broader seafaring community.[161]

Indeed, across almost all occupational groups in Southampton and Bristol, a large number of individuals either routinely or occasionally acted in both the capacity of shipmaster and the capacity of merchant on their voyages. This serves to demonstrate that individuals that engaged in coastal commerce came from eclectic commercial backgrounds and had the skill, means, and desire to participate in the maritime industry, with an operational approach that suited their business models. However, in Bristol, this overlap applied mostly to individuals from outside of the port itself, and primarily to those from Gloucestershire, Worcestershire and the West Midlands. Those traders were most substantially involved in coastal commerce, running numerous trips per year, and tending to operate on established routes carrying the same commodities.

Conversely, Bristol traders were often members of the mercantile elite or craftspeople who utilised coastal trade to accommodate their principal

---

[160] Brown, pp. 90, 109–10.

[161] Although it still often prevails, many historians have now challenged the notion of seafarers as typically drunk and incompetent; however, broad perceptions of coastal commercial activity are often disparaging. See Andrews, 'The Elizabethan Seaman', pp. 245–47; Ian Friel, *Maritime History of Britain and Ireland, c. 400–2001* (London: British Museum Press, 2003), pp. 98–102; Cheryl A. Fury, 'Introduction', in *The Social History of English Seamen, 1485–1649*, ed. by Cheryl A. Fury (Woodbridge: Boydell Press, 2012), pp. 302–03; Fury, 'The Elizabethan Maritime Community', pp. 118–21; Fury, 'Training and Education in the Elizabethan Maritime Community, 1585–1603'; Lambert, 'Tudor Shipmasters and Maritime Communities, 1550–1600'; Craig Lambert and Andrew Ayton, 'The Mariner in Fourteenth Century England', in *Fourteenth Century England*, ed. by Mark Ormrod (Woodbridge: Boydell Press, 2012), pp. 153–77 (pp. 153–56); Ward.

occupations, neither of whom routinely took command of ships themselves, although some members of the Bristol elite did occasionally demonstrate dual skillsets. This activity sits in stark contrast to the activities of those who travelled through Southampton, where various individuals from the port itself, and some of significant social stature, had the skill and desire to act in both capacities some or all of the time. Furthermore, while there is little evidence that members of the Bristol mercantile elite engaged with regularity in coastal commerce, we see various examples in Southampton of wealthy and well-established merchants undertaking extensive coastal activity, with some even becoming career coastal traders.

That being said, the commercial landscape in Hull was slightly more cleanly divided than in Southampton and Bristol and the operational approaches individuals applied to their coastal commercial activity differed from group to group depending on the trade with which they were associated. In the case of trade with Newcastle, the exceptionally low value of coal prompted individuals to routinely act as both shipmaster and merchant and to undertake only single-merchant voyages. On the other hand, those that traded between London and Hull, and those who participated in the sporadic transportation of grains, tended to hire shipmasters and vessels *ad hoc*, in line with the typical operational approach we have seen among members of the mercantile elite in all three case study ports.

Indeed, in both Hull and Bristol, members of the civic elite participated in the transportation of grains and usually hired shipmasters per voyage for those shipments. Grain was a necessary product in every region of the kingdom and during times of dearth the market for grain was especially buoyant. In both Bristol and Hull, this was a strong enough pull for individuals that did not routinely trade along the coast to engage in coastwise voyages, or for those that typically engaged in another form of trade to shift their focus. As we have seen throughout this volume, participation in coastal commercial activity took many forms, and certain commodities attracted particular demographics and behaviours. This can be seen clearly in the opportunistic transportation of grain, where individuals with little interest in domestic exchange would occasionally dabble in particular trades for financial, social or political reasons.

Secondly, in terms of wealth and socio-political influence, we have seen that, across all three case study ports and in Gloucester, merchants were generally wealthier than shipmasters, and occupational merchants wealthier than occupational mariners and craftspeople. That being said, although the richest shipmasters could rarely compete with the wealthiest merchants, a number of shipmasters in all four towns were able to accumulate substantial wealth. In particular, in Southampton, those shipmasters that accumulated the most wealth and social standing were very often also involved in the sale and distribution of alcohol, acting as publicans of various sorts, demonstrating the advantages of dual occupations. Likewise, in Hull, while the shipmasters that worked on the Hull/London trade route were of minimal wealth and influence compared to the mercantile elite for whom they commanded voyages, they were often wealthy enough to pay tax and to invest in vessels, suggesting some degree of affluence. Indeed, in all four ports, traders from a broad array of occupational groups were able to accumulate at least enough wealth to be tax-liable and many were able to accumulate substantially larger sums. Individuals from the full socio-economic spectrum engaged in coastal commerce and, in some cases, it formed a substantial part of their business models and enabled them to establish lucrative maritime careers.

Nonetheless, merchants were undoubtedly the wealthiest individuals to engage in coastal exchange, and those with a primary interest in overseas trade were usually the most affluent. Moreover, occupational merchants tended to be more engaged in local politics than mariners and craftspeople and thus occupied a higher socio-political position. However, this did vary between ports and while members of the mercantile elite in Bristol were largely engaged in overseas trade, those from Gloucester were more focused on coastal activity, owing to the commercial nature of those regions, as discussed in Chapter 2. As a result, there was a stark difference in levels of wealth available to Bristol traders compared to Gloucester traders. Comparing like-for-like, individuals from each occupational group in Bristol were wealthier than individuals from Gloucester. Thus, while some traders in both ports fitted into the category of civic elite within their towns, and the wealthiest Gloucester traders were especially affluent in the context of their wards, they were of a lesser status than their Bristol counterparts.

Likewise, in Southampton, substantial wealth and socio-political influence could also be obtained via a career in coastal trading. This is evidenced best by the case of merchant John Knight, who was able to rise through the political ranks and achieve substantial personal wealth through his role in the supply of Wealdon iron. This contradicts the established narrative that places coastal traders in the lower orders of society, unable to earn a substantial living or to engage in local politics, and highlights the broad range of individuals that found coastal trading to be an appealing form of commercial activity in which to engage.

This was also evident in Hull, where merchants that engaged in trade between London and Hull tended to be both wealthy and politically inclined and can be considered members of the mercantile elite. As trade with London centred on high-value commodities, it tended to attract wealthier and well-established merchants. Some of the individuals involved in coastal trade between London and Hull were of exceptional regional significance, contributing substantial sums of money to the town, becoming mayors, aldermen, and even MPs, and in some cases becoming tied into London politics. In particular, William Gee, Thomas Dalton and Robert Dalton were able to assert much influence in the region and were respected members of the mercantile community. As shown in Chapter 4, these individuals were at the centre of the London trade networks and the sources consulted in this chapter suggest that their desirability as commercial partners owed not just to their exceptional wealth and social standing, but also to their personable approaches to business.

Conversely, individuals that engaged in the Newcastle coal trade fitted into two distinctive groups, based on the frequency of their participation. However, there was very little difference in the socio-economic characteristics of those two factions. In both cases, traders were generally associated with ports in the immediate geographic region, including Hull, Newcastle, York, Keadby and Scarborough, and many appear to have owned or part-owned the vessels on which they traded. These ships typically measured over 30 tons, which was unusually large for coasters in other major ports at this time, as shown in Chapter 2. Thus, on the surface, these traders were in a position to gain substantial wealth and influence; they were clearly skilled mariners as they could command large vessels in difficult waters, but also had sufficient wealth to invest in both their own product and their own vessels. However, although many coal traders appear to have resided in Hull, there is a decided lack of reference to them in local civic sources, suggesting that they were of limited socio-political influence.

Moreover, while several coal traders appeared in the lay subsidy returns, and were thus wealthy enough to be tax-liable, the levels of personal wealth they could achieve were limited. Some coal traders did rank among the wealthiest in their specific wards, but they were all valued substantially lower than individuals that engaged in trade with London. As we have seen throughout, this resulted from the commodities transported and the low value of coal meant that profits per voyage were somewhat limited. While the opportunity to engage in the trade in Newcastle coal was abundant and the investment needed was relatively low, it was not necessarily a sure path to great wealth.

Finally, in terms of inner-town residences, we have seen some degree of occupational clustering in particular wards in both Bristol and Southampton. In Southampton, shipmasters and merchants were both particularly likely to reside in the wards of St Michael/St John and Holy Rood, whereas individuals from non-mercantile and non-maritime occupational groups were spread more broadly across the town. Local histories have identified those two wards as the maritime hubs of the port, and that trend is here supported through quantitative analysis.[162] Likewise, in Bristol, there is some evidence that mariners were especially drawn to the ward of St Ewen's, and much evidence to suggest that

---

[162] Brown, pp. 34–36.

merchants were drawn to the wealthy wards of All Saints and Mary le Port, especially in the case of occupational merchants.

In addition, merchants that were engaged in the transportation of textile products were primarily drawn to Mary Redcliff, which was the traditional centre of the cloth industry. This is also evident among craftspeople, who mostly resided in the middling or poorer wards and often gravitated towards wards containing other individuals from within their occupational groups. This was especially true in the case of brewers, who were particularly likely to congregate in the ward of Holy Trinity. These figures support proposals from maritime historians that seafarers tended to reside in the same areas within ports and form so-called 'proto-sailor towns', and suggest that many merchants occupied those same physical spaces, further complicating the notion that maritime and mercantile communities were markedly separate.[163]

Furthermore, aside from allowing us to observe occupational clustering within the town, residential data also provides a means through which to evaluate the impact of career changes on the personal circumstances of coastal traders. In various cases, movement between wards of different wealth levels coincided with corresponding shifts in lay subsidy valuation and, in some cases, correlated with levels of engagement in specific forms of commercial activity. For example, various brewers moved into Bristol's Holy Trinity ward from other parts of the town and this change in residency generally correlated with increased engagement in the coastal transportation of grains into Bristol and increased interaction with the Gloucestershire mariners at the centre of that trade.

---

[163] Fury, 'The Elizabethan Maritime Community', p. 128; Lambert, 'Tudor Shipmasters and Maritime Communities, 1550–1600'.

6

Conclusions

The aim of this volume has been to provide a broad evaluation of the nature of coastal trading in the years preceding England's establishment as a global maritime empire. In order to achieve this aim, the volume tackled three principal objectives:

1. To establish the commercial nature of coastal trading activity in Bristol, Southampton and Hull in the late sixteenth century.
2. To understand how coastal traders and shipmasters ran their businesses. In particular, how they forged and maintained business networks.
3. To assess the socio-political and socio-economic position of individuals that engaged in coastal trading, and challenge our established notions of what it meant to be a merchant during the Tudor period.

Analysis of diverse national and local sources within the framework of these three core objectives has allowed us to draw far-reaching conclusions regarding the nature of coastal enterprise in three ports of commercial, social and political importance during the 1560s, 1570s and 1580s. However, this volume has also served to highlight the unique character of individual port towns during this period and, in doing so, demonstrates the dangers of studies that focus on a single port and assume that the same characteristics of trade existed elsewhere. Not only did the commercial nature of each port depend heavily on its geographic position and socio-political development over many centuries, but those long-term commercial developments had a huge impact on both the operational nature of the trade undertaken and the socio-political and socio-economic character of the individuals involved.

In other words, although English ports were interconnected, the ways in which individuals engaged in trade through each port hinged on the specific commercial, social and political features of the region. Moreover, individual shipmasters and merchants readily adjusted their business approaches to account for the differences between regions, supporting the assertion that the situation in each port had a direct and measurable impact on the nature of the trade undertaken. Nonetheless, there are a number of overarching trends that can be observed in all three ports that constitute the chief findings of this volume, although regionally specific observations can also be found throughout the chapters above.

This volume has demonstrated that coastwise trade through Southampton, Bristol and Hull was abundant during the latter half of the sixteenth century and that all three ports acted as vital meeting points for the collection and redistribution of goods. In particular, Southampton was central in the supply of arms and defences to the naval port of Portsmouth and the vulnerable Isle of Wight, and in the supply of necessary provisions to the Channel Islands, as well as in the distribution of metal products, including Cornish tin and Sussex iron. Likewise, Bristol played a pivotal role in providing much-needed supplies to the regions inland on the River Severn, was central to the import of leather and cloth products from Wales, and represented an important market for the sale of grain from the surrounding region, as well as for overseas products sourced from various far-reaching domestic ports. Owing to its more limited overseas trade links, the nature of coastal commercial activity through Hull took a slightly different form, and the port principally acted as a gateway to the Humber river system and to the numerous towns in its vast hinterland. This trade largely centred on the transportation of coal and salt from Newcastle and the supply of luxury goods sourced from London, although Hull also provided shipbuilding materials to Whitby. Nonetheless, although the commercial character of Hull was slightly different from Bristol or Southampton, it was an extremely busy provincial port and played a central role in the maritime activity of the region.

Owing to the importance of these ports both within their own regions and within the wider kingdom, a broad array of sources survive that have provided a strong body of data through which to explore engagement in coastal maritime activity. Analysis of this data suggests that coastal commercial enterprise was highly flexible. Even some of the most specialised traders examined here occasionally altered their trading patterns to take advantage of alternative commercial activity. For example, while River Severn traders almost exclusively traded between Bristol and the Severn ports, some would occasionally travel further afield when the opportunity arose. Likewise, those that specialised in the Hampshire trade would opportunistically trade in Sussex iron, and Hull traders across a broad spectrum would occasionally carry Newcastle coal. As a result, historians have traditionally deemed coastal trading to have been poorly organised, chaotic, and undertaken by individuals who were unskilled and lacked business acumen. However, this volume has repeatedly shown that this perceived lack of organisation was the result of a highly adaptive approach that was, in fact, deliberate and premeditated. For example, we have seen that many merchants who typically transported shipments of only their own commodities would occasionally collaborate with other traders in order to reduce risk when carrying high-value cargoes or when travelling on high-risk trade routes. Likewise, on occasions when low-value coal was transported into Southampton or Hull, individuals acted as both shipmaster and merchant in order to reduce outgoings and ensure reasonable profit margins.

Furthermore, this did not just apply to specific commodities, but traders also adjusted for regional differences. For example, in Bristol, where coal production, supply and distribution took a very different form from that in Southampton or Hull, we do not see these same patterns, and coal was instead carried among other products in the same way that any other mixed-cargo voyages were undertaken. Similarly, although Bristol and Southampton both had established ties to Cornish and Devon ports, the commodities traded into and out of those regions varied substantially. Thus, those trading into Cornwall/Devon from Bristol and those trading into Cornwall/Devon from Southampton adopted different approaches to suit the nature of that trade. In addition, both dedicated coastal traders and those that were principally concerned with either overseas activity or non-maritime crafts shifted their network ties to suit the trade in which they wished to participate.

For example, in all three ports, networks shifted and expanded during periods of increased overall trade and individuals that were not dedicated coastal traders were drawn into coastal commerce. These individuals formed network ties within the case study towns or from the towns into which they wished to trade and thus sought out individuals with appropriate backgrounds in order to extend their reach. Even coastal traders with well-established business networks sought out individuals of relevant expertise, resources and contacts when they decided to pursue trade routes outside of their usual *modus operandi*.

Coastal traders also adapted their operational approach with regard to the ships they utilised on particular trade routes. In Southampton and Bristol, larger ships were used on voyages between ports of major commercial significance, where engagement in overseas activity was plentiful. Likewise, the Hull/London trade was undertaken on ships of fairly substantial tonnage and that route also involved the exchange of overseas goods. However, between ports of lesser commercial significance that had fewer overseas trade links, smaller vessels were more common. For example, Southampton's trade with Poole or the Isle of Wight was typically undertaken on much larger ships than trade with Weymouth or Lyme Regis. Likewise, Bristol's trade with the River Severn ports attracted much smaller ships than its trade with Plymouth, Cardiff or Milford Haven.

Moreover, the vessels utilised on specific trade routes were also determined in some cases by the nature of the commodities transported or the geographic character of the region. In particular, the dominance of coal in the North East created a need for exceptionally large vessels on the route from Newcastle to Hull. Likewise, vessels that traded between Southampton and Portsmouth were unusually large, owing to the bulky nature of the ordnance and metals that they typically carried. In contrast, ships that travelled inland from Bristol using the Severn river network were necessarily smaller in order to navigate the region's complex inland waterways.

Importantly, that coastal traders could adapt their operational approach to suit the specific trade in which they wished to engage often owed to the overlap between maritime and mercantile communities. Indeed, the often-perceived barrier between communities of seafarers and merchants has been reinforced by a historiographical bias towards large-scale, wealthy and politically inclined members of the mercantile and maritime elite. However, acknowledgement of individuals that do not fit into that traditional image complicates the established narrative and causes us to question the assumed lack of cohesion between mariners and merchants. Moreover, the frequency with which individuals from non-maritime occupations acted in the capacity of shipmaster or merchant supports the assertion that otherwise disparate groups came together via coastal commerce.

A diverse range of traders were involved in coastwise voyages with varying degrees of regularity, but they often demonstrated similar levels of skill and knowledge and similar networking capabilities. In Southampton, publicans, fishermen and bakers frequently appeared as merchants and shipmasters on coastal voyages, along with a range of individuals from other occupations, including the town's tallow chandler. Likewise, in Bristol, brewers, tanners, shoemakers, maltmakers and trowmen engaged frequently in coastal trading, even beyond the transportation of commodities tied to their primary occupations. Source deficiencies make similar details difficult to ascertain for Hull, but the abundance of traders that casually engaged in coastal commerce for short periods suggests that individuals from other occupational groups were very likely involved.

Thus, in all three ports, persons from a broad occupational spectrum occupied the same trade routes, transported the same commodities, utilised the same vessels, engaged within the same networks, had similar levels of wealth and social status, and had a great deal of overlapping skill and knowledge. Many of the individuals examined here had the ability to command vessels, as well as the contacts and resources to act as merchants. The dividing line between merchant and seafarer in the world of coastal commerce was fine, and individuals could switch between roles as readily as they switched between trades. Individuals from all social levels, with varying access to ships and finance and from a plethora of occupational groups, were involved in coastal commercial activity. Coastal trading was attractive to many and the threshold for participation was often lower than for overseas trade, allowing individuals from the full socio-economic and socio-political spectrum to participate. There were, of course, elite members of the mercantile and maritime communities who rarely deviated from their anticipated activities, but there was a substantial grey area in the middle that was accommodated by the accessible nature of coastal commerce.

That being said, while there was a great deal of overlap in terms of skill, trade routes and commodities, and often a great deal of overlap in networks, there were also physical and societal boundaries between particular groups, even though they occupied the same broader space through their engagement in coastal enterprise. In particular, there is much evidence in Bristol and Southampton that certain wards attracted particular occupational groups. For example, in Southampton, occupational merchants and mariners occupied the wards of Holy Rood and St Michael/St John, and individuals from non-maritime occupations tended to reside elsewhere. In Bristol, individuals associated with the cloth industry tended to congregate in Redcliff ward, and brewers were most commonly found in Holy Trinity. Likewise, merchants and shipmasters tended to congregate in the northern wards, with occupational merchants being most numerous in Bristol's wealthiest areas and occupational mariners appearing to have a slight preference for St Ewen's.

Moreover, within the networks of Gloucestershire/Worcestershire/West Midlands individuals that traded into Bristol, there was a clear divide between mariners, trowmen, and maltmakers, and these groups almost exclusively operated within occupational networks. These networks engaged in the same trade routes, had the same operational approaches, and transported the same commodities, but had a clear preference to form business partnerships with members from their own occupational groups. Likewise, in Hull, there was a stark divide between those that traded between Hull and Newcastle and those that traded between Hull and London. While it is difficult to determine the residences of these individuals, they clearly sat within different socio-economic brackets and engaged in separate business networks. Many coastal traders across all three case study ports did sometimes adapt their networks to access alternative trade routes, but the most prolific coasters very often had a core group that they favoured and these usually remained stable over an extended period.

The combination of a community that was highly flexible in terms of its business approach, but that also frequently clustered into occupational networks, created a mix of strong and weak ties in the network graphs generated. In other words, individuals formed both long-term and short-term business partnerships. As mentioned, individuals elected to engage in coastal commerce in a variety of different ways and, in particular, the frequency with which traders undertook coastwise voyages fluctuated dramatically from trader to trader. Some individuals forged lifelong careers in coastal commerce, while others dipped into coasting opportunistically as an aside to another activity. As discussed in Chapter 3, the relatively low average figures for the voyages undertaken per shipmaster or merchant resulted from this broad spectrum of involvement. There was both a body of individuals dedicated to coastal trading that brought the average up and a substantial body of traders that engaged infrequently, dragging the average down. This did vary between trade routes and we saw particularly large bodies of traders dedicated to Southampton's Channel Island trade, Bristol's River Severn trade, and Hull's trade with Newcastle, but, generally, the range of engagement was diverse.

Moreover, intermittent engagement in coastal commerce often occurred during periods of increased commercial activity through the case study port. In turn, this resulted in the formation of larger and more complex networks, suggesting that propinquity (i.e. physical proximity) within the port played a role in network formation in all three regions. As key commercial centres, Southampton, Bristol and Hull acted as meeting points for traders with aligned business interests. However, as we have established, each port town was unique and the network formation that occurred varied somewhat from region to region. In Southampton, periods of heightened trade resulted in the formation of especially diverse mixed-residency networks as individuals from a broad region came together and forged more extensive network ties. This was particularly evident in the case of Southampton's trade with Sussex and heightened trade on that route resulted in the formation of both short-term and long-term cross-county partnerships.

However, in Bristol, where a large and assertive group of local merchants dominated, increased trade resulted in reduced cross-county integration as the Bristol elite drew traders from previously diverse networks into much larger networks dominated by locals. Analysis of this kind is more difficult to undertake in the case of Hull owing to a lack of residential data in the sources available, however, the size and structure of the networks formed suggest similar trends. In particular, increased levels of trade between London and Hull appeared to lower the threshold of experience required for shipmasters to penetrate the community of elite merchants that dominated that route, creating network ties between individuals that did not generally collaborate.

Those individuals that sat at the centre of coastwise trading also show that it was possible for traders to forge successful careers and gain substantial wealth by specialising in coastal commerce. Although not all traders who had a particular interest in coastal activity became exceptionally wealthy, many were tax-liable and a few were particularly affluent, becoming the richest in their wards and, in some cases, the wealthiest in their towns. Moreover, the fact that overseas traders who were valued upwards of £50 or £100 also engaged in coastal commerce suggests that coastwise voyages could be appealing to even members of the mercantile elite. However, at the other end of the spectrum, some individuals that were very prolific in coastal trade appear to have been of low socio-economic stature. In particular, although abundant, the transportation of coal did not necessarily translate into vast wealth and there was a clear socio-economic divide between Hull traders that travelled into Newcastle and those that travelled into London. This was also true of Bristol's trade with the Severn ports, where career coastal traders were often wealthy in the context of their local towns, but much poorer than their counterparts in Bristol. Yet, even in these cases, many traders dedicated a lifetime to those routes, never seeking higher-reward voyages and remaining committed to those trades.

Each of these points leads to the conclusion that our preconceptions of coastal trading and of coastal traders as small-scale, insignificant, and lacking business acumen or maritime skill have been based on a body of literature that failed to look directly at the individuals to whom those assertions apply. It is true that coastal trading was highly adaptive and, without close source analysis, appears chaotic, but the capability of individuals to adapt should not be confused with a lack of order. Indeed, many opted to pursue a career in coastal trading because they could earn wealth through engagement with a branch of maritime trade that was often more stable than overseas commerce. Some individuals did decide to transition from coastal trading into overseas activity, escalating their business ventures to higher-risk and higher-reward voyages, but this was by no means the case for all coastal traders and many preferred to remain in safer waters.

Moreover, English commercial maritime success relied on both types of individual. Ambitions of commercial expansion could not rely only on large-scale voyages to distant lands but also required an army of smaller-scale traders to continue that trade in domestic waters. Each port contained a body of traders who reached (and in some cases over-reached) for greater affluence and a body of individuals who formed more stable long-term trading patterns within the confines of domestic exchange, and each port required both groups to ensure success in their principal trading activities.

Furthermore, those that engaged in coastal commercial activity hailed from a broad range of backgrounds, socio-economic positions, and occupational groups. Yet individuals from across this spectrum demonstrated a broad range of skills, with many able to act in both the capacity of merchant and shipmaster, bridging the gap between maritime, mercantile and craft communities. Likewise, they demonstrated an extensive corpus of knowledge that allowed them to switch between trade routes and commodities and adapt their operational approach to take full advantage of those opportunities. Many merchants had the skills required to command their own vessels, and many mariners had the motivation and capability to act in the capacity of merchant, running important commodities on key trade routes. This ability to adapt to specific trades also extended to their capacity to adjust their networks and, in many cases, the coming together in a central location allowed for this possibility.

In the broadest sense, this volume has called into question our understanding of the social structure of port towns, and thus of wider Tudor society. The accessible nature of coastal commercial activity meant that individuals from every part of the town and from almost every occupational group engaged in maritime trade, and it is difficult to assert that any individual living in a port could have been immune from the maritime industry. Coastal trading was not the preserve of the rich or formally trained, but was available as a viable option for individuals from all walks of life, regardless of occupational background or level of wealth, calling into question the imagined divide between merchant, mariner, and craftsperson. Moreover, individuals from all communities forged operational approaches that were specific to particular trade routes and commodities, demonstrating that they had knowledge and understanding of the running of a maritime business. Contrary to Ralph Davis' early assertions, English coastal trading was not 'thoroughly humdrum', but involved a great many skilled individuals who had the proficiency, capacity and desire to innovatively adapt to changing markets, ensuring the stability and continuity of the broader maritime industry.[1]

---

[1] Davis, p. 11.

APPENDIX A:
PORT BOOKS ENTERED INTO THE DATABASE

The following table gives a full profile of the port books entered into the database.

	Bristol	**Southampton**	**Hull**
1568	None	30 September – 24 December No significant gaps Customer and controller TNA E190/814/5	28 September – 23 December No significant gaps Customer and controller TNA E190/305/1
1569	1 April – 26 September No significant gaps Customer and controller TNA E190/1128/12	4 January – 22 December No significant gaps Customer and controller TNA E190/814/5 TNA E190/814/6 TNA E190/814/7	3 January – 19 April No significant gaps Customer and controller TNA E190/305/1
1570	29 March – 22 December No significant gaps Customer and controller TNA E190/1128/13 TNA E190/1128/14	2 January – 27 March No significant gaps Customer and controller TNA E190/814/6	2 April – 18 December No significant gaps Customer and controller TNA E190/305/11 TNA E190/305/12

APPENDIX A

(*continued*)

	Bristol	**Southampton**	**Hull**
1571	2 January – 31 May No significant gaps Customer and controller TNA E190/1128/13	None	18 January – 13 December No significant gaps Customer and controller TNA E190/305/11 TNA E190/306/1 TNA E190/306/4
1572	9 April – 7 November No significant gaps Customer and controller TNA E190/1129/1	None	2 January – 12 July Patchy Customer and controller TNA E190/306/1
1573	None	None	1 October – 31 December No significant gaps Customer and controller TNA E190/306/16
1574	None	None	6 January – 30 December No significant gaps Customer and controller TNA E190/306/16 TNA E190/306/17 TNA E190/307/2
1575	None	8 April – 31 December No significant gaps Customer and controller TNA E190/814/11 TNA E190/814/12	4 January – 30 March No significant gaps Customer and controller TNA E190/307/2
1576	16 March – 14 December Customer and controller TNA E190/1129/18 TNA E190/1129/20	2 January – 25 September Customer and controller TNA E190/814/12 TNA E190/815/1	24 April – 4 October No significant gaps Customer and controller TNA E190/307/3

(*continued*)

	Bristol	**Southampton**	**Hull**
1577	2 January – 5 April No significant gaps Customer and controller TNA E190/1129/20 TNA E190/1129/22	11 April – 25 September No significant gaps Customer and controller TNA E190/815/2	7 October – 23 December No significant gaps Customer and controller TNA E190/307/9
1578	None	None	7 January – 26 March No significant gaps Customer and controller TNA E190/307/9
1579	20 August – 23 December No significant gaps Searcher TNA E190/1130/2	27 April – 28 September No significant gaps Customer and controller TNA E190/815/8	2 October – 29 December No significant gaps Customer and controller TNA E190/307/16
1580	2 January – 29 September No significant gaps Searcher TNA E190/1130/2	None	2 January – 7 April No significant gaps Customer and controller TNA E190/307/16

APPENDIX B: COMMODITIES TRADED BETWEEN PORTS

Southampton

Region	Port	Goods shipped into Southampton	Goods shipped out from Southampton
Dorset & Hampshire	Isle of Wight	Various, including French wine, malt and wool	Various, including salt, gunpowder, wine, currants, iron
	Lyme Regis	Green glass	Largely Azores woad and alum, some small quantities of wine and hides
	Poole	Largely wine and Azores woad, some salt, hides, green glass, hops and copper	Various, including lead, wine, Cornish tin, iron, hops, Spanish salt and Normandy glass
	Portsmouth	*None*	Largely iron and ordnance (including minions, falcons and shot) and building materials (including nails and timber)
	Weymouth	Wine (mostly from La Rochelle and Gascony), some green glasses	Firewood

APPENDIX B

Southampton (*continued*)

Region	Port	Goods shipped into Southampton	Goods shipped out from Southampton
London	London	Mixed cargoes, usually including building materials (including ropes, nails, shovels, tar, cables, clapboard, 'iron wares'), ordnance (including gunpowder, cannon, shot), soap, salt and luxury goods (including spices and currants)	Various, including lead, wine (usually French), Cornish tin, firewood, woad, and occasional luxury goods (such as spices or fruit)
Sussex	Sussex (except Chichester)	Iron and ordnance	Miscellaneous goods, including green glass, wine (including Malmsey, Gascon and Rochelle), wool, Spanish salt, bay salt (from Borgneuf), fish, Normandy canvas, Cornish tin, malt, wheat
Sussex	Chichester	Primarily wine, grains (including hops and malt) and animal hides, occasional shipments of iron	
South West	Cornwall	Cornish tin	Mixed cargoes including wheat, malt, bacon, hops, Sussex iron, Normandy glass, canvas, beer, hides, firewood and woad
South West	Devon	Primarily bay salt, some shipments of Cornish tin, millstones and wine	
Other	Channel Islands (Jersey and Guernsey)	*None*	Mostly beer and firewood, occasional shipments of cowhides, calfskins, leather, wheat, bacon, and green glass
Other	Hull	Coal	*None*
Other	Welsh ports (including Neath and Swansea)	Coal	Limited – one shipment found, containing barley

Bristol

Region	Port	Goods shipped into Bristol	Goods shipped out from Bristol
Gloucestershire, Worcestershire & the West Midlands	Bewdley	Manchester cottons and stockings, some calfskins and wine	Primarily wine (especially French, including from Gascony and La Rochelle), plus some shipments of cloth, lead, oil, soap, dry wares, and iron
	Bridgnorth	Mostly wool, some calfskins and wine	
	Worcester	Mostly white cloth, some wine	
	Tewkesbury	Grains (especially barley and wheat)	
	Gloucester	Grains (especially barley and rye)	Mixed cargoes, mostly carrying cloth, iron, oil, wine, soap, and luxury goods (such as pepper or brasil)
East	London	Limited – one shipment found, containing pitch and tar	Lead, wine and brasil
	Dover	*None*	Salt and barley
North	Crostwick	*None*	Frieze cloth and coal
	Millthrop	*None*	Train oil, iron, and pitch and tar
	Workington	Limited – one shipment containing salt, wool and rope	Grains and iron
Somerset	Bridgwater	Iron and wine	Cotton, wool, dry wares, iron, oil, soap and wine
	Minehead	Wool	Mostly iron, some salted fish and other miscellaneous goods

APPENDIX B

Bristol (*continued*)

Region	Port	Goods shipped into Bristol	Goods shipped out from Bristol
Devon	Plymouth	Mostly prunes and oil, some hides	'Smith's coals', grindstones, soap, nails and lead
	Barnstaple	Mixed cargoes, mostly oil and iron, some Spanish wool, luxury goods and wine	Mixed cargoes including grains, calfskins, dry wares, hides, linen, cloth, soap, iron, lead, pewter, wine and cotton
	Bideford	Wine	
Cornwall	Padstow	Cornish tin, salt and salmon	
Wales	Cardiff	Wool, leather and calfskins	Grains (mainly barley and wheat), calfskins, leather, brass, pewter and lead
	Chepstow	Mostly wine, some frieze cloth, leather and oil	Metals (including pewter and brass), linen, grains and haberdasher wares
	Aberthaw	*None*	Mixed cargoes, including cloth, iron, oil, wine, soap, alum, haberdasher wares, dry wares, grains, salt, canvas, linen, and other miscellaneous goods
	Carmarthen	Mostly frieze cloth, some wool, feathers, cotton, brass, lead, calfskins, lambskins and goatskins	
	Milford Haven	Mostly frieze cloth, wool, leather, lambskins and calfskins, some grains and salt	
	Haverfordwest	*None*	
	Tenby	Frieze cloth, lambskins, wool, leather, hides, and some pewter	

Hull

Region	Port	Goods shipped into Hull	Goods shipped out from Hull
East Anglia	King's Lynn	Grains (principally barley, occasionally malt)	Limited - occasional shipments carrying various goods such as lead, barley, butter and feathers
	Dunwich	Herring – white and red (smoked)	*None – returned in ballast?*
	Southwold		
	Great Yarmouth		Various, including coal, wheat and lead
Yorkshire & Lincolnshire[1]	Boston	Various, mostly haberdasher and upholstery wares	Various, including fish, grocery and haberdasher wares, barley, and wheat
	Scarborough	Various, including wine and fish	Various, including wine, salt, soap and grains
	Whitby	Various, including grains, coal and oil	Various, including pitch and tar, grains, hops and soap
Northumberland	Newcastle	Principally coal, some 'white salt', occasional shipments of fish and grains	Grains (limited volumes)
London	London	Various, including iron, oil, wine, 'grocery wares', steel, brasil, madder, hops and 'haberdasher wares'	Various, including lead, iron, ordnance, grains, oil, soap, pewter, feathers, wine and butter

[1] Note that Hull also traded similar commodities with Grimsby, Bridlington and Lincoln.

Hull (*continued*)

Region	Port	Goods shipped into Hull	Goods shipped out from Hull
South	The south coast (including Cornwall, Devon, Dorset, Gloucestershire, Hampshire and Wiltshire)	Grains, including wheat, malt and barley	Various, including white and red (smoked) herring, and salt
	Sussex (including Brighton, Meeching and Rye)	Iron	Various, including wine, coal and wheat
Other	Berwick-upon-Tweed	Herring – white and red (smoked)	Grains, including malt, wheat and hops

APPENDIX C: WEALTH OF MERCHANTS AND MARINERS IN BRISTOL, SOUTHAMPTON AND HULL

The following tables show the lay subsidy valuations of individuals residing in the ports of Southampton, Bristol, Gloucester and Hull that have been identified in the coastal port books.[1]

SOUTHAMPTON MERCHANTS

Merchant	Valuation (goods)	Subsidy	Year of return	Occupation
John Caplein	£16	26s 8d	1571	Merchant
	£10	26s 8d	1598	
Nicholas Caplein	£20	33s 4d	1571	Merchant
John Carewe	£10	16s 8d	1571	Merchant
Bernard Courtney	£10	16s 8d	1571	Merchant/Brewer
John Crook	£50	£4 3s 4d	1571	Merchant/Brewer
Robert Cross	£3	5s	1571	Fishmonger/Publican
Paul Elliott	£10	16s 8d	1571	Tallow chandler
	£6	16s	1594	
John Erintonn	£5	8s 4d	1571	Merchant/Publican
Richard Goddard Senior	£30	50s	1571	Merchant
Richard Goddard Junior	£12	Unclear	1600	Merchant
Reginald House	£10	16s 8d	1571	Merchant/Publican
John Knight	£16	26s 8d	1571	Merchant

[1] TNA E179/174/387, E179/115/355, E179/115/368, E179/115/373, E179/115/386, E179/115/353, E179/115/367, E179/115/382, E179/115/385, E179/203/265, E179/204/274, E179/204/292, E179/204/328; Vick.

APPENDIX C 215

SOUTHAMPTON MERCHANTS (*continued*)

Merchant	Valuation (goods)	Subsidy	Year of return	Occupation
William Nutshaw	£10	16s 8d	1571	Merchant
Alexander Payton	£4	6s 8d	1571	Merchant/Attorney
Average	£14			

SOUTHAMPTON SHIPMASTERS

Shipmaster	Valuation (goods)	Subsidy	Year of return	Occupation
Reginald Barber	£3	5s	1571	Mariner/Publican
John Cotton	£3	Illegible (probably 5s)	1571	Mariner
Thomas Griston	£6	10s	1571	Mariner/Publican
Thomas Hill	£3	5s	1571	Mariner
Peter Janverin	£3	8s	1594	Mariner/Publican
Nicholas Roche	£6	10s	1571	Mariner/Publican
Average	£4			

BRISTOL MERCHANTS

Merchant	Valuation (goods)	Subsidy	Year of return	Occupation
John Adye	£3	3s	1571	Pewterer
Thomas Aldworth	£10	8s 4d	1568	Merchant
Robert Allen	£3	3s	1571	Merchant
Richard Ashurst	£4	3s 4d	1568	Merchant
John Atkins	£3	2s 6d	1568	Merchant
Thomas Balding	£3	2s 6d	1568	Brewer
	£3	3s	1571	
John Ball	£4	3s	1571	Merchant

BRISTOL MERCHANTS (*continued*)

Merchant	Valuation (goods)	Subsidy	Year of return	Occupation
John Barnes[2]	£3	2s 6d	1568	Cardmaker/
	£8	6s 8d	1568	Clothier/ Merchant
James Benbow	£5	5s	1571	Baker
Nicholas Blake	£6	5s	1568	Merchant
William Blast	£8	6s 8d	1568	Brewer/Merchant
	£5	5s	1571	
John Bodell	£4	3s 4d	1568	Vintner/Merchant
	£8	8s	1571	
John Bones	£5	4s 2d	1568	Cardmaker/
	£7	7s	1571	Merchant/ Clothier
John Brown	£8	6s 8d	1568	Merchant/Grocer
	£12	12s	1571	
John Burrow	£3	2s 6d	1568	Pewterer
	£4	4s	1571	
John Bush	£5	Unclear	1560	Tanner/Merchant
	£6	5s	1568	
	£3	4s	1571	
John Carter	£10	8s 4d	1568	Merchant
Dominic Chester	£5	5s	1560	Merchant
	£15	12s 6d	1568	
£15	15s	1571	

[2] Note that two men are listed in TNA E179/115/373 mem.5 as John Barnes (John Barnes Senior and John Barnes Junior). We cannot determine for certain, but since the customs records include both a John Barnes and a John Barnes Junior, it seems likely that both men were engaged in coastal commerce through Bristol, especially given that their operational approach to coastal commerce was practically indistinguishable. Based on this assumption, the valuations for both senior and junior have been included. As they lived within the same ward and were listed with the same occupation, it is of little consequence in terms of residences whether they were the same or separate men.

BRISTOL MERCHANTS (*continued*)

Merchant	Valuation (goods)	Subsidy	Year of return	Occupation
Luke Cocks	£4	4s	1564	Merchant
	£4	3s 4d	1568	
	£5	5s	1571	
Andrew Cotterell	£5	5s	1560	Merchant
	£4	3s 4d	1568	
	£4	4s	1571	
Miles Dickinson	£4	4s	1571	Merchant
John Draper	£4	3s 4d	1568	Merchant
	£6	7s	1571	
Robert Ellis	£3	2s ?d	1568	Tanner
	£5	5s	1571	
Richard Fower	£8	8s	1571	Merchant
Edward French	£3	2s 6d	1568	Grocer
Thomas Griffith	£8	8s	1571	Merchant
Simon Habert	£5	5s	1571	Brewer
Randall Hassell	£10	8s 4d	1568	Merchant/Clothier
Nicholas Hicks	£4	4s	1571	Clothier
William Hicks	£8	6s 8d	1568	Vintner
Giles Hobbs	£5	4s 2d	1568	Vintner
	£8	8s	1571	
Anthony Hodge	£3	2s 5d	1568	Brewer
	£3	3s	1571	
John Holborough	£3	2s 6d	1568	Clothier/ Fishmonger
John Hollister	£5	4s 2d	1568	Merchant
	£6	6s	1571	
John Hopkins	£4	4s	1571	Merchant
William Hopkins	£10	10s	1571	Fisherman/ Fishmonger
Ralph Hurt	£4	4s	1571	Grocer
Griffith Jones	£3	2s 6d	1568	Grocer
Richard Jones	£5	5s	1571	Upholsterer

BRISTOL MERCHANTS (*continued*)

Merchant	Valuation (goods)	Subsidy	Year of return	Occupation
Roger Jones	£8	8s	1571	Merchant
Thomas Kellick	£20	20s	1571	Merchant
Thomas Kirkland	£16	16s	1571	Clothier
Philip Langley	£18	15s	1568	Grocer/Merchant
	£25	25s	1571	
Edward Long	£3	3s	1571	Merchant
George Lymell	£4	4s	1571	Soapmaker
Thomas Melland	£3	3s	1571	Merchant
Thomas Merrick	£4	4s	1571	Merchant
Walter Miles	£3	2s	1568	Haulier
	£4	4s	1571	
William Nicholas	£4	3s 4d	1568	Merchant/Clothier
Lewis Philips	£5	4s 2d	1568	Baker
Thomas Pitt	£10	10s	1564	Draper
	£10	8s 4d	1568	
	£15	15s	1571	
Michael Popwell	£6	6s	1564	Grocer/Merchant
	£8	6s 8d	1568	
	£6	6s	1571	
William Popwell	£30	30s	1560	Merchant
	£98	98s	1564	
	£130	£4 12d	1571	
William Potter	£8	8s	1571	Clothier
Robert Powell	£3	2s 6d	1568	Merchant
John Privett	£10	10s (?)	1568	Tanner
	£8	8s	1571	
Anthony Roberts	£3	3s	1571	Merchant
Edward Roberts	£6	6s	1571	Unknown
John Rowland	£3 (?)	2s 6d	1568	Merchant
	£3	3s	1571	

BRISTOL MERCHANTS (*continued*)

Merchant	Valuation (goods)	Subsidy	Year of return	Occupation
Thomas Rowland	£5	?	1560	Merchant
	£4	4s	1564	
	£5	4s 2d	1568	
William Salter	£6	6s	1571	Merchant
Thomas Sarle	£3	2s 6d	1568	Draper/Merchant
	£8	8s	1571	
Thomas Simons	£5	4s	1568	Merchant
	£3 or £6 (?)	3s or 6s (?)	1571	
Edward Smith	£5	5s	1571	Merchant
Robert Smith	£10	10s	1560	Brewer
	£10	8s 4d	1568	
	£6	6s	1571	
George Snigg	£10	8s 4d	1568	Merchant
	£10	10s	1571	
George Snow	£3	2s 6d	1568	Merchant
John Stone	£15	12s 6d	1568	Brewer
Laurence Sweatman	£4	4s	1571	Merchant
Thomas Taylor	£3	3s	1571	Merchant/Trowman/Mariner
William Tucker	£10	8s 4d	1568	Merchant
	£8	8s	1571	
Thomas Warren	£4	3s 4d	1568	Merchant
	£10	10s	1571	
William Watford	£5	4s 2d	1568	Brewer
	£10	10s	1571	
John Webb	£5	4s 2d	1568	Merchant/Draper
	£4	4s	1571	

BRISTOL MERCHANTS (*continued*)

Merchant	Valuation (goods)	Subsidy	Year of return	Occupation
William Yeoman[3]	£3	2s 6d (?)	1568	Merchant
	£4	4s	1571	
Richard Young	£10	8s 4d	1568	Hooper/Merchant
	£10	10s	1571	
Average	£9			

BRISTOL MERCHANT/SHIPMASTERS

Merchant/ Shipmaster	Valuation (goods)	Subsidy	Year of return	Occupation
Walter Standfast	£8	6s 8d	1568	Merchant
	£8	8s	1571	
John White	£6	Unclear	1560	Merchant/Mariner
	£3	?s 6d	1568	
Average	£6			

BRISTOL SHIPMASTERS

Shipmaster	Valuation (goods)	Subsidy	Year of return	Occupation
Humphrey Hayward	£3	3s	1571	Unknown (probably occupational mariner)
Henry Nelson	£3	3s	1571	Unknown (probably occupational mariner)
Average	£3			

---

[3] Note that two men named William Yeoman appear in the returns for 1568 and 1571, one in Trinity ward and one in Mary le Port. In both cases they appear with the same valuation and subsidy. Therefore, for the purposes of this section it does not matter which is the correct Yeoman, but he has been excluded from the residency section and from Figures 5.2 and 5.3.

GLOUCESTER MERCHANTS

Merchant	Valuation (goods)	Subsidy	Year of return	Occupation
John Brown	£8	8s	1560	Merchant
	£8	8s	1565	
	£7	7s	1572	
Thomas Francombe	£16	16s	1565	Merchant
	£16	16s	1572	
Luke Garnons	£10	10s (?)	1560	Draper
	£15	15s	1572	
Laurence Holiday	100s (£5)	5s	1560	Mercer
	?	5s	1565	
Henry Horn	£6	6s	1565	Maltmaker
	£9	9s	1572	
Thomas Horsforde	£4	4s	1572	Draper
John Moore	£8	8s	1565	Mercer
Richard Stone	£5	8s 4d (?)	1571	Maltmaker
William Willis	£6	6s	1565	Maltmaker
	£7	7s	1572	
Average	£9			

GLOUCESTER MERCHANT/SHIPMASTERS

Merchant/ Shipmaster	Valuation (goods)	Subsidy	Year of return	Occupation
Henry Brown	£3	3s	1572	Mariner
John Long	100s (£5)	5s	1560	Mariner
	£3	3s	1572	
John Payne[4]	100s (£5)	5s	1560	Maltmaker
	100s (£5)	5s	1565	
John Shawe	£4 (?)	5s (?)	1571	Trowman

[4] Note that two men named John Payne appear in the tax records in Gloucestershire, one living in Gloucester's East ward and one in the ward of Hempsted. Given that the John Payne of the East ward was valued in land and John Payne of Hempsted was valued in goods, it seems likely that the Hempsted Payne was the maltmaker that appears in the customs records. TNA E179/115/353 mem.2, 3, E179/115/367 mem.2, 5.

GLOUCESTER MERCHANT/SHIPMASTERS (*continued*)

Merchant/ Shipmaster	Valuation (goods)	Subsidy	Year of return	Occupation
Richard Swanley	100s (£5)	5s	1560	Mariner
	£4	4s	1565	
	£5	5s	1572	
John Taylor	£4	4s	1572	Trowman
Thomas Taylor	100s (£5)	5s	1560	Trowman
Average	£4			

HULL MERCHANTS

Merchant	Valuation (goods)	Subsidy	Year of return	Nature of coastal trading through Hull
George Anderson	£4	4s	1571	Routinely undertook voyages to a range of locations, occasionally traded in Newcastle coal
James Clarkson	£20	33s 4d	1559	London specialist
	£20	20s	1571	
Robert Dalton	£20	33s 4d	1559	London specialist
	£20	20s	1571	
Thomas Dalton	100 marks (£66 13s 4d)	£5 11s 2d	1559	London specialist
	£40 (in lands)	53s 4d (£2 13s 4d)	1571	
Wiliam Gee	£20	33s 4d	1559	London specialist
	£26 14s 4d	26s 8d (£1 6s 8d)	1571	
	£50	£6 13s 4d	1594	
Average	£29			

HULL MERCHANT/SHIPMASTERS

Merchant	Valuation (goods)	Subsidy	Year of return	Nature of coastal trading through Hull
John Thompson	£12	20s	1563	Newcastle specialist
John Trotter	£4	4s	1575	Newcastle specialist
	£3	8s	1594	
Richard Ward	£3	3s	1571	Newcastle specialist
Robert Wardall	£8	13s 4d	1559	Newcastle specialist
	£5	5s	1571	
Average	£6			

HULL SHIPMASTERS

Merchant	Valuation (goods)	Subsidy	Year of return	Nature of coastal trading through Hull
Thomas Emerson	£7	7s	1571	London specialist
Thomas Eratt	£3	3s	1571	London specialist
Walter Hall	£5	8s 4d	1563	Primarily commanded voyages between London and Hull, occasionally traded in Newcastle coal
	£3	3s	1571	

HULL SHIPMASTERS (*continued*)

Merchant	Valuation (goods)	Subsidy	Year of return	Nature of coastal trading through Hull
Robert London	£3 10s	3s 6d	1571	Primarily commanded voyages between London and Hull, occasionally traded in Newcastle coal
Thomas Thisstle	£5	8s 4d	1559	London specialist
Roger Watson	£3	3s	1571	London specialist
Average	£4			

APPENDIX D: INDICATIVE VOYAGES SHOWING DIFFERENCE IN VALUE BETWEEN HULL'S NEWCASTLE TRADE AND HULL'S LONDON TRADE

The following indicative voyages have been used to assess the difference in value between Hull's trade with Newcastle and Hull's trade with London. These are the only voyages for which a valuation has been attempted, but are comparable to the vast majority of shipments undertaken on those routes. As the market value of goods fluctuated significantly year to year (or sometimes even month to month), these valuations were compiled using the customs valuations in the Book of Rates and as calculated by previous scholars. Using these figures it is possible to directly compare different types of goods and allows us to roughly assess the potential profits that could be gained from carrying different commodities within the confines of the same sized vessels.[1]

Voyages between London and Hull

- On 10 December 1570, the 30-ton *Robert* of Hull entered Hull from London carrying a shipment including 5 tons of iron, 6 tons of olive oil, 6 bales of madder, 1 last of black soap, 5 bales of copperas and alum, an unknown quantity of soap, and three additional commodities that could not be identified. Even without being able to value the unknown goods or those with unclear quantities, this shipment was very likely worth upwards of £200.[2]
- On 21 November 1571, the 30-ton *James* of Hull entered Hull from London carrying a shipment including 7 lasts of soap, 2 tons of grocery wares, 3 tons of copperas, 4 tons of Seville olive oil, 20 pieces of raisins, 2 barrels of steel, 2 butts of sack wine, an unknown quantity of hops, an unknown quantity of brasil, and six additional commodities that could not

---

[1] The valuations were obtained using Flavin and Jones, 'A Glossary of Commodities, Weights and Measures Found in the Sixteenth-Century Bristol Customs Account'; Jones, 'The Bristol Shipping Industry in the Sixteenth Century', p. 146; Thomas S. Willan, 'A Tudor Book of Rates' (Manchester: The University Press, 1962), p. 17.

[2] TNA E190/305/11 fol.4v.

be identified. This shipment was more difficult to value as many of the commodities were noted using non-standard units. Nonetheless, the olive oil, raisins and steel alone accumulate a value of more than £85. Were it possible to value the other goods, this shipment would very likely exceed a value of £100, and probably substantially more.[3]

Voyages between Newcastle and Hull

- On 4 November 1570, the 30-ton *Swallow* of Newcastle entered Hull from Newcastle carrying 20 Newcastle chaldrons of coal. The value of coal is especially difficult to determine, given the varying qualities, units, and types. Nonetheless, using the highest possible figures, this shipment was unlikely to be valued at more than £26 and, using the lowest possible figures, the value unlikely exceeded £10.[4]
- On 30 November 1571, the 30-ton *Matthew* of York entered Hull from Newcastle carrying 16 chaldrons of coal. Using the same measures, this shipment was likely valued at between £9 and £21.[5]
- On 25 October 1577, the 30-ton *John Baptist* of York entered Hull from Newcastle carrying 22 chaldrons of coal. This shipment was probably valued at between £11 and £29.[6]

---

[3] TNA E190/306/1 fol.20r.
[4] TNA E190/305/11 fol.1r.
[5] TNA E190/306/1 fol.11v.
[6] TNA E190/307/9 fol.1r.

BIBLIOGRAPHY

Manuscript sources

The National Archives of the United Kingdom, Kew (TNA)

Exchequer: King's/Queen's Remembrancer: Memoranda Rolls and Enrolment Books (E159)
Exchequer: King's/Queen's Remembrancer: Particulars of Account and other records relating to Lay and Clerical Taxation (E179)
Exchequer: King's/Queen's Remembrancer: Port Books (E190)
PROB: Wills and Letters of Administration, Records of the Prerogative Court of Canterbury
State Papers: Domestic, Elizabeth I (SP12)
State Papers: Domestic, Addenda, Edward VI to James I (SP15)

Hull History Centre, Hull (HHC)

C/BRD/1: Papers relating to the sale of property and land by the Corporation
C/BRI/20: Commission for gaol delivery
C/BRS/48: Documents relating to shipping and the provision of ships for government service
C/BRV/44: Litigation Papers: Mayor and Burgesses of Hull vs Robert Brooke and other Merchants of London
C/BRX/4: Agreement between Hull and York concerning Trade and Carriage of Goods
C/DMT/5: The Tyndall Wildridge Collection: Other Corporation of Hull Records, 1446–1835
C/DMT/10: The Tyndall Wildridge Collection: Miscellaneous letters, 1858–1877
C/DMT/35: The Tyndall Wildridge Collection: Miscellaneous original documents, 1522–1894
C/DSN/1: Court Books (Minutes)
C/WG: Gee's Hospital, Hull records
C/WW/296: Hull Weigh House accounts: 1561–1563
U/DDBH/3/12: Papers of the Baines Family: Deighton (East Riding), 1158–1873
U/DDCB/12: Papers of the Burton Family (incorporating the Robinson Family of County Durham) of Cherry Burton: Various Townships 1586–1804
U/DDFA/6: Papers of the Forbes Adam/Thompson/Lawley (Barons Wenlock) Family of Escrick: Hull 1556

U/DDHA/2: Papers of the Langdale Family (incorporating Stourton and Harford) of Houghton Hall and Holme-on-Spalding-Moor: Beverley and Molescroft, 1312–1770
U/DDSY/52: Papers of the Sykes family of Sledmere: Owstwick
U/DDWB/11/1: Papers of the Wickham-Boynton Family (incorporating Griffith) of Burton Agnes: Hull 1592–1636
U/DX28/7: Kingston upon Hull Bench Books (nineteenth-century transcription)

Bristol Record Office, Bristol (BRO)

00565: Parcel of old Wills, 1348–1700
26166: Deeds and documents relating to properties belonging to Christchurch, City
BristolPlans/Arranged: Plans arranged and numbered after deposit at Bristol Record Office
AC/D: Records of the Smyth family of Ashton Court: Deeds
P.AS/D: Records of the Anglican parish of All Saints, City: Deeds

Printed primary sources

Butler, Cheryl, *The Remembrance Books of Richard Goddard 1583, John Crook 1584 and Andrew Studeley 1586* (Southampton: Southampton Record Series, 2021)

George, Edwin, and Stella George, eds, *Bristol Probate Inventories, Part 1: 1542–1650*, 54 (Bristol: Bristol Record Society, 2002)

Hearnshaw, Fossey, ed., *Southampton Court Leet Records, A.D. 1550–1577*, 1 (Southampton: Southampton Record Series, 1905)

——, ed., *Southampton Court Leet Records, A.D. 1578–1602*, 1 (Southampton: Southampton Record Series, 1906)

——, ed., *The Charters of the Borough of Southampton*, XI (Southampton: Southampton Record Series, 1910)

Lang, Sheila, and Margaret McGregor, eds, *Tudor Wills Proved in Bristol, 1546–1603*, 44 (Bristol: Bristol Record Society, 1993)

Lewis, Edward A., ed., *The Southampton Port and Brokage Books 1448–9*, 36 (Southampton: Southampton Record Series, 1993)

Loomte, Albert J., 'An Armada Pilot's Survey of the English Coastline, October 1597', *The Mariner's Mirror*, 49 (1963), pp. 288–300

Merson, Allan, ed., *The Third Book of Remembrance of Southampton, 1514–1602*, I and II (Southampton: Southampton Record Series, 1965)

Roberts, Edward, and Karen Parker, eds, *Southampton Probate Inventories, 1447–1575*, 34 (Southampton: Southampton Record Series, 1991)

Smith, Lucy T., ed., *The Maire of Bristowe Is Kalendar by Robert Ricart, Town Clerk of Bristol 18 Edward IV*, V (Westminster: Camden New Series, 1872)

Vick, Douglas F., ed., *Central Hampshire Lay Subsidy Assessments, 1558–1603; Fawley Division, Southampton, Isle of Wight and Winchester* (Farnham: D. F. Vick, 1987)

Welch, Edwin, ed., *The Admiralty Court Book of Southampton, 1566–1585*, XIII (Southampton: Southampton Record Series, 1968)

Willan, Thomas S., ed., *A Tudor Book of Rates* (Manchester: The University Press, 1962)

Online primary sources

Butler, Cheryl, *The Southampton Tudor Project: From Records to Revels*, http://www.tudorrevels.co.uk/records.php (27 August 2019)
Dasent, John R., *Acts of the Privy Council of England*, vol. 11: 1578–1580 (London: British History Online, 1895), www.british-history.ac.uk/acts-privy-council/vol11 (accessed 16 September 2019)
——, *Acts of the Privy Council of England*, vol. 12: 1580–1581 (London: British History Online, 1896), www.british-history.ac.uk/acts-privy-council/vol12 (accessed 16 September 2019)
Green, Mary A. E., *Calendar of State Papers Domestic: Elizabeth*, vol. 1: 1558–1560 (London: British History Online, 1869), www.british-history.ac.uk/cal-state-papers/domestic/edw-eliz/1595-7/pp48-68 (accessed 27 August 2019)
Jones, Evan T., *Bristol 'Particular' Accounts and Port Books of the Sixteenth Century, 1503–1601* (UK Data Service, 2009), dx.doi.org/10.5255/UKDA-SN-6275-1
Lambert, Craig, and Gary Baker, *The Medieval and Tudor Ships Project* (2017), www.medievalandtudorships.org (accessed 18 April 2019)
UK Public General Acts, *Lieutenancies Act 1997*, www.legislation.gov.uk/ukpga/1997/23/data.pdf (accessed 15 August 2019)
——, *Local Government Act 1888*, http://www.legislation.gov.uk/ukpga/1888/41/pdfs/ukpga_18880041_en.pdf (accessed 15 August 2019)
——, *Local Government Financial Statistics England, No. 20, 2010, Presented to Parliament Pursuant to Section 168(4) of the Local Government Act, 1972*, www.gov.uk/government/statistics/local-government-financial-statistics-england-no-20-2010 (accessed 5 December 2019)

Secondary sources

Alsop, James D., 'Tudor Merchant Seafarers in the Early Guinea Trade', in *The Social History of English Seamen, 1485–1649*, ed. by Cheryl A. Fury (Woodbridge: Boydell Press, 2012), pp. 75–115
Andrews, Kenneth R., *Elizabethan Privateering: English Privateering during the Spanish War, 1585–1603* (Cambridge: Cambridge University Press, 1964)
——, 'The Elizabethan Seaman', *The Mariner's Mirror*, 68 (1982), pp. 245–62
——, *Trade, Plunder and Settlement: Maritime Enterprise and the Genesis of the British Empire, 1480–1630* (Cambridge: Cambridge University Press, 1984)
Appleby, John C., 'Neutrality, Trade and Privateering, 1500–1689', in *A People of the Sea: The Maritime History of the Channel Islands*, ed. by Alan G. Jamieson (London: Methuen, 1986), pp. 59–105
Ashford, Philip, 'The West Somerset Woollen Trade, 1500–1714', *Proceedings of the Somerset Archaeology and Natural History Society*, 151 (2008), pp. 165–80
Baker, Gary Paul, 'Domestic Maritime Trade in Late Tudor England c. 1565–1585:

A Case Study of King's Lynn and Plymouth', in *The Routledge Companion to Marine and Maritime Worlds, 1400–1800*, ed. by Claire Jowitt, Craig Lambert and Steve Mentz (London: Routledge, 2020)

Barker, Rosalin, *The Rise of an Early Modern Shipping Industry: Whitby's Golden Fleet, 1600–1750* (Woodbridge: Boydell Press, 2011)

Bearman, Peter S., *Relations into Rhetorics: Local Elite Social Structure in Norfolk, England, 1540–1640* (New Brunswick, NJ: Rutgers University Press, 1993)

Bennett, Judith M., *Ale, Beer, and Brewsters in England: Women's Work in a Changing World, 1300–1600* (Oxford: Oxford University Press, 1996)

Berry, Charlotte, '"To Avoide All Envye, Malys, Grudge and Displeasure": Sociability and Social Networking at the London Wardmote Inquest, c.1470–1540', *The London Journal*, 42 (2017), pp. 201–17

Bindoff, Stanley T., 'Dalton, Thomas (1516/17–91), of Kingston-upon-Hull, Yorks.', in *The History of Parliament: the House of Commons 1509–1558*, www.historyofparliamentonline.org/volume/1509-1558/member/dalton-thomas-151617-91 (27 August 2019)

Blackmore, Robert, 'Keep Calm and Ignore the Armada', *BBC History Magazine* (September 2023)

Blake, J. B., ' The Medieval Coal Trade of North East England: Some Fourteenth-Century Evidence', *Northern History*, 2 (1967), pp. 1–26

Boddie, John Bennett, *Seventeenth Century Isle of Wight County, Virginia: A History of the County of Isle of Wight, Virginia, during the Seventeenth Century, Including Abstracts of the County Records* (Chicago: Genealogical Publishing Company, 1973)

Bowden, Peter J., 'Wool Supply and the Woollen Industry', *The Economic History Review*, 9 (1956), pp. 44–58

——, *Wool Trade in Tudor and Stuart England* (Oxon: Taylor & Francis, 2013)

Boyle, Jennifer, 'Treading the Digital Turn: Mediated Form and Historical Meaning', *Journal for Early Modern Cultural Studies*, 13:4 (2013), pp. 79–90

Brenner, Robert, 'The Social Basis of English Commercial Expansion, 1550–1650', *The Journal of Economic History*, 32 (1972), pp. 361–84

——, *Merchants and Revolution: Commercial Change, Political Conflict, and London's Overseas Traders, 1550–1653* (London: Verso, 2003)

Britnell, Richard, *The Commercialisation of English Society, 1000–1500* (Manchester: Manchester University Press, 1996)

——, 'Urban Demand in the English Economy, 1300–1600', in *Trade, Urban Hinterlands and Market Integration c.1300–1600*, ed. by James A. Galloway (London: Centre for Metropolitan History, 2000), pp. 1–21

Broadberry, Stephen, Bruce Campbell, Alexander Klein, Mark Overton and Bas van Leeuwen, *British Economic Growth 1270–1870* (Cambridge: Cambridge University Press, 2015)

Brown, Henry P., and Sheila V. Hopkins, 'Seven Centuries of the Prices of Consumables, Compared with Builders' Wage-Rates', *Economica*, 23 (1956), pp. 296–314

Brudner, Lilyan A., and Douglas R. White, 'Class, Property, and Structural Endogamy: Visualizing Networked Histories', *Theory and Society*, 26 (1997), pp. 161–208

Burkhardt, Mike, 'Networks as Social Structures in Late Medieval and Early Modern Towns: A Theoretical Approach to Historical Network Analysis', in *Commercial Networks and European Cities, 1400–1800*, ed. by Andrea Caracausi and Christof Jeggle, vol. 32 (London: Pickering and Chatto Publishers, 2014), pp. 13–44

Burwash, Dorothy, *English Merchant Shipping 1460–1540* (Toronto: University of Toronto Press, 1947)

Campbell, Bruce M. S., 'The Population of Early Tudor England: A Re-Evaluation of the 1522 Muster Returns and 1524 and 1525 Lay Subsidies', *Journal of Historical Geography*, 7 (1981), pp. 145–54

Caracausi, Andrea, and Christof Jeggle, eds, *Commercial Networks and European Cities, 1400–1800*, 32 (London: Pickering and Chatto Publishers, 2014)

Carson, Edward, *The Ancient and Rightful Customs: A History of the English Customs Service* (Bristol: Faber and Faber, 1972)

Carus-Wilson, Eleanora M., 'The Merchant Adventurers of Bristol in the Fifteenth Century', *Transactions of the Royal Historical Society*, 11 (1928), pp. 61–82

——, 'The Iceland Trade', in *Studies in English Trade in the 15th Century*, ed. by Eileen E. Power and Michael M. Postan (London: Routledge, 1933), pp. 155–82

——, 'The Overseas Trade of Bristol', in *Studies in English Trade in the 15th Century*, ed. by Eileen E. Power and Michael M. Postan (London: Routledge, 1933), pp. 183–247

——, *Medieval Merchant Venturers: Collected Studies* (London: Methuen, 1954)

Carvajal de la Vega, David, 'Merchant Networks in the Cities of the Crown of Castile', in *Commercial Networks and European Cities, 1400–1800*, ed. by Andrea Caracausi and Christof Jeggle, vol. 32 (London: Pickering and Chatto Publishers, 2014), pp. 137–52

Childs, Wendy, *The Trade and Shipping of Hull, 1300–1500* (Yorkshire: East Yorkshire Local History Society, 1990)

Clark, Peter, 'The Alehouse and the Alternative Society', in *Puritans and Revolutionaries: Essays in Seventeenth Century History*, ed. by Donald Pennington and Keith Thomas (Oxford: Clarendon Press, 1978), pp. 47–72

Clay, John William, ed., *Dugdale's Visitation of Yorkshire, with Additions*, III (Exeter: W. Pollard & Co., 1917)

Coleman, Olive, 'Trade and Prosperity in the Fifteenth Century: Some Aspects of the Trade of Southampton', *The Economic History Review*, 16 (1963), pp. 9–22

Colson, Justin, 'Web Databases for Late Medieval Social and Economic History: England's Immigrants and the Overland Trade Project', *Reviews in History* (2015), http://www.history.ac.uk/reviews/review/1820 (accessed 27 August 2019)

Colson, Justin, and Arie van Steensel, 'Urban Communities in Medieval and Early Modern Europe', in *Cities and Solidarities: Urban Communities in Pre-Modern Europe*, ed. by Justin Colson and Arie van Steensel (Oxon: Routledge, 2017), pp. 1–24

——, eds, *Cities and Solidarities: Urban Communities in Pre-Modern Europe* (Abingdon: Routledge, 2017)

Cornwall, Julian, 'English Population in the Early Sixteenth Century', *The Economic History Review*, 23 (1970), pp. 32–44

Croft, Pauline, 'Trading with the Enemy 1585–1604', *The Historical Journal*, 32 (2009), pp. 281–302

Dalton, Heather, *Merchants and Explorers: Roger Barlow, Sebastian Cabot, and Networks of Atlantic Exchange 1500–1560* (Oxford: Oxford University Press, 2016)

Davis, Ralph, *The Trade and Shipping of Hull, 1500–1700* (Yorkshire: East Yorkshire Local History Society, 1964)

Deane, Phyllis, and W. A. Cole, *British Economic Growth, 1688–1959: Trends and Structure* (Cambridge: Cambridge University Press, 1967)

Dietz, Frederick C., 'Elizabethan Customs Administration', *The English Historical Review*, 45 (1930), pp. 35–57

Dimmock, Spencer, 'Urban and Commercial Networks in the Later Middle Ages: Chepstow, Severnside, and the Ports of Southern Wales', *Archaeologia Cambrensis*, 152 (2003), pp. 53–68

Dixon, Hepworth, *Robert Blake, Admiral and General at Sea: Based on Family and State Papers* (London: Chapman and Hall, 1852)

Dowell, Stephen, *A History of Taxation and Taxes in England from the Earliest Times to the Year 1885*, III: Direct Taxes and Stamp Duties (London: Longmans, Green and Co., 1888)

Drake, Barbara, 'The Development of an Urban Site 1455–1750, the Island and Lower Part of Westgate Street', *Gloucestershire History*, Special Extra Edition (1990), pp. 2–17

Düring, Marten, 'From Hermeneutics to Data to Networks: Data Extraction and Network Visualization of Historical Sources', *The Programming Historian* (2015), https://programminghistorian.org/lessons/creating-network-diagrams-from-historical-sources (accessed 27 August 2019)

Durkee, Dana, 'A *Cursus* for Craftsmen? Career Cycles of the Worsted Weavers of Late-Medieval Norwich', in *Cities and Solidarities: Urban Communities in Pre-Modern Europe*, ed. by Justin Colson and Arie van Steensel (Oxon: Routledge, 2017), pp. 151–69

Dyer, Alan, *Decline and Growth in English Towns 1400–1640*, New Studies in Economic and Social History (Cambridge: Cambridge University Press, 1995)

Dyer, Florence, 'The Elizabethan Sailorman', *The Mariner's Mirror*, 10 (1924), pp. 133–46

East, William G., 'The Port of Kingston-upon-Hull during the Industrial Revolution', *Economica* (1931), pp. 190–212

——, 'The Historical Geography of the Town, Port, and Roads of Whitby', *The Geographical Journal*, 80 (1932), pp. 484–97

Engerman, Stanley, and Patrick O'Brien, 'The Industrial Revolution in Global Perspective', in *The Cambridge Economic History of Modern Britain*, ed. by Roderick Floud et al. (Cambridge: Cambridge University Press, 2004)

Erikson, Emily, *Between Monopoly and Free Trade: The English East India Company, 1600–1757* (Woodstock: Princeton University Press, 2014)

Erikson, Emily, and Peter Bearman, 'Malfeasance and the Foundations for Global Trade: The Structure of English Trade in the East Indies, 1601–1833', *American Journal of Sociology*, 112 (2006), pp. 195–230

Erikson, Emily, and Samila Sampsa, 'Social Networks and Port Traffic in Early Modern Trade', *Social Science History*, 39 (2015)

Evans, Chris, Owen Jackson and Göran Rydén, 'Baltic Iron and the British Iron Industry in the Eighteenth Century', *The Economic History Review*, 55 (2002), pp. 642–65

Farr, Grahame, 'Severn Navigation and the Trow', *The Mariner's Mirror*, 32 (1946), pp. 66–95

Fischer, David H., *Champlain's Dream* (New York: Simon & Schuster, 2008)

Fisher, Franz J., 'Commercial Trends and Policy in Sixteenth-Century England', *The Economic History Review*, 10 (1940)

Flavin, Susan, and Evan T. Jones, *Bristol's Trade with Ireland and the Continent 1503–1601: The Evidence of the Exchequer Customs Accounts* (Dublin: Four Courts Press for the Bristol Record Society, 2009)

———, 'A Glossary of Commodities, Weights and Measures Found in the Sixteenth-Century Bristol Customs Account', *University of Bristol, ROSE* (2009), pp. 1–120

Fleming, Peter, 'Time, Space and Power in Later Medieval Bristol', *Working Paper*, University of the West of England (2013), www.eprints.uwe.ac.uk/22171/2/TimeSpacePowerFinalVersion%20%283%29.pdf (accessed 2 April 2019)

Forrest, Mark, 'The Development of Dorset's Harbours in the Fourteenth and Fifteenth Centuries', *Proceedings of the Dorset Natural History & Archaeological Society*, 138 (2017), pp. 17–33

Friel, Ian, *Maritime History of Britain and Ireland, c. 400–2001* (London: British Museum Press, 2003)

Fury, Cheryl A., 'Training and Education in the Elizabethan Maritime Community, 1585–1603', *The Mariner's Mirror*, 85 (1999), pp. 147–61

———, *Tides in the Affairs of Men: The Social History of Elizabethan Seamen, 1580–1603* (Westport, CT: Greenwood Press, 2002)

———, 'The Elizabethan Maritime Community', in *The Social History of English Seamen, 1485–1649*, ed. by Cheryl A. Fury (Woodbridge: Boydell Press, 2012), pp. 117–39

———, 'Introduction', in *The Social History of English Seamen, 1485–1649*, ed. by Cheryl A. Fury (Woodbridge: Boydell Press, 2012), pp. 1–4

———, ed., *The Social History of English Seamen, 1485–1649* (Woodbridge: Boydell Press, 2012)

Gadd, Stephen, 'Illegal Quays: Elizabethan Customs Reforms and Suppression of the Coastal Trade of Christchurch, Hampshire', *The Economic History Review*, 71 (2018), pp. 727–46

Galloway, James A., 'One Market or Many? London and the Grain Trade of England', in *Trade, Urban Hinterlands and Market Integration c.1300–1600*, ed. by James A. Galloway (London: Centre for Metropolitan History, Institute of Historical Research, 2000), pp. 23–42

———, ed., *Trade, Urban Hinterlands and Market Integration, c.1300–1600: A Collection of Working Papers Given at a Conference Organised by the Centre for Metropolitan History and Supported by the Economic and Social Research Council, 7 July 1999* (London: Centre for Metropolitan History, Institute of Historical Research, 2000)

Grant, Alison, 'Breaking the Mould: North Devon Maritime Enterprise, 1560–1640', in *Tudor and Stuart Devon: The Common Estate and Government: Essays Presented to Joyce Youings*, ed. by Todd Gray, Margery Rowe and Audrey Erskine (Exeter: University of Exeter Press, 1992), pp. 119–40

Gras, Norman S., *The Early English Customs System: A Documentary Study of the Institutional and Economical History of the Customs from the Thirteenth to the Sixteenth Century* (Cambridge, MA: Harvard University Press, 1918)

Greenhill, Basil, 'The Story of the Severn Trow', *The Mariner's Mirror*, 26 (1940), pp. 286–92

Haggerty, John, and Sheryllynne Haggerty, 'Visual Analytics of an Eighteenth-Century Business Network', *Enterprise and Society*, 11 (2010), pp. 1–25

——, 'The Life Cycle of a Metropolitan Business Network: Liverpool 1750–1810', *Explorations in Economic History*, 48 (2011), pp. 189–206

Hair, Paul E. H., 'The Experience of the Sixteenth-Century English Voyages to Guinea', *The Mariner's Mirror*, 83 (1997), pp. 3–13

Hair, Paul E. H., and J. D. Alsop, *English Seamen and Traders in Guinea, 1553–1565: The New Evidence of Their Wills* (Lewiston, NY: E. Mellen Press, 1992)

Hare, John, 'Miscellaneous Commodities', in *Southampton and Its Region – English Inland Trade 1430–1540*, ed. by Michael Hicks (Oxford: Oxford University Press, 2015), pp. 161–71

Hasler, P. W., 'Aldworth, Thomas II (d.1599), of Bristol, Glos.', in *The History of Parliament: The House of Commons 1558–1603*, www.historyofparliamentonline.org/volume/1558-1603/member/aldworth-thomas-ii-1599 (27 August 2019)

——, 'Dalton, Thomas (1517–91), of Kingston-upon-Hull, Yorks.', in *The History of Parliament: The House of Commons 1558–1603*, www.historyofparliamentonline.org/volume/1558-1603/member/dalton-thomas-1517-91 (27 August 2019)

——, 'Garnons, Luke (d.1615), of Southgate Street, Gloucester', in *The History of Parliament: The House of Commons 1558–1603*, www.historyofparliamentonline.org/volume/1558-1603/member/garnons-luke-1615 (27 August 2019)

——, 'Langley, Philip (c.1525–92), of Bristol', in *The History of Parliament: The House of Commons 1558–1603*, www.historyofparliamentonline.org/volume/1558-1603/member/langley-philip-1525-92 (27 August 2019)

Hatcher, John, *The History of the British Coal Industry*, I (New York: Clarendon Press, 1993)

Hicks, Michael, 'The Trading Calendar', in *Southampton and Its Region – English Inland Trade 1430–1540*, ed. by Michael Hicks (Oxford: Oxford University Press, 2015), pp. 35–42

——, ed., *Southampton and Its Region – English Inland Trade 1430–1540* (Oxford: Oxford University Press, 2015)

Hipkin, Stephen, 'The Structure, Development, and Politics of the Kent Grain Trade, 1552–1647', *The Economic History Review*, 61 (2008), pp. 99–139

Hodgett, Gerald A. J., *Tudor Lincolnshire*, History of Lincolnshire (Lincoln: History of Lincolnshire Committee, 1975)

Hoskins, William G., 'Harvest Fluctuations and English Economic History, 1480–1619', *The Agricultural History Review*, 12 (1964), pp. 28–46

Howell, Martha C., *Commerce before Capitalism in Europe, 1300–1600* (Cambridge: Cambridge University Press, 2010)

Hoyle, Richard, *Tudor Taxation Records: A Guide for Users* (London: PRO Publications, 1994)

——, 'Taxation and the Mid-Tudor Crisis', *The Economic History Review*, 51 (1998), pp. 649–75

'Hull in the 16th and 17th Centuries', in *A History of the County of York East Riding*, ed. by Keith J. Allison (London: Victoria County History, 1969), http://www.british-history.ac.uk/vch/yorks/east/vol1/pp90-171 (accessed 22 August 2019), pp. 90–171

Hutton, Charles, *A Philosophical and Mathematical Dictionary: Containing an Explanation of the Terms, and an Account of the Several Subjects Comprised under the Heads Mathematics, Astronomy, and Philosophy Both Natural and Experimental; with an Historical Account of the Rise, Progress and Present State of These Sciences; Also Memoirs of the Lives and Writings of the Most Eminent Authors Both Ancient and Modern Who by Their Discoveries or Improvement Have Contributed to the Advancement of Them* (London: C. Hutton, 1815)

Irwin, Geoffrey, 'Pots and Entrepots: A Study of Settlement, Trade and the Development of Economic Specialization in Papuan Prehistory', *World Archaeology*, 9 (1978), pp. 299–319

James, Tom B., 'The Town of Southampton and Its Foreign Trade 1430–1540', in *Southampton and Its Region – English Inland Trade 1430–1540*, ed. by Michael Hicks (Oxford: Oxford University Press, 2015), pp. 11–24

Jamieson, Alan G., ed., *A People of the Sea: The Maritime History of the Channel Islands* (London: Methuen, 1986)

Jenkins, Philip, 'Wales', in *The Cambridge Urban History of Britain*, ed. by David M. Palliser, vol. 2 (Cambridge: Cambridge University Press, 2000), pp. 133–50

Jones, Evan T., 'River Navigation in Medieval England', *Journal of Historical Geography*, 26:1 (January 2000), pp. 67–68

——, *Inside the Illicit Economy: Reconstructing the Smugglers' Trade of Sixteenth Century* (Farnham: Ashgate, 2012)

——, 'The Shipping Industry of the Severn Sea', in *The World of the Newport Medieval Ship: Trade, Politics and Shipping in the Mid-Fifteenth Century*, ed. by Evan T. Jones and Richard G. Stone (Melksham: University of Wales Press, 2018), pp. 135–59

Jowitt, Claire, and Daniel Carey, eds, *Richard Hakluyt and Travel Writing in Early Modern Europe* (Oxon: Taylor & Francis, 2016)

Kadushin, Charles, *Understanding Social Networks: Theories, Concepts, and Findings* (Oxford: Oxford University Press, 2012)

Kahl, William F., *The Development of London Livery Companies: An Historical Essay and a Select Bibliography* (Cambridge, MA: Baker Library, Harvard Graduate School of Business Administration, 1960)

Keene, Derek, 'Changes in London's Economic Hinterland as Indicated by Debt Cases in the Court of the Common Pleas', in *Trade, Urban Hinterlands and Market Integration c. 1300–1600*, ed. by James A. Galloway (London: Centre for Metropolitan History, Institute of Historical Research, 2000), pp. 59–81

Kermode, Jenny, *Medieval Merchants: York, Beverley and Hull in the Later Middle Ages* (Guildford: Cambridge University Press, 2002)

Korsch, Evelyn, 'The Scerimans and Cross-Cultural Trade in Gems: The Armenian Diaspora in Venice and Its Trading Networks in the First Half of the Eighteenth Century', in *Commercial Networks and European Cities, 1400–1800*, ed. by Andrea Caracausi and Christof Jeggle (London: Pickering and Chatto Publishers, 2014), pp. 223–40

Kowaleski, Maryanne, 'The Expansion of the South-Western Fisheries in Late Medieval England', *The Economic History Review*, 53 (2000), pp. 429–54

——, *Local Markets and Regional Trade in Medieval Exeter* (Cambridge: Cambridge University Press, 2003)

——, 'The Shipmaster as Entrepreneur in Medieval England', in *Commercial Activity, Markets and Entrepreneurs in the Middle Ages: Essays in Honour of Richard Britnell*, ed. by Ben Dodds and Christian D. Liddy (Woodbridge: Boydell Press, 2011), pp. 165–82

Lambert, Craig, *Shipping the Medieval Military: English Maritime Logistics in the Fourteenth Century* (Woodbridge: Boydell Press, 2011)

——, 'Tudor Shipmasters and Maritime Communities, 1550–1600', in *The Routledge Research Companion to Marine and Maritime Worlds, 1400–1800: Oceans in Global History and Culture*, ed. by Claire Jowitt, Craig Lambert and Steve Mentz (London: Routledge, 2020)

Lambert, Craig, and Andrew Ayton, 'The Mariner in Fourteenth Century England', in *Fourteenth Century England*, ed. by Mark Ormrod, vol. VII (Woodbridge: Boydell Press, 2012), pp. 153–77

Lambert, Craig, and Gary Paul Baker, 'An Investigation of the Size and Geographical Distribution of the English, Welsh, and Channel Islands Merchant Fleet: A Case Study of 1571–72', in *The Maritime World of Early Modern Britain*, ed. by Richard Blakemore and James Davey (London: Amsterdam University Press, 2020)

Lang, Heinrich, 'Networks and Merchant Diasporas: Florentine Bankers in Lyon and Antwerp in the Sixteenth Century', in *Commercial Networks and European Cities, 1400–1800*, ed. by Andrea Caracausi and Christof Jeggle (London: Pickering and Chatto Publishers, 2014), pp. 107–20

Latimer, John, *The History of the Society of Merchant Venturers of the City of Bristol; with Some Account of the Anterior Merchants' Guilds* (Bristol: Arrowsmith, 1903)

Laughton, L. G. Carr, and Michael Lewis, 'Early Tudor Ship-Guns', *The Mariner's Mirror*, 46 (1960), pp. 242–85

Lemercier, Claire, 'Formal Network Methods in History: Why and How?', in *Social Networks, Political Institutions, and Rural Societies*, ed. by Georg Fertig (Turnhout, Belgium: Brepols, 2015), pp. 281–310

Lewis, Edward A., ed., *The Welsh Port Books (1550–1603): With an Analysis of the Customs Revenue Accounts of Wales for the Same Period*, Cymmrodorion Record Series, 41 (London: Honourable Society of Cymmrodorion, 1927)

Liddy, Christian D., *War, Politics and Finance in Late Medieval English Towns: Bristol, York and the Crown, 1350–1400* (Woodbridge: Boydell Press, 2005)

Loades, David, *The Mid-Tudor Crisis, 1545–1565* (Basingstoke: Macmillan, 1992)

——, *England's Maritime Empire: Seapower, Commerce, and Policy, 1490–1690* (Harlow: Pearson Education, 2000)

——, 'The English Maritime Community, 1500–1650', in *The Social History of English Seamen, 1485–1649*, ed. by Cheryl A. Fury (Woodbridge: Boydell Press, 2012), pp. 5–26

Lobel, Mary D., and Eleanora M. Carus-Wilson, 'Bristol', in *Historic Towns: The Atlas of Historic Towns: Volume 2: Bristol: Cambridge: Coventry: Norwich*, ed. by Mary D. Lobel, vol. 2 (Yorkshire: Scolar Press, 1969), pp. 1–27

MarineTraffic, *Voyage Planner* (2018), www.marinetraffic.com/en/voyage-planner/ (accessed 27 July 2018)

The Maritime Museum, Southampton, *Southampton in 1620 and the "Mayflower": An Exhibition of Documents by the Southampton City Record Office to Celebrate the 350th Anniversary of the Sailing of the "Mayflower" from Southampton in 1620*, 1 (Southampton: Southampton City Record Office, 1970)

Marsden, Peter V., and Nan Lin, eds, *Social Structure and Network Analysis* (London: Sage Publishing, 1982)

Masschaele, James, 'Transport Costs in Medieval England', *The Economic History Review*, 46 (1993), pp. 266–79

Mate, Mavis E., *Trade and Economic Developments, 1450–1550: The Experience of Kent, Surrey and Sussex* (Woodbridge: Boydell Press, 2006)

Merson, Allan, 'Elizabethan Southampton ', in *Collected Essays on Southampton*, ed. by J. B. Morgan and Philip Peberdy (Southampton: Southampton County Borough Council, 1961), pp. 57–75

Moore, John S., 'Demographic Dimensions of the Mid-Tudor Crisis', *The Sixteenth Century Journal*, 41 (2010), pp. 1039–63

Murphy, Margaret, 'Feeding Medieval Cities: Some Historical Approaches', in *Food and Eating in Medieval Europe*, ed. by M. Carlin and J. Rosenthal (London: Hambledon, 1998)

Nash, Peter, 'The Maritime Shipping Trade of Scarborough, 1550 to 1750', *Northern History*, 49 (2012), pp. 202–22

Nef, John U., *The Rise of the British Coal Industry* (London: Taylor & Francis, 2013)

O'Brien, Patrick, 'Exports and the Growth of the British Economy, 1688–1802', in *Slavery and the Rise of the Atlantic System*, ed. by Barbara Solow (Cambridge: Cambridge University Press, 1991)

O'Brien, Patrick, Derek Keene, Marjolein Hart and Herman van der Wee, eds, *Urban Achievement in Early Modern Europe: Golden Ages in Antwerp, Amsterdam and London* (Cambridge: Cambridge University Press, 2001)

Oldland, John, 'The Allocation of Merchant Capital in Early Tudor London', *The Economic History Review*, 63 (2010), pp. 1058–80

——, 'The Economic Impact of Clothmaking on Rural Society, 1300–1550', in *Medieval Merchants and Money*, ed. by Martin Allen and Matthew Davies (London: University of London, School of Advanced Study, Institute of Historical Research, 2016), pp. 229–52

Padgett, John F., and Christopher K. Ansell, 'Robust Action and the Rise of the Medici', *American Journal of Sociology*, 98 (1993), pp. 1259–319

Padgett, John F., and Paul D. McLean, 'Organizational Invention and Elite

Transformation. The Birth of Partnership Systems in Renaissance Florence', *American Journal of Sociology*, 111 (2006), pp. 1463–568

Parker, Leanna T., 'Southampton's Sixteenth-Century Illicit Trade: An Examination of the 1565 Port Survey', *International Journal of Maritime History*, 27 (2015), pp. 268–84

Patarino, Vincent, 'The Religious Shipboard Culture of Sixteenth and Seventeenth-Century English Sailors', in *The Social History of English Seamen, 1485–1649*, ed. by Cheryl A. Fury (Woodbridge: Boydell Press, 2012), pp. 141–92

Pearce, Cathryn, *Cornish Wrecking, 1700–1860: Reality and Popular Myth* (Woodbridge: Boydell Press, 2010)

Platt, Colin, *Medieval Southampton: The Port and Trading Community, A.D. 1000–1600* (London: Routledge, 1973)

Ramsay, George D., 'The Distribution of the Cloth Industry in 1561–2', *The English Historical Review*, 57 (1942), pp. 361–69

——, 'The Smugglers' Trade: A Neglected Aspect of English Commercial Development', *Transactions of the Royal Historical Society*, 2 (1952), pp. 131–57

——, *English Overseas Trade during the Centuries of Emergence: Studies in Some Modern Origins of the English Speaking World* (London: Macmillan, 1957)

Ramsey, Peter, *Tudor Economic Problems* (London: Victor Gollancz, 1963)

Reeves, Richard, *To Inquire and Conspire, New Forest Documents 1533–1615*, New Forest Records Series, V (Hampshire: New Forest Centre, 2008)

Rigby, Stephen H., 'Urban Population in Late Medieval England: The Evidence of the Lay Subsidies', *The Economic History Review*, 63 (2010), pp. 393–417

Rosenthal, Naomi, Meryl Fingrutd, Michele Ethier, Roberta Karant and David McDonald, 'Social Movements and Network Analysis: A Case Study of Nineteenth-Century Women's Reform in New York State', *American Journal of Sociology*, 90 (1985), pp. 1022–54

Rudder, Samuel, *The History and Antiquities of Gloucester: Including the Civil and Military Affairs of That Antient City; with a Particular Account ... Of the Cathedral Church; and All Other Public Establishments, from the Earliest Period to the Present Time* (Cirencester: S. Rudder, 1781)

Ruddock, Alwyn, 'Alien Merchants in Southampton in the Later Middle Ages', *The English Historical Review*, 61 (1946), pp. 1–17

——, 'London Capitalists and the Decline of Southampton in the Early Tudor Period', *The Economic History Review*, 2 (1949), pp. 137–51

——, *Italian Merchants and Shipping in Southampton, 1270–1600*, Southampton Record Series, I (Southampton: University College, 1951)

——, 'Merchants and Shipping in Medieval Southampton', in *Collected Essays on Southampton*, ed. by J. B. Morgan and Philip Peberdy (Southampton: Southampton County Borough Council, 1961)

Sacks, David Harris, *The Widening Gate: Bristol and the Atlantic Economy, 1450–1700*, 15 (California: University of California Press, 1991)

Scammell, Geoffrey V., 'English Merchant Shipping at the End of the Middle Ages: Some East Coast Evidence', *The Economic History Review*, 13 (1961), pp. 327–41

——, 'Manning the English Merchant Service in the Sixteenth Century', *The Mariner's Mirror*, 56 (1970), pp. 131–54

——, *Seafaring, Sailors and Trade, 1450–1750: Studies in British and European Maritime and Imperial History* (Aldershot: Variorum, 2003)

'Section 4.1: The History of the Salmon and Sea-Trout Net Fisheries of the Tweed and the Eye', in *Tweed & Eye Fisheries District Fisheries Management Plan*, 5th edn (Melrose: The Tweed Foundation, 2014)

Stephens, William B., 'The Cloth Exports of the Provincial Ports, 1600–1640', *The Economic History Review*, 22 (1969), pp. 228–48

——, 'English Wine Imports, c. 1603–40, with Special Reference to the Devon Ports', in *Tudor and Stuart Devon: The Common Estate and Government: Essays Presented to Joyce Youings*, ed. by Todd Gray, Margery Rowe and Audrey Erskine (Exeter: University of Exeter Press, 1992), pp. 141–72

Stone, Lawrence, 'State Control in Sixteenth-Century England', *The Economic History Review*, 17 (1947), pp. 103–20

Stone, Richard G., 'The Overseas Trade of Bristol before the Civil War', *International Journal of Maritime History*, 23 (2011), pp. 211–39

Sutton, Anne F., *The Mercery of London: Trade, Goods and People, 1130–1578* (Oxon: Ashgate, 2005)

Syvret, Marguerite, and Joan Stevens, *Balleine's History of Jersey* (Gloucestershire: History Press Limited, 2011)

Tavener, L. E., 'The Port of Southampton', *Economic Geography*, 26 (1950), pp. 260–73

Thornton, Tim, *The Channel Islands, 1370–1640: Between England and Normandy* (Woodbridge: Boydell Press, 2012)

Thrush, Andrew, and John P. Ferris, 'Gee, William (?1565–1611), of York Minster Yard and Bishop Burton, Yorks.', in *The History of Parliament: The House of Commons 1604–1629*, www.historyofparliamentonline.org/volume/1604-1629/member/gee-william-1565-1611 (27 August 2019)

Tittler, Robert, 'The English Fishing Industry in the Sixteenth Century: The Case of Great Yarmouth', *Albion: A Quarterly Journal Concerned with British Studies*, 9 (1977), pp. 40–60

——, 'The Vitality of an Elizabethan Port: The Economy of Poole, 1550–1600', *Southern History*, 7 (1985), pp. 95–118

Trinder, Barrie, *Barges and Bargemen: A Social History of the Upper Severn Navigation 1660–1900* (Chichester: Phillimore & Co., 2005)

van den Heuvel, Charles, Scott B. Weingart, Nils Spelt and Henk Nellen, 'Circles of Confidence in Correspondence', *Nuncius*, 31 (2016), pp. 78–106

Vanes, Jean, ed., *Documents Illustrating the Overseas Trade of Bristol in the Sixteenth Century* (Kendal: Bristol Record Society, 1979)

Walton, Steven A., 'State Building through Building for the State: Foreign and Domestic Expertise in Tudor Fortification', *Osiris*, 25 (2010), pp. 66–84

Ward, Robin, *The World of the Medieval Shipmaster: Law, Business and the Sea c.1350–c.1450* (Woodbridge: Boydell Press, 2009)

White, Douglas R., and H. Gilman McCann, 'Cites and Fights', in *Social Structures: A Network Approach*, ed. by Barry Wellman and Steven Berkowitz (Cambridge: Cambridge University Press, 1998), pp. 380–400

Whitley, Edythe J. R., *Red River Settlers: Records of the Settlers of Northern*

Montgomery, Robertson, and Sumner Counties, Tennessee (Baltimore: Genealogical Publishing Company, 1980)
Willan, Thomas S., *The English Coasting Trade: 1600–1750* (Manchester: The University Press, 1967)
——, *The Inland Trade: Studies in English Internal Trade in the Sixteenth and Seventeenth Centuries* (Manchester: Manchester University Press, 1976)
Williams, Neville, *The Maritime Trade of the East Anglian Ports, 1550–1590* (Gloucestershire: Clarendon Press, 1988)
Woodward, Donald, 'Short Guide to Records: 22. Port Books', *History*, 55 (1970), pp. 207–10
——, 'Ships, Masters and Shipowners of the Wirral 1550–1650', *The Mariner's Mirror*, 63 (1977), pp. 233–48
Y., B., *A Sure Guide to Merchants, Custom-House Officers, &C., or the Modern Practice of the Court of Exchequer; in Prosecutions Relating to His Majesty's Revenue of the Customs* (London: E. and R. Nutt and R. Gosling, 1730)

Unpublished theses, dissertations and conference papers

Basford, Helen Victoria, 'The Isle of Wight in the English Landscape: Medieval and Post-Medieval Rural Settlement and Land Use on the Isle of Wight' (unpublished doctoral thesis, University of Bournemouth, 2013)
Brown, James, 'The Landscape of Drink: Inns, Taverns and Alehouses in Early Modern Southampton' (unpublished doctoral thesis, University of Warwick, 2007)
Bryson, Alan, 'The Legal Quays: Sir William Paulet, First Marquis of Winchester', Tudor Ports of London Conference (2008)
Colson, Justin, 'Local Communities in Fifteenth Century London: Craft, Parish and Neighbourhood' (unpublished doctoral thesis, Royal Holloway, University of London, 2011)
Harreld, Donald, 'Merchants and International Trade Networks in the Sixteenth Century', XIV International Economic History Congress (2006)
Higgins, Alexander 'The Establishment of the Head Port of Gloucester, 1565–1584' (unpublished MPhil thesis, University of Bristol, 2012)
Hunter, Judith, 'Legislation, Royal Proclamations and Other National Directives Affecting Inns, Taverns, Alehouses, Brandy Shops and Punch Houses 1552 to 1757' (unpublished doctoral thesis, University of Reading, 1994)
Inwood, Joe, 'The Chesters of Bristol: A Tudor Merchant Dynasty' (unpublished BA thesis, University of Bristol, 2006)
Jones, Evan T., 'The Bristol Shipping Industry in the Sixteenth Century' (unpublished doctoral thesis, University of Edinburgh, 1998)
Kermode, Jenny, 'The Merchants of York, Beverley and Hull in the Fourteenth and Fifteenth Centuries' (unpublished doctoral thesis, University of Sheffield, 1990)
Lamb, David Frank, 'The Seaborne Trade of Southampton in the Seventeenth Century' (unpublished doctoral thesis, University of Southampton, 1971)
Lee, James Matthew, 'Political Communication in Early Tudor England: The

Bristol Elite, the Urban Community and the Crown, c.1471–c.1553' (unpublished doctoral thesis, University of the West of England, Bristol, 2006)

Stone, Richard G., 'The Overseas Trade of Bristol in the Seventeenth Century' (unpublished doctoral thesis, University of Bristol, 2012)

Taylor, Duncan, 'The Maritime Trade of the Smaller Bristol Channel Ports in the Sixteenth Century' (unpublished doctoral thesis, University of Bristol, 2009)

Wiggs, Joan L., 'The Seaborne Trade of Southampton in the Second Half of the Sixteenth Century' (unpublished MA thesis, University of Southampton, 1955)

INDEX

Aberthaw 45 n.71, 48–49, 211
Alderney *see* Channel Islands
Aldworth, Thomas 155, 160, 215
Alum 24, 208, 211, 225
Anderson, George 68, 154, 222
Antwerp 6, 50, 58 n.2
armigers 154–55
Arundel 32
Aware, John 107, 139 n.7
Azores 24, 59, 208

bacon 34, 209
bakers 104, 113–14, 148–50, 199, 216, 218
Balding, Thomas 110, 188–89, 215
Ball, Richard 106
Barber, Reginald 92, 101, 150, 176–77, 215
barley *see* grain
Barnstaple 33–35, 73, 115–16, 211
Basford, Alan 126–27
Baston, Edward 109
Bat, Blaise 126–27
beer 34, 42, 73, 143, 146, 148–50, 174, 209
Benbow, James 104, 216
Bennett, Robert 73
Berwick-upon-Tweed 28, 36–37, 39–40, 64, 130, 152, 154–55, 213
Bewdley 22, 26, 107, 139 n.9, 140 n.10, 210
Bideford 33–34, 73, 211
Biston, Richard 59, 86, 89–90, 96–97, 182
Blake, Nicholas 188, 216
Blake, Ralph 131
Blake, Robert 133
Blast, William 110, 112, 175, 188, 216
Bodell, John 188, 216
Bones (Bonnar), John 115–16, 216
Bordeaux 50, 163

Boston 28, 30, 68, 212
brasil 32, 210, 212, 225
brass 211
brewers 65, 70, 103–04, 109–10, 112–14, 134, 148–50, 174–76, 186, 188–90, 195, 199–200, 214–17, 219
Bridgnorth 22, 26, 107 n.71, 210
Bridgwater 33 n.39, 34–35, 45, 60, 133, 210
Bridlington 30, 212 n.1
Brighton 62, 213
Brook, John 107, 139 n.8
Brook, Roger 107, 139 n.8
Brown, Thomas 104, 139 n.6, 139 n.9
Brown, Valentia 155
Burnham 64
Burrow, John 115, 216
Bush, John 116, 216
butter 31, 48, 123, 126, 212

Cade, Anthony 110
Calman, Nicholas 129
canvas 34, 117, 209, 211
Caper, John 107
Caper, Richard 107, 139 n.6
Caplein, Edmund 89
Caplein, John (junior) 85, 89, 162 n.76, 214
Caplein, John (senior) 85, 89
Caplein, Nicholas 97, 163, 214
Cardiff 45, 48, 66, 148, 198, 211
cardmakers 115–16, 148, 190, 216
Carmarthen 45 n.71, 47, 74, 115, 140 n.10, 158 n.62, 166, 211
Cavil, John 176–77
Chamberlain, James 104, 106, 139 n.8
Channel Islands 19–20, 24, 41–44, 54, 56, 84, 86, 92–93, 98, 101–02, 149, 177, 197, 201, 209
Chapman, Thomas 112
Chator, John 113

INDEX

Chepstow   45 n.71, 47–48, 115, 159–60, 211
Chester, Dominic   185–86, 216
Chichester   32, 62, 98, 209
Child, William   106
Christian, John   144
Clark, John   131
Clarkson, James   126–29, 155, 168–70, 222
cloth   6, 12, 14, 24–25, 34–35, 45–46, 66, 117, 138, 145–46, 165, 184–89, 195, 197, 200, 210–11
clothiers   106, 117, 145, 159, 188, 190, 216–18
coal   7, 15, 23, 27–29, 36–40, 49–52, 54–55, 57, 60, 63–64, 66, 68, 73–77, 82, 84, 86, 131–32, 137, 142–43, 151–54, 167, 169, 171–74, 192, 194, 197–98, 201, 209–10, 212–13, 222–24, 226
Cocks, Luke   188, 217
Cocks, Thomas   104
Collins, William   128, 153
copper   208
Corbet, Peter   171
Cornwall   20, 26, 33–37, 41, 53, 61, 69–70, 72, 74, 83, 85–87, 99, 118, 129–30, 132, 150, 198, 209, 211, 213
Cotton, John   97–98, 133, 158, 163–64, 215
cotton(s)   26, 34, 210–11
Courtney, Bernard   59 n.5, 89–90, 93, 149, 214
Courtney, Thomas   149
Courtney, William   93, 149
Crook, John   59 n.5, 69, 82, 86, 89–91, 97, 133, 150, 162–63, 176–77, 182, 214
currants *see* dried fruit

Dalton, Robert   126, 128, 168–70, 194, 222
Dalton, Thomas   126, 168–70, 194, 222
Dartford   69
Davies, Robert   106
Davies, Thomas   84, 86
Davies, William   84
Dee, River   26
Demarest, Gerald   84
Devart, Hugh   84–86
Devon   20, 26, 33–37, 53, 61, 73–75, 86, 93, 109, 113, 116, 118, 132, 149, 198, 209, 211, 213
Dibden   164, 180
Dorset   20, 22–25, 33, 36–37, 71–72, 82, 86, 92, 208, 213
Dower, Thomas   114
drapers   106, 112, 145–46, 159, 161, 164–65, 185, 188, 190, 218–19, 221
dried fruit   24, 34–35, 131, 208–09, 211, 225–26
dry wares   34, 145, 210–11
Duffield, Robert   130–31, 173
Dunwich   27–28, 212

East Anglia   27–29, 64, 68, 129–30, 132, 212
Edward, John   109
Eire, Robert   84–85, 89 n.25, 92–93, 97, 101
Eire, Thomas   84–85, 92–93
Elliott, Paul   98–99, 162 n.76, 180, 214
Emerson, Thomas   125, 127, 157, 167, 223
Eratt, Thomas   124 n.95, 127–28, 167, 223
Estur, family   98
Etrier, Richard   90, 98
Exeter   23–24, 33 n.39, 34
Eyre, Robert *see* Eire, Robert
Eyre, Thomas *see* Eire, Thomas

feathers   31, 123, 130, 211–12
firewood *see* wood
fish   15, 27–30, 34–35, 39–40, 131–32, 154, 209–13
Fisher, Thomas   166
fishermen   97, 180, 191, 199, 217
fishmongers   148, 190, 214, 217
France   5, 10, 24–25, 35, 42, 54, 61, 98, 101, 130, 163, 186
Francombe, Thomas   165, 221

Garnons, Luke   112, 146 n.27, 165, 221
Gascony   14, 23, 208, 210
Gdansk   50
Gee, William   125–29, 134, 155, 167 n.92, 168–70, 194, 222
geographic features
    of Bristol   14, 23, 26, 62, 66, 69–70, 72, 104
    of Hull   16, 22, 152
    of Southampton   11–12, 23–24, 65, 71–73

glass   24–25, 34, 66, 72, 84, 208–09
Gloucester   14 n.32, 22, 25–26, 113, 117, 138–40, 145, 149, 159, 164–65, 178, 192–93, 210, 221–22
Gloucestershire   20, 22–23, 26, 33, 37, 65–66, 69–70, 77, 103–07, 109, 112–13, 145, 148–49, 165, 175, 178, 186, 188 n.155, 191, 195, 200, 210, 213, 221 n.4
Goddard, John   84
Goddard, Richard (junior)   59 n.5, 163, 214
Goddard, Richard (senior)   163, 214
Goole   27
grain   26–28, 31–32, 34–40, 42, 52–54, 61, 64, 70, 104, 107, 109, 112–14, 126–27, 130–31, 146–50, 153–56, 165, 175, 186, 192, 195, 197, 209–13
Great Yarmouth   21, 27–29, 40, 123, 129, 134, 212
Grimsby   30, 212 n.1
grindstones   34, 211
Griston, Thomas   94 n.41, 158, 176, 215
grocers   114–15, 145–46, 159–60, 188, 190, 216–18
Guernsey *see* Channel Islands
gunpowder   24, 62 n.16, 208–09

haberdasher wares   30, 68, 131, 167, 211–12
Habert, Simon   104, 188–89, 217
Hall, Walter   124 n.95, 127, 167, 173 n.111, 223
Hampshire   20, 22–23, 33, 36–37, 42, 62, 71–72, 82, 84, 86–87, 89–96, 98–101, 177, 197, 208, 213
Harman, John   94, 101, 133
Harrison, William   131
Hassowle, Laurence   131
Hastings   32, 62
hauliers   188, 218
Haverfordwest   45 n.71, 48–49, 74, 211
Hawkins, John   5
Hawkins, William   60
Hedley, Francis   171
Helston   33–34, 85, 87
herring *see* fish
hides/skins   34, 47, 148, 166, 208–11
Hill, Thomas   158, 215
Historical Network Research *see* Social Network Analysis

Hobbs, Francis   141, 142–43, 145
Hobbs, Nicholas   115
Hodge, Anthony   110, 175, 186, 188, 217
Holford, John   90, 97–99, 133, 164, 180
Holiday, Laurence   117, 221
Holy Island   152
Hooper, Samuel   107, 109
hoopers   148, 220
hops   24, 34, 61, 130, 150, 186, 208–09, 212–13, 225
House, Reginald   182, 214
Humber, River   16, 18–19, 22–23, 51–52, 54, 64, 152–53, 197

Iberia/Iberian Peninsula   5, 9, 12, 14, 163, 186
Iceland   14
Ilfracombe   33 n.39, 113
Instow   115
Ireland   5, 12, 14, 26, 53, 59, 66 n.26, 109, 144 n.22, 158 n.63
iron   10, 24–25, 31–35, 39, 53, 61–63, 69, 82, 91–95, 97, 101, 115, 130 135, 137, 145, 161, 166 n.90, 161, 193, 197, 208–13, 225
Isle of Wight   12, 22, 24, 32–33, 59–63, 65, 69, 94–98, 101, 197, 198, 208

James, Richard   113
Janverin, Peter   102–03, 176–77, 215
Jersey *see* Channel Islands
Johnson, Richard   114

Keadby   27–28, 64, 130, 153, 173, 194
Kent   25, 93
Kent, Noel   93
King, Thomas   112
King's Lynn   21, 27–29, 64, 123, 129, 131–32, 134, 154, 212
Kitching, Robert   110
Knight, John   94–95, 97, 161–62, 193, 214
Krithe, Thomas   127

La Rochelle   23, 50, 60–62, 97, 163, 208–10
Lake, Emery   182
Langley, Philip   160–61, 218
lead   24, 31, 34, 39, 60, 72 n.38, 75, 89–90, 126–27, 157, 166, 202, 208–12
Lepe   62

Lewis, John 113
Lewis, Richard 114
Lewis, Thomas 117
Limbery, Roger 84
Lincoln 30, 130, 212 n.1
Lincolnshire 30, 64–66, 68, 212
linen 34, 117, 211
London 1, 5, 10–11, 13, 14, 16, 20–21, 23, 25, 27–28, 30–33, 35–39, 41, 50, 52–55, 59–61, 63–66, 68–69, 72, 74–77, 83–84, 86–90, 93, 97–98, 119–29, 131–35, 137, 142, 150–53, 156, 163, 166–70, 172–74, 182, 192–94, 197–98, 200–02, 209–10, 212, 222–26
Looe 129
Low Countries 5, 9, 130
Lowe, Thomas 104, 106
Lundy, William 94, 96–98
Lyme Regis 22, 24–25, 65–66, 71–72, 84, 198, 208
Lymington 11

madder 212, 225
malt 24, 34, 93, 130, 149, 208–09, 212–13
maltmakers 103–10, 134, 148–49, 155, 178, 190, 199–200, 221
Manchester 26, 210
Marshall, Adam 106–07
Meeching 32, 62, 92–94, 213
Megg, William 92 n.33, 126–28, 131, 155
Melcombe Regis 22, 24
mercers 117, 164–65, 221
Mersey 26
Milford Haven 45–46, 49, 66, 115, 198, 211
millstones 34, 209
Minehead 33–35, 53, 210
Moore, George 104–05
Moore, John 117, 221
Morell, David 182

nails 34, 61, 208–09, 211
Nelson, Henry 158, 220
Netherlands 58
new draperies *see* cloth
New Forest 12, 24, 42
Newcastle 11, 20, 23, 27–28, 36–39, 49–54, 63–64, 66, 68, 73, 77, 82, 84, 119, 129–32, 137, 142–43, 151–54, 166–67, 171, 173, 192, 194, 197–201, 212, 222–26
Newhaven 32
Newport 22, 45 n.71, 48, 62 n.17, 96, 115, 160
Norfolk 29, 37, 80, 153
Norris, John 173
Norway 50
Norwich 28–29

oil 31, 34–35, 39, 74, 91, 117, 131, 159, 167, 210–2, 225–26
ordnance 25, 31–32, 53, 62, 199, 208–09, 212
Ouse, River 22, 27, 51–52, 54
overland trade 10, 13, 14, 26, 51
overseas trade
    of Bristol 12, 57, 116–17,160, 165
    of England 5–9, 67–68, 71, 197
    of Hull 15, 50–51, 64
    of Southampton 10–11, 24–25, 57, 59–62, 69, 97–98, 162–63

Padstow 33–34, 60, 211
Palmer, Laurence 87, 90
Palmer, Tristan 104, 106–07
Parrett, William 173
Payton, Alexander 182, 215
Pembroke 45 n.71
Pembrokeshire 47
Percy, Richard 153
Pert, Richard 106
Peter, David 166
pewter 31, 34, 126, 211–12
pewterers 115, 148, 188, 215–16
Philips, John 115
Philips, Lewis 114, 218
pitch and tar 30, 39, 131, 210, 212
Pitt, Thomas 106, 185–86, 218
Plymouth 23, 33 n.39, 34, 36, 60, 61 n.14, 62 n.17, 69, 74, 198, 211
Poole 22, 24, 41, 59–61, 65, 69, 98, 144, 177, 198, 208
Popwell, Michael 159, 218
Popwell, William 159–60, 218
port books
    coverage and record keeping 1–3, 18–19, 41–42, 51–52, 57, 103, 119, 137–38, 205–07
    establishment of 1–3
Portsmouth 22, 25, 32, 60–62, 197–98, 208

prunes *see* dried fruit
publicans 90, 103, 148, 150, 174, 176–77, 179, 191–92, 199, 214–15

Rackes, Ralph 129, 171
Railson, Matthew 126–27
raisins *see* dried fruit
risk management 37–39, 62, 66, 71–75, 83–84, 117, 131–32, 152, 172–73, 197–98
Rawson, unknown 131
Raymond, Owen 60
Richard, Thomas 104, 124 n.95
Roberts, Edward 188, 218
Roche, Nicholas 150, 158, 166, 176, 215
Rochester 28
Rowden, Thomas 126–27
Rowland, Thomas 161, 219
Ryde 22
Rye 32, 62, 210, 213

Saddler, John 106–07
Sallarwaye, Hugh 104, 106–07, 139 n.7, 139 n.9
salmon *see* fish
salt 7, 10, 23–24, 29–30, 34–35, 39–40, 52, 61, 63, 126, 131, 144, 166 n.90, 197, 208–13
Sarle, Thomas 146 n.27, 161, 219
Scarborough 30, 152–53, 194, 212
Selby 27–28
servants 85, 89 n.23, 182
Severn, River 14, 20, 22–23, 25–26, 48, 66, 69–70, 77, 103–04, 106–07, 109–10, 112–13, 134, 139 n.9, 144, 149, 197–99, 201–02
Shoreham-by-Sea 32
Shynge (Shining?), William 110
Simons, John 73, 115
Smart, William 93
Smith, Robert 113, 174, 185, 188–89, 219
smuggling 1–3, 12–14, 16, 42, 46–47, 54, 160
Smyth, Thomas 135
soap 31, 34–35, 60, 75, 117, 123, 131, 148, 166 n.90, 209–12, 218, 225
soapmakers 148, 218
Social Network Analysis (methods of) 79–82
Society of Merchant Venturers of Bristol 159–61

Somerset 33–35, 114, 210
Southwold 27–28, 212
Sowter, John 149
Spain 5, 35, 61 n.14, 160, 186
spices 32, 72, 209
St Davids 33 n.39, 115
St Ives 33–35, 60
Standfast, Walter 158, 220
Stone, Richard 106, 221
Stone, John 174, 188 n.155, 219
Strange, Philip 115
Sussex 20, 24–25, 31–34, 36 n.45, 39, 41, 50, 53, 62–63, 69, 82, 91–94, 97, 100–02, 112, 133, 135, 150, 197, 201, 209, 213
Swanley, family 109–14, 174–75, 178, 186, 188–89
Swanley, Richard 109, 112–13, 178, 222
Swanley, Thomas 110–12, 186, 189

tallow chandlers 99, 180, 199, 214
tanners 66, 148, 190, 199, 216–18
Tenby 45 n.71, 47, 112, 117, 211
Tewkesbury 22, 26, 65, 70, 114, 140 n.10, 210
Thompson, John 124 n.95, 172, 223
tin 10, 24, 32–35, 61–62, 69, 72, 82–89, 92, 99–100, 131–32, 135 ,197, 208–09, 211
Trent, River 22, 27, 52
trowmen 69–70, 103–11, 114, 134, 138–40, 142, 145, 149, 178, 190, 199–200, 219, 221–22

upholsterers 148, 190, 217
upholstery wears 30, 212

Venard, John 84
vintners 109, 145, 159, 188, 190, 216

Walwine, Richard 110
Ward, Richard 131, 223
Wardall, Robert 172, 223
Water, William 69
Watford, Richard 112
Watford, William 110, 112, 175, 186, 188, 219
Watson, Richard 110
Watson, Roger 125, 167, 224
Watson, William 110–12
Waymer, John 130
Wells-next-the-sea 64

West Midlands 22–23, 77, 103, 106–07, 145, 191, 200, 210
Weymouth 22–24, 65, 72–73, 198, 208
wheat *see* grain
Whitby 30, 68, 154, 197, 212
White, John 84–87, 90, 100, 135, 185, 220
William, John 117
Willmott, Richard 182
Wilson, John 109
Wiltshire 33, 36–37, 85, 92, 213
wine 10, 12, 23–25, 30–32, 34–35, 39, 47–48, 54, 59–62, 70, 72, 74–75, 98, 123, 131, 138, 144–46, 159–60, 165–67, 190, 208–13, 225

woad 24, 34, 59–60, 208–09
wood 24, 32, 34, 42, 73, 143, 208–09
wool 6, 14, 24, 33–35, 45, 53, 145, 208–11
Worcester 22, 26, 107 n.70, 109, 140, 210
Worcestershire 22–23, 65, 69–70, 77, 103–07, 114, 145, 191, 200, 210

Yare, River 29
York 2, 22–23, 27, 51, 64, 129, 153, 171, 173, 194, 226
Yorkshire 16, 30, 54, 65–6, 68, 129, 212